Deliberate Injustice

Leaving Them Behind Through Indifferent and Incompetent
Leadership In Urban Education

A Case History of Systemic Failure

José Rosado

ISBN 978-1-4958-1425-9

Published April 2017

INFINITY PUBLISHING
1094 New DeHaven Street, Suite 100
West Conshohocken, PA 19428-2713
Toll-free (877) BUY BOOK
Local Phone (610) 941-9999
Fax (610) 941-9959
Info@buybooksontheweb.com
www.buybooksontheweb.com

DEDICATION

This book is dedicated to all of those people that strive to make a positive impact on the lives of our young people by protecting their rights and advocating for appropriate services. In the field of education, these people adhere to ethical standards and school code regardless of the challenging behaviors a student may present.

It's important to note that many of our young people arrive at our schools having experienced failure and/or hardships in their home and/or community. As such, they arrive at our schools often feeling angry. Others are diagnosed with emotional, learning and/or mental health disorders.

Nonetheless, all of these students at one time or another had hopes, dreams, goals, and aspirations. And as educators we are called upon to reinforce, and where necessary reignite, the hopes, dreams, goals, and aspirations of these young people.

For the vast majority of our disadvantaged and troubled young people, education is their only legitimate and viable option to break the negative cycles, which often lead to generational hardships.

Unfortunately, as some of these students may act out in school, they are often met with consequences outlined in the school's student code of conduct rather than provided appropriate services and interventions. This is often true for special education students as well. Even though they have additional due process rights and protections.

As an educator, one should be bound by ethical conduct and serving the best interests of our students. However, the reality is that many often fall short of our ethical duties and responsibilities and unfortunately adhere to the status quo of displacing disadvantaged and/or troubled students with alternative education placements, suspensions and/or expulsions.

For those that risk alienating their colleagues, risk being insubordinate to a supervisor, risk taking a chance on a student, risk being suspended and/or fired in an effort to stand against injustice and protect the rights of the students you serve... This book is dedicated to you!

CONTENTS

Relevant Quotes

❮——◆——❯

"A child miseducated is a child lost."
John F. Kennedy

"If you are neutral in situations of injustice, you have chosen the side of the oppressor."
Desmond Tutu

"The root cause of poverty is social injustice and the bad government that abets it."
Colin Powell

"Life's most persistent question is – What are you doing for others?"
Martin Luther King Jr.

"The way to right wrongs is to turn the light of truth upon them."
Ida B. Wells

"I think that one thing that people are missing is that we are never going to be able to fix this country's (American) economy in the long run until we fix our public education system."
Michelle Rhee

INTRODUCTION

"In theses days, it is doubtful that any child may reasonably be expected to succeed in life if he is denied the opportunity of an education. Such an opportunity, where the state has undertaken to provide it, is a right that must be made available on equal terms." [1]

These are the words of Chief Justice Earl Warren, supporting his opinion in the landmark 1954, United States Supreme Court Case Brown v. Board of Education.

These words, along with the legislation they supported, must have seemed like the beginning of an era, which would bring fairness, justice and equality for all. However, at the onset of the No Child Left Behind Act of 2001, nearly half a century after segregation was banned in our public schools, the inequalities within our public education system remained rampant. And while we have laws that support equal opportunity for all students, many practices within our public education system, especially in urban schools, lend themselves to leaving students behind. Unfortunately, those being left behind or otherwise being displaced by our schools are more likely to feed into the school-to-prison pipeline and further increase our prison population and mass incarceration in the United States.

Over the past few years the issue of mass incarceration has increasingly become the topic of much debate. Politicians, civil rights advocates, law-enforcement officials, as well as educators, scholars and pundits have all offered their thoughts and insights. Mass incarceration in the United States was even a topic of discussion during the 2016, presidential campaign. Much was discussed and debated regarding the emphasis and impact of legislation and the criminalization of certain acts.

The roots of mass incarceration in the United States can be traced back to the early 1970's with President Richard Nixon's declaration of "An all-out global war on the drug menace" and the establishment of the Drug Enforcement Administration in 1973. [2]

President Ronald Reagan declared illicit drugs to be a threat to our national security in 1982, and in 1988, he created the Office of National Drug Control Policy. A primary focus of this office was the coordination of drug-related legislative policy. [3]

The political escalation of the war on drugs and get tough on crime was ramped up by the 1994, "Clinton Crime Bill" (Violent Crime Control and Law Enforcement Act). This law, signed by President Bill Clinton, increased federal penalties for many crimes, created a variety of new federal crimes, authorized the establishment of "boot camps" for youthful offenders and provided $9.7 billion for states to build and operate prisons. [4]

Given the political emphasis and resources placed on the war on drugs and crime since the 1970's, it should come as no surprise that the prison population in the United States increased by 500% over the last forty years. By 2014, legislation, along with law enforcement policies and practices, led to the incarceration of 2.2 million people in the United States. [5] Those incarcerated are predominately Black and Latino. And although African Americans comprise 13% of the United States population, African Americans account for nearly 40% of those incarcerated in state or federal prison for drug law violations. Similarly, Latinos comprise 17% of the United States population, but account for 37% of those incarcerated in federal prisons for drug offenses. [6]

Eventually, the get tough on crime policies and practices, which dominated our legislation and fueled mass incarceration filtered into our public schools and spurred the zero-tolerance policies and strict student codes of conduct beginning in the 1990's and continuing today. The correlation between the two have had a devastating impact on many of the more than 7 million children in this country that have a family member incarcerated, on probation or parole. [7]

These students, as well as others facing life stressors in their homes such as: family dysfunction, parental substance abuse, neglect, verbal and/or physical abuse, family mental health issues and poverty/financial stress; often take on a sense of failure. This sense of failure is compounded for many of them by life stressors in their community such as: crime, violence, drug and alcohol abuse, gangs, teen-pregnancy, high unemployment and other factors.

So it comes to be for many of our most vulnerable and disadvantaged students that they arrive at school with two strikes against them, only to find themselves in public schools with inadequate resources, strict zero-tolerance policies which focus on out of school suspensions, expulsions, alternative education placements, school-based arrests and a disregard for due process rights and the protection of students with special education needs.

As such, although federal legislation and initiatives such as the No Child Left Behind Act (passed by congress in 2001, and signed into law by President George W. Bush in 2002) [8], Race to the Top (a $4.35 billion competitive grant funded by the American Recovery and Reinvestment Act of 2009 and announced by President Barack Obama) [9], and the Every Student Succeeds Act (2015) [10], have been passed with the intent of establishing common standards, increasing educator effectiveness and closing the achievement gap, the inequalities persist.

Furthermore, the mounting data indicates that the road to mass incarceration in the United States now goes directly through our urban school districts across our country. Based on the following statistics, a case could be made to support the position that the school-to-prison pipeline is being fed by school administrators and teachers' unions' in urban districts:

- 40% of students expelled from U.S. schools each year are Black
- 70% of students involved in "in-school" arrests or referred to law-enforcement are Black or Latino
- 68% of all males in state and federal prisons do not have a high school diploma [11]

Much can and needs to be done to address the high rate of school failure in this country, especially in our urban schools. We must recognize that the economic viability of our communities, and our country as a whole, is only as vibrant as the quality of education our young people receive in our schools. As such, it should be in all of our best interest to strive toward providing a high quality education for all students. Essential to this end must be the presence and commitment of qualified and ethical educational leaders in our schools.

The cycle of mass incarceration and school failure, linked by the school-to-prison pipeline, is firmly established and very complex. It is also very lucrative for those with a financial interest in keeping the poor and uneducated poor and uneducated. The private prison industry along with contracted prison services is a multi-billion dollar industry in this country. Those with financial interests in theses private prisons and contracted prison services want to keep the pipeline flowing. Although I will not elaborate further on the structure of our prison system in this book, I offer this information as a small piece of background knowledge so that the reader can appreciate some of the systemic challenges we face as we confront mass incarceration in our country and begin the dialogue of criminal justice reform.

Many have and continue to argue that we are also very much in need of education reform in this country as well. Given the high rate of school failure and the ever-present achievement gap between our more affluent students and our disadvantaged students, it would be difficult to argue against comprehensive education reform in the United States.

Given the many concerns regarding our public education system, identifying and agreeing on a starting point would be difficult. As previously mentioned, our federal government has passed legislation and provided financial incentives to address the concerns and increase student success in our schools (the No Child Left Behind Act of 2001, the Race to the Top grants of 2009, and the Every Student Succeeds Act of 2015). Comprehensive education reform may be necessary and may eventually take place in our country. However, in the meantime our students and our communities would be best served if our educational leaders adhered to the legislation and policies already in place to protect the rights of students including our most vulnerable students and our special education needs students.

The focus of this book is to provide the reader with information, including a complaint filed by the Education Law Center – PA with the United States Department of Justice, alleging the violation of student's rights in public schools in the state of Pennsylvania. Further, this book will provide the reader with a case history, including sworn depositions and other legal documents from the federal law suite I filed against my former employer – The Allentown School District - after the superintendent and other administrators engaged in retaliatory actions against me for reporting alleged legal and ethical violations to the Pennsylvania Department of Education which led to sanctions against the district.

It will be up to each individual reader to determine whether any legal and/or ethical violations were committed, and if so, is it possible that the violations lend themselves to school failure, the school-to-prison pipeline and mass incarceration in the United States.

NOTE: Documents used for the purpose of this book including: ELC – PA "Formal Complaint", memorandums, teacher and student statements, investigation reports and sworn depositions have not been edited for grammar, punctuation and/or spelling.

CALLING ON THE D.O.J.

Unfortunately, the concern regarding the violation of student's rights, more specifically the rights of some of our most vulnerable students, is apparently widespread and systemic, at least in numerous public school districts in the state of Pennsylvania. The concern, based in part on anecdotal information and statistical data, was such that it led the Education Law Center – PA to file a "Formal Complaint" with the United States Department of Justice. The complaint alleges that the Pennsylvania Department of Education is "neglecting" specific duties and responsibilities pertaining to protecting the rights of African American students and students with disabilities. Although this complaint was filed prior to their administration, it is now the responsibility of Governor Tom Wolf and Secretary of Education Pedro Rivera to address the concerns they have inherited. Following, I provide excerpts from the Education Law Center – PA complaint:

August 7, 2013

Anurima Bhargava
Chief, Educational Opportunities Section
Civil Rights Division
U.S. Department of Justice
950 Pennsylvania Avenue, N.W.
Educational Opportunities Section, PHB
Washington, D.C. 20530
Anurima.bhargava@usdoj.gov

Re: Formal Complaint Regarding the Pennsylvania Department of Education's Ongoing Violations of Section 504 of the Rehabilitation Act of 1973, Title II of the Americans with Disabilities Act, and Title VI of the Civil Rights Act of 1964.

Dear Ms. Bhargava,

This Complaint, filed by the Education Law Center of Pennsylvania ("ELC"), alleges that the Pennsylvania Department of Education's policies and practices regarding Alternative Education of Disruptive Youth ("AEDY") programs have resulted in the disproportionate placement of students with disabilities and African American students in AEDY disciplinary placements. ELC asserts that AEDY programs are significantly more limited and inferior to traditional public school programs and that students placed in these disciplinary settings are denied equal opportunities to access quality educational experiences. ELC files this Complaint against the Pennsylvania Department of Education ("PDE") on behalf of students with disabilities and African American students who were placed and continue to be placed in AEDY programs on a disproportionate basis in violation of Section 504 of the Rehabilitation Act of 1973 ("Section 504"), Title II of the Americans with Disabilities Act of 1990 ("Title II"), and Title VI of the Civil Rights Act of 1964 ("Title VI"), and their respective implementing regulations.

I.   INTRODUCTION

The Education Law Center is a non-profit legal advocacy organization dedicated to insuring that all Pennsylvania children have access to a quality public education. ELC's work has focused on addressing the educational needs of the most vulnerable children who historically have been at a disadvantage in the public education system, including economically-disadvantaged children, minority children, children with disabilities, English language learners, children experiencing homelessness, children in foster homes and institutions, and others. Through individual advocacy, class action litigation, and legislative initiatives, ELC has advocated on behalf of thousands of students and regularly represents students who are unfairly disciplined in school districts across Pennsylvania. ELC is recognized as a statewide and national expert in education law and school climate issues.

ELC alleges that as a result of PDE's policies and practices, including its approval of AEDY programs, numerous school districts in Pennsylvania are discriminating against students with disabilities through their misuse of AEDY placements. The disproportionate and frequent placement of students with disabilities in such disciplinary settings violates regulations implementing Title II and Section 504. ELC alleges, in part, that PDE has neglected its ultimate responsibility for ensuring that every local education agency in Pennsylvania complies with Section 504, including its prohibition against discrimination…

By turning a blind eye towards overwhelming evidence of the disparate impact on students with disabilities, PDE has violated its duties under both Section 504 and Title II. In addition, though not the subject of this Compliant, PDE is also neglecting its duties under the Individuals with Disabilities Education Act ("IDEA") to ensure that all children with disabilities in AEDY programs receive a free, appropriate public education.

ELC independently alleges that as a result of PDE's policies and practices, including its approval of numerous AEDY programs in particular school districts, PDE is responsible for the overrepresentation of African American students in AEDY programs. The disproportionate placement of these students in disciplinary settings violates regulations implementing Title VI. This Complaint seeks to enforce the rights of African American students who are disproportionately harmed by the AEDY placement policies of PDE and individual districts…

Furthermore, ELC asserts that PDE has chosen to ignore the rampant use of "non-AEDY" disciplinary placements of students. While little is known about these placements, given that PDE does no monitoring of these programs, it is likely that these programs are also disproportionately and adversely impacting students with disabilities and African American students. We specifically ask the Department to investigate the extent to which public schools in Pennsylvania are utilizing these non-authorized disciplinary programs, whether students placed in these programs receive a quality education, and whether particular subgroups of students are placed in these programs at a disproportionate rate.

In response to these allegations, ELC respectfully requests that the Department of Justice Educational Opportunities Section:

- Fully investigate all claims asserted in this Complaint:
- Direct PDE to improve its guidance and establish clear criteria for the placement of students into AEDY programs as well as their transition back to regular schools;
- Ensure that PDE actively monitors all AEDY programs across the state to ensure that students with disabilities and African American students are afforded proper procedural protections, including due process procedures and manifestation hearings;
- Direct PDE to perform quarterly compliance reviews of school districts' alternative school policies and procedures to ensure that school districts do not discriminate against student with disabilities and African American students;
- Direct PDE to review the records of all students with special education needs and African American students currently placed in AEDY programs;
- Direct PDE to promote and provide resources and technical assistance for the implementation of evidence-based practices to reduce disruptive behavior and protect the rights of students with disabilities and African American students by reducing disparate placement in AEDY programs;
- Direct PDE to develop a process and protocol to determine and document the placement of students into AEDY programs, to ensure that all student files are appropriately reviewed each semester, and that students successfully transition back into regular education;
- Direct PDE to develop less discriminatory alternatives to AEDY placements that can be implemented in school districts, such as positive behavior intervention supports (PBIS);
- Direct PDE to ensure that students in AEDY programs receive a quality public education that is equivalent to or better than academic and extra-curricular opportunities afforded to students in the regular education environment;
- Direct PDE to monitor and report rates of graduation for all students placed into AEDY during high school;
- Direct PDE to develop and implement a process for an administrative appeal whereby students who believe they have been improperly placed into an AEDY program can have their placements independently reviewed by PDE and reversed where appropriate; and
- Direct PDE to prohibit school entities from operating or placing students in non approved and unregulated disciplinary settings.

II. JURISDICTION

PDE is Pennsylvania's state education agency ("SEA") and is a recipient of federal financial assistance and is therefore subject to the antidiscrimination prohibitions of Title VI, Title II, and Section 504. The Department of Justice is the appropriate venue for this Complaint, as the DOJ Educational Opportunities Section has the primary responsibility for enforcing Title II and Title VI provisions with respect to recipients of federal education funds. The Complaint is timely because the policies and practices of PDE and districts which unnecessarily cause a disparate impact on students with disabilities and African American students are ongoing and continuing.

III. FACTUAL BACKGROUND

A. History of AEDY in Pennsylvania – Inferior Programs by Design

Pennsylvania's Alternative Education for Disruptive Youth programs were created in 1997, when the Pennsylvania General Assembly enacted the state's first law on alternative education. The law, Act 30, created a state-level grant program through which districts, intermediate units, and a consortium of schools could apply for supplemental funding to operate AEDY programs to serve students in middle school and high school...

> Under the law, a "disruptive student" is defined as any student who, "to a marked degree," exhibits:
> (1) A disregard for school authority;
> (2) Display of or use of controlled substances on school property or during school-affiliated activities;
> (3) Violent or threatening behavior on school property or during school-related activities;
> (4) Possession of a weapon on school property;
> (5) Commission of a criminal act on school property;
> (6) Misconduct that would merit suspension or expulsion; or
> (7) Habitual truancy.

It is important to note that, under state law, school districts do not have the legal authority to punish incoming students for conduct that occurred while the student was enrolled in another district. However, school districts frequently place students newly arriving in their district into an AEDY program based on alleged conduct from a previous school district, prior placement in a juvenile justice facility, or even involvement in the child welfare system. ELC believes these practices may contribute to the disparities by race and disability...

B. Evaluations of AEDY Programs – Evidence of Drastically Inferior Programs

ELC has gathered a plethora of anecdotal information about AEDY programs through our parent hotline. The experiences of these students and families indicate that many AEDY programs offer significantly subpar academic instruction. ELC has fielded complaints from parents and students that the academic rigor expected in AEDY programs is well below that expected of students in traditional middle and high schools. Many programs provide nearly all "computer based" instruction. Moreover, some parents have reported that the academic instruction consists of completing worksheets all day long. Others have complained that their high school student was receiving elementary-level math work and that all students in grade 7-12 were receiving the same academic instruction...

The State has been on notice for many years of the problems raised in the Complaint. In 2010, ELC issued a lengthy report, which questioned the quality and effectiveness of AEDY programs and the impact of such placements on the ability of students to graduate, and provided PDE with recommendations for improvements. ELC's report also raised particular longstanding concerns: the overrepresentation of students of color and students with disabilities in AEDY programs and the extent to which students with special education needs receive a free and appropriate public education. Other reports about Pennsylvania's AEDY programs, issued prior to ELC's report, also noted the large percentage of students with disabilities in AEDY programs and raised questions about whether these students were receiving appropriate services.

C. Overrepresentation of Students with Disabilities in AEDY Programs

Alarmed by the large percentage of students with disabilities in AEDY programs, ELC testified before the state legislature in 2009 and before PDE's Bureau of Special Education in 2011. Our testimony to the state legislature recommended that PDE "monitor overrepresentation of students with disabilities in alternative education programs and deny funding to school districts accordingly." ELC's testimony explained; "PDE should direct the Bureau of Special Education to closely monitor all AEDY programs that serve children with disabilities as part of its cyclical monitoring to determine whether the schools and the sending school districts are fully complying with the IDEA's procedural and substantiate requirements. PDE has not heeded these requirements. In fact, PDE's Bureau of Special Education does very minimal monitoring of AEDY programs, including little to no oversight of the provision of a free appropriate public education ("FAPE") to students with Individual Education Programs ("IEP"), despite their clear duty as an SEA to ensure a FAPE for all children.

Based on the failure of PDE to publish annual reports, ELC's long history of receiving complaints about AEDY programs, and the State's lack of response to our efforts to bring the disproportionality problem to its attention, ELC decided to request recent data from PDE to reexamine the percentage of students with disabilities and the percentage of African American students referred to AEDY programs. Based on these requests, ELC received data regarding the 2008-2009, 2009-2010, 2010-2011, and 2011-2012 school years. To the extent available, we examined the number of students with disabilities and the number of African American students sent to AEDY programs and compared this data to the overall percentage of these student cohorts in individual school districts.

ELC's examination of the data revealed that students with disabilities continue to be dramatically overrepresented in AEDY programs across the state. In public schools in Pennsylvania as a whole, 15% of students are identified as students with disabilities. In recent years, however, the percentage of students with disabilities sent to AEDY programs has increased to almost three times the state average. In 2008-2009, 37.88% of the students sent to AEDY across the state were students with disabilities. The disproportionate number increased over the next three years: from 41.26%, in 2009-2010; to 42.63%, in 2010-2011; to 43.66% in 2011-2012. Thus, over the last four school years, while the total number of students sent to AEDY programs statewide has actually decreased, the percentage of students with disabilities served in these programs has increased...

> Individual Districts with Extremely High Disparate Impact on Students with Disabilities

ELC further examined data regarding students with disabilities sent to AEDY programs by each individual school district in Pennsylvania. We found that the vast majority of school districts across the state have a significantly higher percentage of students with disabilities in their AEDY programs as compared to the percentage of students with disabilities in their district as a whole. In 2010-2011, the most recently available statewide data, ELC identified 82 districts where students with disabilities comprised 50% or more of their AEDY population...

In each of these districts, the percentage of students with disabilities in the AEDY programs was more than double the rate of students with disabilities in the district. In all but three districts, the rate was more than triple...

D. Overrepresentation of African American Students in AEDY Programs

The percentage of African American students referred to AEDY programs statewide shows that state and local AEDY referral policies have had a disparate impact on African American students. The statewide percentage of African American students in all Pennsylvania public schools has remained steady at just under 16%. During the school years we studied, the percentage of African American students referred to AEDY programs has remained significantly more than two times that percentage. During the 2008-2009 school year, African American students comprised 38.5% of all students sent to AEDY programs. During the 2009-2010 school year, African American students comprised 36.1% of all students sent to AEDY programs. During the 2010-2011 school year, African American students comprised 35.3% of all students sent to AEDY programs.

E. Oversight for "Non-AEDY" Disciplinary Programs

An additional long-standing ELC concern has been the proliferation of "non-AEDY" disciplinary programs that operate in schools throughout Pennsylvania and that receive no oversight from PDE. ELC is concerned that the discriminatory impact of these programs on students with disabilities and African American students is even higher than in approved

AEDY disciplinary programs. Additionally, ELC believes that these "non-AEDY" alternative programs are of no better quality than the approved AEDY programs. While PDE has provided insufficient monitoring of AEDY programs, PDE has provided zero monitoring of these non-AEDY disciplinary programs. Because they do not call themselves "AEDY," there is no required approval process by PDE. No one at PDE, or anywhere else, conducts any monitoring of these programs. No one knows (1) whether these disciplinary programs are providing students with due process prior to placement, either for nondisabled students or for students with disabilities; (2) whether they are providing students with the full curriculum required for all regular education students under 22 Pa Code 4; (3) whether students receive the full hours of instruction, 900 hours a year for elementary students and 990 hours a year for middle and high school students; (4) whether these programs are staffed with highly-qualified teachers; or (5) whether these programs are discriminating against students with disabilities or students of color...

Just as in AEDY programs, students in these alternative disciplinary programs are segregated from the rest of the student body, often in the basement or on a separate floor of the school. However, because the program is physically located in the same building as the rest of the school, PDE has determined that these programs do not require AEDY approval or oversight.

ELC is aware that a number of these schools do not afford students due process protections prior to placement. We believe that, in addition to segregating students, these programs provide a narrower curriculum with fewer hours of academic instruction. These are clearly "disciplinary programs, and all students have an entitlement to due process prior to placement. In addition, students with disabilities should have procedural protections that ensure they are not being punished for conduct that is either caused by their disability or the result of a failure of their school to provide appropriate educational accommodations. At the very least, to protect against discrimination, PDE should be monitoring these programs and requiring school districts and charter schools to report data related to the placement of students by disability and by race.

IV. LEGAL CLAIMS

A. PDE's Policies and Practices Discriminate Against Students with Disabilities in Violation of Title II and Section 504

Title II provides that "no qualified individual with a disability shall, by reason of such disability, be excluded from participation in or be denied the benefits of the services, programs or activities of a public entity, or be subjected to discrimination by any such entity...

Section 504 also sets forth that a recipient of federal financial assistance cannot exclude students with disabilities from participation in or deny them the benefits of its schools, or otherwise subject them to discrimination because of their disabilities...

ELC contends that PDE's actions with regard to AEDY programs violate both Title II and Section 504. ELC's analysis reveals that a series of school districts across the state are utilizing AEDY referral policies that have the effect of subjecting students with disabilities to discrimination on the basis of disability. The discriminatory effect of these policies is demonstrated by the data PDE collects. Our analysis discloses that students with disabilities are overrepresented in a series of districts and that this overrepresentation is widespread...

It is unclear why students with disabilities are being referred to AEDY programs on a disproportionate basis. After all, the law mandates that students with disabilities receive extra support and special education services, mandates greater procedural safeguards to protect against discriminatory placements, and also requires the development of functional behavioral assessments and behavioral interventions including positive support plans. Specifically, Section 504 and the IDEA prohibit schools from placing a student in AEDY if the behavior is a manifestation of, or related to, his/her disability. The IDEA imposes specific requirements to fully implement this mandate...

PDE's failure to monitor AEDY programs and hold districts accountable has resulted in an overrepresentation of students with disabilities in AEDY programs. This overrepresentation has subjected these students to the collateral consequences that accompany removals to AEDY programs, including exclusion from the regular education system, multiple disruptions in their education program, and barriers to graduation. Research shows that disciplinary removals from regular school are associated with significantly higher dropout rates and a negative effect on timely graduation. ELC has worked with many students returning from AEDY programs who struggle when placed back in their traditional school, and far too many eventually drop out. Unfortunately, there is little evidence to rely on besides anecdotes. In fact, even though AEDY programs have existed in Pennsylvania for fifteen years, PDE has not collected any data on the outcomes of students placed in AEDY programs who are eventually transitioned back to their school districts. PDE tracks and reports how many students return to the regular school after being placed in AEDY, but does not track long term outcomes for these students. Because PDE does not track student length of stay in AEDY programs or link these students to other longitudinal data, it is unknown how many students cycle in and out of these programs during their high school careers and how many students languish in these programs for most of high school.

Based on annual data, the statistics regarding the percentage of students statewide who eventually transition back to a traditional middle school or high school are quite alarming. During the last three years for which there is data from PDE and despite the requirement for semester reviews, less than 23% of students sent to AEDY returned to a regular school classroom. Although this statistic is not currently captured, we believe that many students may drop out of high school. Thus, based on available data, the discriminatory impact of PDE's AEDY policies and practices not only results in placing students with IEP's in inferior programs, but may significantly increase the likelihood that these students eventually drop out of school.

B. PDE's Policies and Practices Discriminate Against African American Students in Violation of Title VI

Title VI prohibits discrimination on the basis of "race, color, or national origin… under any program or activity receiving Federal financial assistance." The purpose of Title VI is to ensure that public funds are not spent in a way as to encourage, subsidize, or result in racial discrimination. The Supreme Court has held that such regulations may validly prohibit practices that have a disparate impact on protected groups, even if the actions or practices are not intentionally discriminatory. Hence, Title VI prohibits government practices that have the effect – even if not the intent – of discriminating by race. Under this "disparate impact" theory, if a recipient of federal funding disparately harms students of color, those policies are unlawful unless they are justified by educational necessity and there are no less discriminatory means of achieving the same educational goals.

We contend that PDE, as a recipient of federal funds, has acted in violation of Title VI regulations by employing practices and procedures that, while facially neutral, have a disparate impact on African American students and that such practices lack a "substantial legitimate justification." PDE has propagated a system where African American students are overrepresented in inferior district-run AEDY programs. PDE has allowed numerous school districts to employ practices, which have contributed to the dramatic overrepresentation of African American students. For example, Williamsport's AEDY program data demonstrates that although African American students represent approximately 18.1% of the Williamsport student population, African American students account for 60.6% of all Williamsport students sent to AEDY programs…

PDE bears some responsibility for the overrepresentation of African American students in district-run AEDY programs because PDE has failed to review and sufficiently monitor the placement of students in AEDY programs, failed to establish and articulate sufficiently narrow criteria governing the placement of students in these programs, and failed to encourage and support less discriminatory means of achieving the same educational goals.

In terms of monitoring, PDE has collected data about AEDY programs for numerous years, but has not taken concerted efforts to address the overrepresentation of African American students in districts they identify. Additionally, PDE has propagated a discriminatory system as a result of the criteria used to define "disruptive youth." Currently, forty percent of all students referred to AEDY programs are referred for behavior that "disregards school authority or violates a school rule," the most subjective and vague category among the seven delineated. This category allows the greatest degree of discretion and thus allows the most room for potential discrimination…

V. CONCLUSION

Based on the foregoing, we request that the Department of Justice: (1) accept jurisdiction and fully investigate these claims; (2) perform district-wide compliance reviews of identified school districts, including their referral policies and practices to determine if they discriminate against students with disabilities, African American students, or other minority students; (3) compel PDE to overhaul its monitoring practices regarding local AEDY programs, including involving PDE's Bureau of Special Education in compliance reviews, requiring the collection of longitudinal data on students placed in AEDY programs, including graduation rates; and (4) develop policies and issue guidance as set forth herein on page three. In addition, we specifically ask the Department to investigate the extent to which public schools in Pennsylvania are utilizing non-authorized disciplinary programs similar to AEDY, whether students place in these programs receive a quality education, and whether particular subgroups of students are placed in these programs at a disproportionate rate.

Respectfully submitted,

David Lapp, Esq.
Education Law Center – PA
1315 Walnut Street, Suite 400
Philadelphia, PA 19107

Nancy Potter, Esq.
Education Law Center - PA
429 Fourth Avenue, Suite 702
Pittsburgh, PA 15219

Marnie Kaplan–Stoneleigh Fellow
Education Law Center

THE DIRECTIVE

On the morning of November 2, 2011, my supervisor, Susan Lozada informed me that Dr. Mayo; Interim Superintendent of Schools for the Allentown School District wanted to meet with us. Going into the meeting that morning we had no idea what the nature of the meeting was. However, Dr. Mayo made the concern very clear to us immediately upon the onset of the meeting. Dr. Mayo shared with us that he was hearing from principals and assistant principals that I was "blocking" the placement of students into the district's alternative education programs. Both Susan and I assured him that was not true. We made it clear to him that our alternative education programs had to comply with Pennsylvania Department of Education policies and expectations, especially in regards to proper documentation of interventions and protecting the due process rights of students. I proceeded to inform him of a regional AEDY (Alternative Education for Disruptive Youth) meeting I attended a few days prior where Drew Schuckman, State Coordinator of AEDY emphasized the requirement of completing and documenting AEDY mandated interventions and procedural safeguards prior to placing a student in an AEDY program. The mandates and safeguards included: documented interventions made by the home school, Student Assistant Program (SAP) services, adherence to due process rights for all students and a Manifestation Determination Review (MDR) procedural safeguard for special education students. Mr. Schuckman also emphasized that Pennsylvania School Code governs the AEDY programs.

We shared with Dr. Mayo that we had communicated the AEDY mandates and procedural safeguards with the principals and assistant principals, and provided specific feedback regarding incomplete referrals and the required documentation and/or signatures (due process) which were missing.

Upon sharing this information with Dr. Mayo, he replied, "We are operating under a state of emergency." He then looked at me and said, "I want you to expedite the process." Both Susan and I objected to the directive and made it clear to him that moving the students into the AEDY programs without proper documentation and compliance with due process would be illegal and/or unethical. Nevertheless, Dr. Mayo stated, "I want those students moved into alternative education."

Given the directive issued to me by Dr. Mayo, I now had a dilemma. I could comply with the directive and be complicit or I could refuse and be insubordinate.

The decision I made was to accept the referrals made by the principals and assistant principals as they were, move the students into the alternative education (AEDY) programs and then report the violations to Mr. Schuckman and the Pennsylvania Department of Education.

So on December 7, 2011, after the students had been reassigned to the alternative education program, their intakes had been completed and the students were attending, I contacted the Pennsylvania Department of Education to report the violations. After speaking with and explaining the situation to Mr. Gonzalez, a colleague of Mr. Schuckman, Mr. Gonzalez asked me if I clearly understood the seriousness of the allegations I was making and the potential consequences of reporting the violations. I told him that I did understand the situation. Mr. Gonzalez told me that he would inform Mr. Schuckman of my allegations against the district and ask Mr. Schuckman to contact me. Soon after my conversation with Mr. Gonzalez, Mr. Schuckman called my office. During our conversation I shared with him the meeting Susan and I had with Dr. Mayo including specific details of the conversation and the directive that was made. Upon sharing the information, Mr. Schuckman stated, "So you are self reporting violations within your own program?" I responded, "Yes I am." Mr. Schuckman then informed me that he would schedule a "formal compliance visit" to the school.

The following day, December 8, 2011, I received an email from Mr. Schuckman regarding the formal compliance visit. Upon receiving the email, I shared the email with my supervisor Susan Lozada and Dr. Mayo.

In the following pages, I have provided the email I received from Mr. Schuckman, as well as other documents relevant to my reporting the alleged violations and the findings of said allegations as determined by Mr. Schuckman.

Rosado, Jose (Sr.)

From:	Schuckman, Drew <dschuckman@pa.gov>
Sent:	Thursday, December 08, 2011 3:00 PM
To:	Rosado, Jose (Sr.)
Cc:	agonzalez@csc.csiu.org
Subject:	AEDY Compliance Monitoring Visit-December 13, 2011 (Allentown City SD-IBEAM Academy)
Importance:	High

Mr. Rosado:

Please consider this correspondence as notification that the Pennsylvania Department of Education will be conducting a formal compliance monitoring visit of the IBEAM Academy Alternative Education Program operated by the Allentown City School District at 10:00 AM on Tuesday, December 13, 2011.

We are conducting this monitoring with limited notification due to allegations made by various stakeholders pertaining to various non-compliant operations of this Alternative Education for Disruptive Youth Program.

The district is responsible to have appropriate administrative representation present.

Please have all required program documentation and student files available for review.

If additional clarification is required please contact me at the number listed below.

Sincerely,

Drew Schuckman-State Coordinator AEDY
Bureau of Teaching and Learning
Division of School Options and Safety
Pennsylvania Department of Education
333 Market Street-Harrisburg, PA 17126
Phone: 717-705-6908 Fax: 717-783-4392
dschuckman@pa.gov
www.education.state.pa.us

Notice: On **Friday, July 29th**, the commonwealth will be adding @pa.gov as the primary email domain for all state employees. For example: dschuckman@state.pa.us will now be dschuckman@pa.gov The email addresses ending in @state.pa.us will continue to function so that emails will never be interrupted. We appreciate your cooperation as we take a small step to increase the usability and consistency of the commonwealth's online communications.

1

From: Hartman, Deborah W.
Sent: Friday, December 09, 2011 5:45 PM
To: Togno, Nicole; Kemp, Theresa; Cunningham, Matthew;
             Bennis, Jennifer
Cc: Rosado, Jose (Sr.)
Subject: Compliance Audit

Tuesday – the state auditors are visiting IBEAM I am not certain what they will be reviewing. But, in advance please make certain your student's files are in order. That includes the current IEPs, RR, NOREPs etc. and progress monitoring. They may observe your classrooms and interview students and faculty.

I will be at IBEAM during their visit.

Debby Hartman

Rosado, Jose (Sr.)

From:	Schuckman, Drew <dschuckman@pa.gov>
Sent:	Friday, December 23, 2011 1:39 PM
To:	Rosado, Jose (Sr.)
Cc:	agonzalez@csc.csiu.org; Fitzgerald, Adam
Subject:	AEDY Compliance Monitoring-Allentown City SD-Final Report (IBEAM Academy) December 2011-ATTENTION REQUIRED!
Attachments:	Allentown SD (I-BEAM Academy) FINAL AEDY Monitoring Report December 2011.doc; Allentown SD 2011-2012 (IBEAM ACADEMY) Corrective Action Plan Notifcation-December 2011.doc; Allentown SD (I-BEAM Academy) 2011-20112 AEDY Corrrective Action Plan Matrix December 20111.doc

Importance:	High

Follow Up Flag:	Follow up
Due By:	Friday, January 20, 2012 4:00 PM
Flag Status:	Flagged

Dear Mr. Rosado:

The final monitoring report for the Allentown City School District (IBEAM) and required corrective action plan documentation is attached. Please review all comments listed keeping in mind that a response will be necessary for all items noted as AREAS REQUIRING IMMEDIATE ATTENTION. Please respond appropriately by submitting your corrective action plan matrix and signature document as outlined in the correspondence provided.

Please work with appropriate staff members to ensure understanding and implementation of required corrective action steps.

A hard copy of this documentation will be mailed to the district administration offices this afternoon.

Please contact me if you require additional clarification.

Drew Schuckman-State Coordinator AEDY
Bureau of Teaching and Learning
Division of Curriculum
Pennsylvania Department of Education
333 Market Street-Harrisburg, PA 17126
Phone: 717-705-6908 Fax: 717-783-4392
dschuckman@pa.gov
www.education.state.pa.us

1

Allentown City School District (I-BEAM Academy)
Corrective Action Notification

A Corrective action Plan is needed because of the following deficiencies or non-compliant program components:

1. District has placed students in this program that do not qualify for AEDY placement. The AEDY Program is a disciplinary exclusion program and must serve no other purpose.

2. District placed students in this program without implementing required behavioral interventions. All interventions must be implemented PRIOR to consideration for AEDY Program placement.

3. District did not comply with due process requirements in some cases when placing students in this program.

4. Student referral forms relative to required interventions were incomplete and many were completely blank. This documentation must be present in order to execute placement in this program.

5. District placed at least one child in this program whose behavior was determined to be a manifestation of their disability. Students whose behavior is a manifestation of a disability may not be placed in this program as the AEDY Program is a disciplinary exclusion. This program must not be used as special education.

6. Special Education students referred to an AEDY program must have a documented, accurately conducted Manifestation Determination prior to referral to an AEDY placement. All other required procedural safeguards must be implemented prior to the change of educational placement. The district affirmed understanding of these requirements in the submitted AEDY Program application; however, the process described in the application was not followed.

7. Required behavior assessment for students as stated in the AEDY Program application was not implemented. Documentation to verify the implementation of required behavior assessment was not present in any student file.

8. District did not document the statutory required periodic review team meetings for each individual student.

   *See official monitoring report for specific items to be addressed and for additional comments.

This form and a completed Corrective Action Plan Matrix must be mailed to Drew Schuckman, State Coordinator, Alternative Education, 333 Market Street – 5th Floor, Harrisburg, PA 17126 **no later that January 23, 2012**.

* The signatures below indicate understanding of all non-compliant areas and assurance that a Corrective Action Plan has been implemented.

_____   _____
Mr. Jose Rosado   Date
Allentown School District

_____   _____
Dr. C. Russell Mayo   Date
Superintendent
Allentown School District

Rosado, Jose (Sr.)

From:	Rosado, Jose (Sr.)
Sent:	Monday, January 23, 2012 3:44 PM
To:	'dschuckman@pa.gov'
Cc:	agonzalez@csc.csiu.org; Lozada, Susan
Subject:	ASD - AEDY Corrective Action Plan for Non- Compliance
Attachments:	Secondary Principals Meeting 011812.docx; Behavior Chart - WAHS.doc; Threat Assessment Flowchart.pdf; Alternative Education Option Graphic.docx; Positive Behavior Support Plan for Children 011812.docx; Alt Education Application 2011-2012 - 011812.docm; ASD 2011-2012 AEDY Corrrective Action Plan.doc
Importance:	High

Dear Mr. Schuckman:

On behalf of the Allentown School District and as principal of the IBEAM Academy, I am submitting to you our AEDY Corrective Action Plan in response to your monitoring visit on December 13, 2011 and our Non-compliant Status.

In addition to the Corrective Action Plan, I have also provided supporting documents relative to our plan. I will also review our application on egrant to assure that all of the information is accurate and current.

I have placed hard copies of these documents along with the signed signature form (Dr. Mayo – Superintendent, Jose Rosado, Principal) in the mail to your attention.

I trust that you will find that we have taken the appropriate measures to address the areas of non-compliance. If you have any questions regarding the Corrective Action Plan or any other concerns related to the IBEAM Academy or our other AEDY programs, please contact me.

Thank You!

Jose Rosado
Director of Community & Student Services
Allentown School District
31 S. Penn Street, P.O. Box 328
Allentown, PA 18105
Phone: 484-765-4074
Fax: 484-765-4076
rosadojo@allentownsd.org

1

Allentown School District (I-BEAM Academy) AEDY Corrective Action Plan Matrix *(MAIL TO PDE BY 1/23/2012)*

Area of Non-Compliance	Action to be taken	Person Responsible	Target Date for Completion
• District has placed students in this program that do not qualify for AEDY placement. The AEDY Program is a disciplinary exclusion program and must serve no other purpose.	• Any non-AEDY qualifying special education student (3 students) who were participating in the AEDY sections of the IBEAM program have been placed into special education alternative education programs or returned to their home school.	J. Rosado, Director of Community & Student Services D. Hartman, Director of Special Education S. Lozada, Executive Director of Community & Student Services	• December 14, 2011/meeting with Acting Superintendent and Interim Chief Academic Officer • December 16, 2011/ meeting with special education facilitators • December 21, 2011/meeting with secondary principals and Acting Superintendent • December 23, 2011/meeting with school psychologists • January 6, 2012/meeting with Acting Superintendent – review of Corrective Action Plan • January 7, 2012/complete removal of 3 students • January 18, 2012/meeting with all principals and assistant principals
• District placed students in this program without implementing required behavioral interventions. All interventions must be implemented PRIOR to consideration for AEDY Program placement.	• Conduct file audit to determine what was missing from each student's referral process. Any missed items will be implemented. • Interventions will be implemented and documented during the student's initial	J. Rosado, Director of Community & Student Services S. Lozada, Executive Director of Community &	• December 14, 2011/meeting with Acting Superintendent and Interim Chief Academic Officer • December 16, 2011/ meeting with special education facilitators

23

Allentown School District (I-BEAM Academy) AEDY Corrective Action Plan Matrix *(MAIL TO PDE BY 1/23/2012)*

	45 day placement. • Revise referral process to include building principal checklist for interventions and due process procedures. • Train all administrators in disciplinary due process and AEDY referral process.	Student Services	• December 21, 2011/meeting with secondary principals and Acting Superintendent • December 23, 2011/meeting with school psychologists • January 6, 2012/meeting with Acting Superintendent – review of Corrective Action Plan • January 18, 2012/meeting with all principals and assistant principals
• District did not comply with due process requirements in some cases when placing students in this program.	• Conduct file audit to determine what was missing from each student's referral process. Any missed items will be implemented. • All families were informed of their rights during intake in alternative site. • Revise referral process to include building principal checklist for interventions and due process procedures. • Train all administrators in disciplinary due process and AEDY referral process.	J. Rosado, Director of Community & Student Services S. Lozada, Executive Director of Community & Student Services	• December 14, 2011/meeting with Acting Superintendent and Interim Chief Academic Officer • December 16, 2011/ meeting with special education facilitators • December 21, 2011/meeting with secondary principals and Acting Superintendent • December 23, 2011/meeting with school psychologists • January 6, 2012/meeting with Acting Superintendent – review of Corrective Action Plan • January 18, 2012/meeting with all principals and

Allentown School District (I-BEAM Academy) AEDY Corrective Action Plan Matrix *(MAIL TO PDE BY 1/23/2012)*

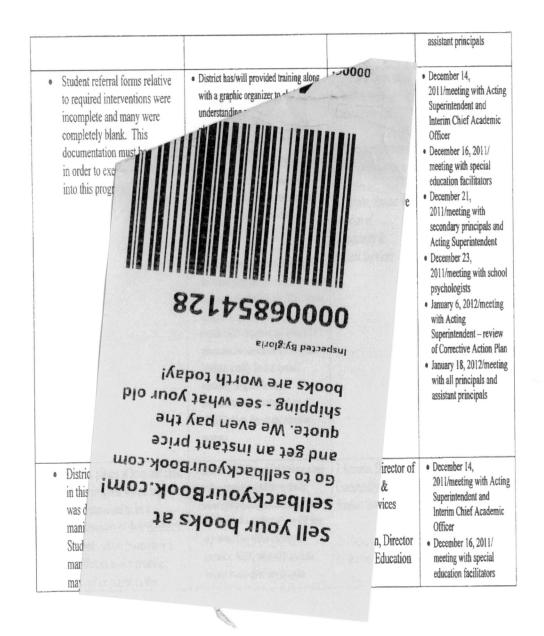

			assistant principals
• Student referral forms relative to required interventions were incomplete and many were completely blank. This documentation must b... in order to exe... into this progr...	• District has/will provided training along with a graphic organizer to ... understanding ...	00000	• December 14, 2011/meeting with Acting Superintendent and Interim Chief Academic Officer • December 16, 2011/ meeting with special education facilitators • December 21, 2011/meeting with secondary principals and Acting Superintendent • December 23, 2011/meeting with school psychologists • January 6, 2012/meeting with Acting Superintendent – review of Corrective Action Plan • January 18, 2012/meeting with all principals and assistant principals
• Distric... in this ... was d... mani... Stud... man... ma...		irector of & vices n, Director Education	• December 14, 2011/meeting with Acting Superintendent and Interim Chief Academic Officer • December 16, 2011/ meeting with special education facilitators

Sell your books at
sellbackyourBook.com!
Go to sellbackyourBook.com
and get an instant price
quote. We even pay the
shipping - see what your old
books are worth today!

Inspected By:gloria

000068541728

Allentown School District (I-BEAM Academy) AEDY Corrective Action Plan Matrix (MAIL TO PDE BY 1/23/2012)

program as the AEDY Program is a disciplinary exclusion. This program must not be used as a special education.	without a detailed list of interventions with clear timelines of student participation. • District offers an onsite fulltime, self-contained programs for special education students at the IBEAM site. This District operated special education program is not an AEDY program, but is the LRE placement for students with disabilities. Students qualify for this special education program through a reevaluation/IEP process and are NOREPed into the special education program.	S. Lozada, Executive Director of Community & Student Services	• December 21, 2011/meeting with secondary principals and Acting Superintendent • December 23, 2011/meeting with school psychologists • January 6, 2012/meeting with Acting Superintendent – review of Corrective Action Plan • January 18, 2012/meeting with all principals and assistant principals
• Special Education students referred to an AEDY program must have a documented, accurately conducted Manifestation Determination prior to referral to an AEDY placement. All other required procedural safeguards must be implemented prior to the change of educational placement. The district affirmed understanding of these requirements in the submitted AEDY Program application; however, the	• The MDR process for referral to an AEDY program will be reviewed and revised to be fully compliant with the stated application process.	J. Rosado, Director of Community & Student Services D. Hartman, Director of Special Education S. Lozada, Executive Director of Community & Student Services	• December 14, 2011/meeting with Acting Superintendent and Interim Chief Academic Officer • December 16, 2011/ meeting with special education facilitators • December 21, 2011/meeting with secondary principals and Acting Superintendent • December 23, 2011/meeting with school psychologists • January 6, 2012/meeting with Acting

Allentown School District (I-BEAM Academy) AEDY Corrective Action Plan Matrix (MAIL TO PDE BY 1/23/2012)

process described in the application was not followed.			Superintendent – review of Corrective Action Plan • January 18, 2012/meeting with all principals and assistant principals
• Required behavior assessment for students as stated in the AEDY Program application was not implemented. Documentation to verify the implementation of required behavior assessment was not present in any student file.	• Referral process will require behavior assessment for students during home school intervention period. The behavior assessment will be implemented, if student is placed in AEDY program, during 30 day review. • District has/will provide training along with a graphic organizer to clarify understanding and procedures for the placement of a student into any alternative education program, including AEDY programs. • District will revise the periodic review form to incorporate the documentation of the behavior assessment.	J. Rosado, Director of Community & Student Services D. Hartman, Director of Special Education S. Lozada, Executive Director of Community & Student Services	• December 14, 2011/meeting with Acting Superintendent and Interim Chief Academic Officer • December 16, 2011/ meeting with special education facilitators • December 21, 2011/meeting with secondary principals and Acting Superintendent • December 23, 2011/meeting with school psychologists • January 6, 2012/meeting with Acting Superintendent – review of Corrective Action Plan • January 18, 2012/meeting with all principals and assistant principals
• District did not document the statutory required periodic review team meetings for each individual student.	• District will revise the periodic review form to incorporate the documentation of the behavior assessment. • District will re-title the alternative	J. Rosado, Director of Community & Student Services D. Hartman, Director of Special Education	• December 14, 2011/meeting with Acting Superintendent and Interim Chief Academic Officer • December 16, 2011/ meeting with special

Allentown School District (I-BEAM Academy) AEDY Corrective Action Plan Matrix *(MAIL TO PDE BY 1/23/2012)*

	education form used for periodic review.		education facilitators
	• District will implement the process for the quarterly meetings on student progress to become fully compliant with the required periodic review team meetings.	S. Lozada, Executive Director of Community & Student Services	• December 21, 2011/meeting with secondary principals and Acting Superintendent • December 23, 2011/meeting with school psychologists • January 6, 2012/meeting with Acting Superintendent – review of Corrective Action Plan • January 18, 2012/meeting with all principals and assistant principals

COMMONWEALTH OF PENNSYLVANIA
DEPARTMENT OF EDUCATION
333 Market Street
Harrisburg, PA 17126-0333

Division of Planning
Bureau of Teaching and Learning

Phone: (717) 772-2813
FAX: (717) 783-4392
TTY: (717) 783-8445

April 26, 2013

Mr. Jose Rosado
Director of Community and Student Services
Allentown City School District
31 S. Penn Street, PO Box 18105
Allentown, PA 18105

Dear Mr. Rosado:

The Pennsylvania Department of Education (PDE) conducted a follow up compliance monitoring visit of the I-BEAM AEDY Program on April 23, 2013. This monitoring was conducted to verify the district's compliance with AEDY Statute and PDE AEDY Guidelines as a result of corrective action findings from a compliance monitoring visit conducted in December of 2011. The district was placed in corrective action status and required to submit a corrective action plan to the PDE. The district outlined actions to be taken to address each corrective action item.

A determination has been made to **remove the district from corrective action status**. The district has taken necessary steps to ensure program compliance.

Please contact the AEDY Program Office if additional clarification or support is necessary. We may be reached at 717-705-6908.

Sincerely,

Drew Schuckman
State Coordinator-Alternative Education

Cc: File

THE REFERRALS

Prior to the 2011-2012 school year, the Allentown School District AEDY middle school program consisted of one classroom in each of the four middle schools. Students assigned to the Alternative Learning Center (ALC) in each school received instruction from one teacher for all of the content areas, regardless of teacher content area certification, with no specifications for grade level instruction for students in different grades. This practice did not comply with Pennsylvania Department of Education AEDY standards. As a result, I recommended to my supervisor Susan Lozada that we remove the ALC program (classroom) from the "home schools" and centralize them by creating a district-wide program. My recommendation was supported. As a result, the ALC teacher and a paraprofessional from each middle school were reassigned to my staff. Under the new structure, students were placed in grade level sections and received grade level curriculum and instruction.

Middle school principals, assistant principals and counselors were all informed of the AEDY referral process and expectations moving forward. As expected, some voiced their displeasure with the change by contacting me or going directly to the superintendent.

Although the school board approved the change and the process and expectations were made clear, the home schools continued to send incomplete AEDY referrals to me for student placement into the program.

At the high school level, incomplete referrals continued to be made even after the AEDY compliance monitoring visit. When asked during his deposition, "Do you think that students had certain due process rights?" Dr. Mayo responded, "Students always have due process rights. It's fundamental." When asked, "And do you know if the principals were following them?" He responded, "I know the principals would have been following the due process rights, yes. I know they would have." When asked during his deposition regarding the documentation of due process, "Well, if there was a problem did you check to see if there was such an instance?" Dr. Mayo responded "Well, I had the word of our principals that I had spoken with, and their concern, and the collective concern of several of the staff..."

As the referrals will show, Dr. Mayo was not accurate. Was he being indifferent? Was he incompetent? Or was he not being truthful?

From: Rosado, Jose (Sr.)
Sent: Friday, August 26, 2011 8:23 AM
To: Derrick, Frank; Elliott, Susan M; Kruger, Kristin; Gabryluk, Karen P
Cc: Lozada, Susan; Hartman, Deborah W
Subject: ALC Placements

Principals,

I will need the following information/documents for those students that you will "grandfather" into the ALC Program at the start of the 2011-2012 school year:

- Copy of your "In-House" ALC Referral for each student
- Student's Discipline history for 10-11
- Interventions
- SAP Referral
- Signed Due Process Form

Please note – IEP students may not be placed in the ALC program at this time (based on last years discipline record) without consulting and having the approval of Deb Hartman.

Please inform parents – during the Due Process Meeting – of the ALC dress code. Students must adhere to the following dress code:

- Full-length dress pants (Solid Color) no restrictions on color of pants. No Jeans
- Solid color shirt with buttons and a collar (may be long sleeve, short sleeve or polo shirt as long as it has buttons and a collar)
- Must wear a belt and maintain shirt tucked in
- Sneakers, shoes or boots

Please forward student information/documents to me at the Admin. Bldg. as soon as you are able.

The 2011-2012 referral and other required documents will be forwarded to you in the next few weeks. These documents will be used to make New Referrals for this school year based on our new CSP.

Thanks,
Jose Rosado
Director of Community & Student Services
Allentown School District

From: Rosado, Jose (Sr.)
Sent: Thursday, September 01, 2011 9:35 AM
To: Derrick, Frank; Elliott, Susan M; Kruger, Kristin; Gabryluk, Karen P
Cc: Lozada, Susan; Hartman, Deborah W
Subject: RE: ALC Placements

Hello Principals,

I have received several incomplete ALC referrals. You should have shared my previous email with your assistant principals regarding the information/documents that must be included with the referrals.

The Due Process Form is very important. The home school must inform the parent/guardian of the placement prior to the student being placed in the ALC.

Please make sure that parents/guardians are being informed and afforded due process.

The parents do not have to agree with the placement, but we must inform them and document the notice via the due process form.

Jose Rosado
Director of Community & Student Services
Allentown School District

Rosado, Jose (Sr.)

From: Kitchenman, Patricia
Sent: Thursday, September 01, 2011 3:41 PM
To: Derrick, Frank
Cc: Rosado, Jose (Sr.)
Subject: ALC Referrals

Good Afternoon!

As per Jose Rosado the following students ALC referrals are not complete and cannot be accepted until the missing items are provided.

~~J.F. 100049~~--No Due Process documentation; no ALC referral, no SAP referral

~~J.G. 200902~~--No Due Process documentation; no SAP referral

~~R.M. 103409~~--No Due Process documentation; no SAP referral

The letter that was sent to these students was sent prematurely. The information needs to be given to the parents via the Due process meeting.

Please forward this informantion to Jose Rosado. If you have any questions please contact Jose.

Pat Kitchenman
ALC Counselor/Lead Person

1

34

Rosado, Jose (Sr.)

From:	Kitchenman, Patricia
Sent:	Thursday, September 01, 2011 3:51 PM
To:	Kruger, Kristin
Cc:	Rosado, Jose (Sr.)
Subject:	ALC Referrals

Good Afternoon!

As per Jose Rosado the following students ALC referrals are not complete and cannot be accepted until the missing items are provided.

~~2.6 112357~~--No Due Process documentation

~~WIO 109784~~--No Due Process documentation;no ALC referral;no intervention documentation

~~WIR 107786~~-No Due Process documentation; no SAP referral;no ALC referral;no discipline history;no intervention documentation

~~JM 212718~~--No Due Process documentation

Please forward this informantion to Jose Rosado. If you have any questions please contact Jose.

Pat Kitchenman
ALC Counselor/Lead Person

1

ALC Referral Form

School: _Trexler Middle_   Referral Date: _March 15, 2011_

Student Name: ████████████████   D.O.B.: ████████████

Grade: _6_   Homeroom: _121_   House: _Villanova_

Ethnic Code: *(circle one)*

1-American Indian/Alaskan Native; 2-Asian/Pacific Islander, 3-African American; ④-Hispanic; 5-White

Reason(s) for referral (Please check all that apply);

✓ frequent school suspensions

___ overt threat of violent behavior   ✗ Due Process

___ physical act(s) of violence   Form Incomplete

___ poses a clear threat to the welfare o

✓ behavior interferes with the learnin   ✗ NO S.A.P.

___ creates an unsafe school environme   Referral/Interventions

✓ disrupts the overall education envir

___ other (specify) _____

Which of these behaviors listed is of greatest concern to the team? _disruption_
of overall education environment

ALC Referral Form

School: __Trexler Middle School__ Referral Date: __4/1/11__

Student Name: __████████████████__ D.O.B.: __████████████__

Grade: __6__ Homeroom: __108__ House: __P.S.U.__

Ethnic Code: *(circle one)*

1-American Indian/Alaskan Native; 2-Asian/Pacific Islander; (3-)African American; 4-Hispanic; 5-White

Reason(s) for referral (Please check all that apply);

__✓__ frequent school suspensions

__✓__ overt threat of violent behavior

__✓__ physical act(s) of violence

__✓__ poses a clear threat to the welfare of other stud

__✓__ behavior interferes with the learning of other s

__✓__ creates an unsafe school environment

__✓__ disrupts the overall education environment

__✓__ other (specify) __Insubordinate on all accounts__

✱ NO S.A.f.
Referral /
Services

Which of these behaviors listed is of greatest concern to the team? __Creates an__
__Unsafe school environment__

37

ALC Referral Form

School: __Trexler MS__   Referral Date: __11·11·10__

Student Name: ███████████   D.O.B.: ████████

Grade: __6__   Homeroom: __116__   House: __Villanova Wildcats - House 1__

Ethnic Code: *(circle one)*

1-American Indian/Alaskan Native; 2-Asian/Pacific Islander, 3-African American; 4-Hispanic; 5-White

Reason(s) for referral (Please check all that apply);

_____ frequent school suspensions

_____ overt threat of violent behavior   *✗ Due Process*

_____ physical act(s) of violence   *Form Incomplete*

_____ poses a clear threat to the welfare of oth(

✓ behavior interferes with the learning of (*✗ NO S.A.P.*

✓ creates an unsafe school environment   *Services/Interventions*

✓ disrupts the overall education environme

✓ other (specify) __Attendance i__

Which of these behaviors listed is of greatest concern to the team? __By refusing to__
follow directions - defiant of classroom = school rules - walks (without permission)
halls - chronic attendance issues - disrespectful to teachers & staff
Provokes other students to model his behavior - disrespect + defiance

ALTERNATIVE EDUCATION REFERRAL

Program: _____ Middle School (ALC)

✓ High School (IBEAM/CIS)

School: William Allen HS

Date: _____

Student Name: ████████

Grade: 10

D. O. B: ████████

Student ID Number: ████████

Counselor- ████████

Parent/Guardian: ████████

Address: ████████

Phone: ████████

Language spoken in the home: English

Student's Dominant Language: English

Ethnic Background (Please Circle One):

1. American Indian or Alaskan Native
2. Asian or Pacific Islander
3. Black (Non-Hispanic)
4. Hispanic
5. White (Non-Hispanic)

rec'd 1/31/11

All referrals must meet the following established criteria:

- Regular Education Student*
- Minimum of Three (3) suspensions for the current school yea
- Considered disruptive as defined by Act 30, section 19-1901
- Interventions (completed, attempted, offered/denied). The att
  levels of Interventions (Administrative, Guidance Referral ar

*A Manifestation Determination Conference must be held for an I.E.]

REASON(S) FOR REFERRAL (Please check all that apply):
Students enrolled in this program must be considered disruptive as
Identify and provide documentation (suspension documents) that ap

* No
DUE
PROCESS
Brng in?
or wait
for due process?

*Schedule Intake

_____ Commission of a criminal act on school property
_____ Display/Use of controlled substance on school prope
_____ Violent behavior on School Property
_____ Threatening behavior on school property
___✓___ Misconduct Meriting Suspension or Expulsion
___✓___ Disregard for School Authority/Persistent Violation of Policy

PLEASE NOTE - Students will continue to be enrolled at the home school until an intake has been completed by the alternative education program staff.

VW

VERIFICATION OF DUE PROCESS HEARING FOR PLACEMENT

Please complete this form and forward to the Director of Community and Student Services. An intake will not be scheduled at the alternative education site until this is completed.

Student Name: _____   School: _____

Grade: _____   Parent Name: _____   Phone Number: _____

A due process meeting was held at the following date and time for the purpose of student placement in an alternative education program.

Informal Hearing Scheduled: _____   _____
                                                          Date   Time

Parent Contacted to attend: _____   _____
                                                          Date   Time

---

Result of the due process meeting:

☐ The student will be placed in the _____ alternative education program.

☐ The student will remain in his/her home school.

☐ Other: _____

_____   _____
           Signature   Administrator-Required

_____   _____
           Signature   Parent – Optional

_____   _____
           Signature   Student – Optional

4

ALTERNATIVE EDUCATION REFERRAL

Program: _____ Middle School (ALC)
___X__ High School (IBEAM/CIS)

School:___William Allen High School____

Date:_____11-9-11_____

Student Name:___███████_____

Grade:_____11_____

D. O. B:___███████_____

Student ID Number:__308379_____

Parent/Guardian:___███████___

Address:___███████_____

Phone:___███████_____

Language spoken in the home:_____English_____

Student's Dominant Language:__English_____

Ethnic Background (Please Circle One):

1. American Indian or Alaskan Native
2. Asian or Pacific Islander
3. Black (Non-Hispanic)
4. Hispanic
5. White (Non-Hispanic)

All referrals must meet the following established criteria:

- Regular Education Student*
- Minimum of Three (3) suspensions for the current schoo|
- Considered disruptive as defined by Act 30, section 19-1|
- Interventions (completed, attempted, offered/denied). Th|
  levels of Interventions (Administrative, Guidance Referr|

* A Manifestation Determination Conference must be held for an|

REASON(S) FOR REFERRAL (Please check all that apply): |
Students enrolled in this program must be considered disruptive |
Identify and provide documentation (suspension documents) tha|

Handwritten notes:

Ⓧ Interventions
— Blank   i. All three

Ⓧ Due Process   Placement
— Blank

_____ Commission of a criminal act on school property
_____ Display/Use of controlled substance on school property
_____ Violent behavior on School Property
_____ Threatening behavior on school property
_____ Misconduct Meriting Suspension or Expulsion
___X___ Disregard for School Authority/Persistent Violation of Policy

PLEASE NOTE - Students will continue to be enrolled at the home school until an intake has been completed by the alternative education program staff.

41

Behavior (please describe)	Intervention w/ Dates & Notes Administrative	Result
	• Parent Conference – Review Behavior/Discuss Expectations_____ • Reflection documents, apology, behavior contract, conflict agreements_____ • Connect student to school activities_____ • Involve teachers in meetings, mentors, conferences_____ • Address physical, Environmental Concerns_____ • Probation (if applicable)_____	

	Guidance Referral ____ ____ ____ ____ ____
	• Could be made by teacher/administrator or other staff
	• Referral must be related to disciplinary issues and discipline referrals
	• Must be completed by guidance counselor
	• Possible Outcomes:
	  1. Referral to Group_____
	  2. SAP Referral_____
	  3. Individual, group or Community Based Counseling_____
	  4. Schedule Modification_____
	  5. Peer Mediation_____
	  6. Conflict Resolution strategies_____
	  7. Mentoring_____
	  8. Check in/out_____
	  9. Parent Contact_____
	  10. Student created Action Plan_____	

	SAP Referral ____ ____ ____ ____ ____
	• Parent Contact_____
	• Possible Outcomes:
	  1. Contact without outside agencies_____
	  2. Mental Health Evaluation_____
	  3. Individual or Group Counseling_____
	  1. Community Based Services_____	

	Other: ____ ____ ____ ____ ____	

VERIFICATION OF DUE PROCESS HEARING FOR PLACEMENT

Please complete this form and forward to the Director of Community and Student Services. An intake will not be scheduled at the alternative education site until this is completed.

Student Name: _____   School: _____

Grade: ____   Parent Name: _____   Phone Number: _____

A due process meeting was held at the following date and time for the purpose of student placement in an alternative education program.

Informal Hearing Scheduled: _____   _____
                               Date   Time

Parent Contacted to attend: _____   _____
                               Date   Time

Result of the due process meeting:

☐   The student will be placed in the _____ alternative education program.

☐   The student will remain in his/her home school.

☐   Other: _____

_____   _____
          Signature   Administrator-Required

_____   _____
          Signature   Parent – Optional

_____   _____
          Signature   Student – Optional

4

ALTERNATIVE EDUCATION REFERRAL

Program: _____ Middle School (ALC)
_____ High School (IBEAM/CIS)

School: Wm Allen HS

Date: 11-15-11

Student Name: ███████████

Grade: 9

D. O. B: ███████████

Student ID Number: ███████████

Parent/Guardian: ███████████

Address: ███████████

Phone: ███████████

Language spoken in the home: English

Student's Dominant Language: English

Ethnic Background (Please Circle One):

1. American Indian or Alaskan Native
2. Asian or Pacific Islander
3. Black (Non-Hispanic)
4. Hispanic
5. White (Non-Hispanic)

All referrals must meet the following established criteria:

- Regular Education Student*
- Minimum of Three (3) suspensions for the current s
- Considered disruptive as defined by Act 30, section
- Interventions (completed, attempted, offered/denied)
  levels of Interventions (Administrative, Guidance R

⊗ NO S.A.P. Referral / Services

leted. All three
ted.

* A Manifestation Determination Conference must be held fo

. Ed. Placement

REASON(S) FOR REFERRAL (Please check all that appl
Students enrolled in this program must be considered disru
Identify and provide documentation (suspension documents

[ ] Commission of a criminal act on school pro
[ ] Display/Use of controlled substance on school property
[✓] Violent behavior on School Property
[✓] Threatening behavior on school property
[✓] Misconduct Meriting Suspension or Expulsion
[✓] Disregard for School Authority/Persistent Violation of Policy

7 (5).
e referral...

PLEASE NOTE - Students will continue to be enrolled at the home school until an intake has been completed by the alternative education program staff.

12-02-11 22:37 RCVD

Behavior (please describe)	Intervention w/ Dates & Notes	Result
	Administrative	
	• Parent Conference – Review Behavior/Discuss Expectations _11-1?-11_ • Reflection documents, apology, behavior contract, conflict agreements_____ • Connect student to school activities_____ • Involve teachers in meetings, mentors, conferences_____ • Address physical, Environmental Concerns _New seating assignment_ 11-14-11 • Probation (if applicable)_____	

	Guidance Referral ___10-27-11___
	 • Could be made by teacher/administrator or other staff
	 • Referral must be related to disciplinary issues and discipline referrals
	 • Must be completed by guidance counselor
	 • Possible Outcomes:
	   1. Referral to Group_____
	   2. SAP Referral_____
	   3. Individual, group or Community Based Counseling_____
	   4. Schedule Modification_____
	   5. Peer Mediation ___10-27-11___
	   6. Conflict Resolution strategies_____
	   7. Mentoring_____
	   8. Check in/out_____
	   9. Parent Contact _9/9, 9/12, 9/20_
	   10. Student created Action Plan_____	

	SAP Referral ___10-27-11___ _NO SAP Koffer_
	 • Parent Contact_____
	 • Possible Outcomes:
	   1. Contact without outside agencies_____
	   2. Mental Health Evaluation_____
	   3. Individual or Group Counseling_____
	   1. Community Based Services_____	

	Other: ___ ___ ___ ___ ___	

2

45

ALTERNATIVE EDUCATION REFERRAL

Program: _____ Middle School (ALC)

✓ High School (IBEAM) CIS)

School: Wm Allen HS	Parent/Guardian: ▮▮▮▮
Date: 11-15-11	Address: ▮▮▮▮
Student Name: ▮▮▮▮	Phone: ▮▮▮▮
Grade: 9	Language spoken in the home: English
D.O.B: ▮▮▮▮	Student's Dominant Language: English
Student ID Number: ▮▮▮▮	Ethnic Background (Please Circle One):

1. American Indian or Alaskan Native
2. Asian or Pacific Islander
3. Black (Non-Hispanic)
4. Hispanic
5. White (Non-Hispanic)

All referrals must meet the following established criteria:

- Regular Education Student*
- Minimum of Three (3) suspensions for the current
- Considered disruptive as defined by Act 30, sectio
- Interventions (completed, attempted, offered/denie
  levels of Interventions (Administrative, Guidance

✗ Interventions Page
- Not Included/Missing

npleted. All three
inted.

* A Manifestation Determination Conference must be held

lt. Ed. Placement

REASON(S) FOR REFERRAL (Please check all that ap

Students enrolled in this program must be considered disr

Identify and provide documentation (suspension documen

✗ Due Process Page
- Not Included/Missing

-C (5).

'he referral...

_____	Commission of a criminal act on school pr
_____	Display/Use of controlled substance on school property
_____	Violent behavior on School Property
_____	Threatening behavior on school property
✓	Misconduct Meriting Suspension or Expulsion
✓	Disregard for School Authority/Persistent Violation of Policy

PLEASE NOTE - Students will continue to be enrolled at the home school until an intake has been completed by the alternative education program staff.

12-14-11 15:13 RCVD

46

ALTERNATIVE EDUCATION REFERRAL

Program: _____ Middle School (ALC)
/ _____ High School (IBEAM/CIS)

School: _LED_

Date: 11/17/11

Student Name: ███████████████████

Grade: 9

D. O. B: ███████████

Student ID Number: ████████

Parent/Guardian: ███████████████
Address: ███████████████████████

Phone: ███████████████████

Language spoken in the home: _____

Student's Dominant Language: _____

Ethnic Background (Please Circle One):

1. American Indian or Alaskan Native
2. Asian or Pacific Islander
3. Black (Non-Hispanic)
4. Hispanic
5. White (Non-Hispanic)

ll referrals must meet the following established criteria:

- Regular Education Student*
- Minimum of Three (3) suspensions for the current
- Considered disruptive as defined by Act 30, section
- Interventions (completed, attempted, offered/denie   completed. All
  three levels of Interventions (Administrative, Guid   cumented.

A Manifestation Determination Conference must be held f   lt. Ed.
acement

⊗ NO
Due Process
— Blank

EASON(S) FOR REFERRAL   (Please check all that app
udents enrolled in this program must be considered disr   C (5).
entify and provide documentation (suspension document   he referral...*

_____	Commission of a criminal act on school pro
_____	Display/Use of controlled substance on school property
_____	Violent behavior on School Property
_____	Threatening behavior on school property
_____	Misconduct Meriting Suspension or Expulsion
X	Disregard for School Authority/Persistent Violation of Policy

EASE NOTE - Students will continue to be enrolled at the home school until an intake has
en completed by the alternative education program staff.

Rec'd 11/17/11

VERIFICATION OF DUE PROCESS HEARING FOR PLACEMENT

Please complete this form and forward to the Director of Community and Student Services. An intake will not be scheduled at the alternative education site until this is completed.

Student Name: _____   School: _____

Grade: ____   Parent Name: _____   Phone Number: _____

A due process meeting was held at the following date and time for the purpose of student placement in an alternative education program.

Informal Hearing Scheduled: _____   _____
                              Date   Time

Parent Contacted to attend: _____   _____
                              Date   Time

Result of the due process meeting:

☐   The student will be placed in the _____ alternative education program.

☐   The student will remain in his/her home school.

☐   Other: _____

_____	_____
Signature	Administrator-Required
_____	_____
Signature	Parent – Optional
_____	_____
Signature	Student – Optional

TEAM MEMBERS – "Please Print Clearly"

4

ALTERNATIVE EDUCATION REFERRAL

Program: _____ Middle School (ALC)
_____ High School (BEAM/CIS)

School: WAHS	Parent/Guardian: ███████
Date: 11/18/11	Address: ███████
Student Name: ███████	Phone: ███████
Grade: 10	Language spoken in the home: English
D.O.B: ███████	Student's Dominant Language: English
Student ID Number: ███████	Ethnic Background (Please Circle One):
███████ -Counselor	1. American Indian or Alaskan Native 2. Asian or Pacific Islander 3. Black (Non-Hispanic) 4. Hispanic Rec'd 11/21/11 5. White (Non-Hispanic)

All referrals must meet the following established criteria:

- Regular Education Student*
- Minimum of Three (3) suspensions for the current school year. (Attach suspension documents)
- Considered disruptive as defined by Act 30, section 19-1901-C (5)
- Interventions (completed, attempted, offered/denied). The attached intervention sheet must be completed. All three levels of Interventions (Administrative, Guidance Referral and S.A.P. Referral) must be documented.

* A Manifestation Determination Conference must be held for an I.E.P. student being considered for an Alt. Ed. Placement

REASON(S) FOR REFERRAL   (Please check all that apply):
*Students enrolled in this program must be considered disruptive as Defined by Act 30, Section 19-1901-C (5).
Identify and provide documentation (suspension documents) that applies to each behavior resulting in the referral...*

_____	Commission of a criminal act on school property
_____	Display/Use of controlled substance on school property
_____	Violent behavior on School Property
_____	Threatening behavior on school property
✓	Misconduct Meriting Suspension or Expulsion
✓	Disregard for School Authority/Persistent Violation of Policy

No Due Process

**PLEASE NOTE - Students will continue to be enrolled at the
been completed by the alternative education program staff.**

VERIFICATION OF DUE PROCESS HEARING FOR PLACEMENT

Please complete this form and forward to the Director of Community and Student Services. An intake will not be scheduled at the alternative education site until this is completed.

Student Name: ███████████████████   School: WAHS

Grade: 10   Parent Name: ███████████████   Phone Number: ███████████

A due process meeting was held at the following date and time for the purpose of student placement in an alternative education program.

Informal Hearing Scheduled: _____   _____
                               Date   Time

Parent Contacted to attend: _____   _____
                               Date   Time

Result of the due process meeting:

☐ The student will be placed in the _____ alternative education program.

☐ The student will remain in his/her home school.

☐ Other: _____

_____   _____
Signature   Administrator-Required

_____   _____
Signature   Parent – Optional

_____   _____
Signature   Student – Optional

4

ALTERNATIVE EDUCATION REFERRAL

Program: __X__ Middle School (ALC)
_____ High School (IBEAM/CIS)

School: _Harrison-Morton_

Date: _November 30, 2011_

Student Name: ███████

Grade: _6th_

D. O. B: ███████

Student ID Number: ███████

Parent/Guardian: ███████
Address: ███████

Phone: ███████

Language spoken in the home: _English_

Student's Dominant Language: _English_

Ethnic Background (Please Circle One):

1. American Indian or Alaskan Native
2. Asian or Pacific Islander
3. Black (Non-Hispanic)
4. (Hispanic)
5. White (Non-Hispanic)

All referrals must meet the following established criteria:

- Regular Education Student*
- Minimum of Three (3) suspensions for the current sc
- Considered disruptive as defined by Act 30, section
- Interventions (completed, attempted, offered/denied
  three levels of Interventions (Administrative, Guidan

**⊗ NO
Due Process
- Blank**

ompleted. All
ımented.

Ed.

* **A Manifestation Determination Conference must be held for**
Placement

REASON(S) FOR REFERRAL (Please check all that appl
Students enrolled in this program must be considered disrup
Identify and provide documentation (suspension documents

(5).
referral...

_____ Commission of a criminal act on school prop___
_____ Display/Use of controlled substance on school property
_____ Violent behavior on School Property
__X___ Threatening behavior on school property
_____ Misconduct Meriting Suspension or Expulsion
__X___ Disregard for School Authority/Persistent Violation of Policy

PLEASE NOTE - Students will continue to be enrolled at the home school until an intake has
been completed by the alternative education program staff.

12-19-11 19:53 RCVD

VERIFICATION OF DUE PROCESS HEARING FOR PLACEMENT

Please complete this form and forward to the Director of Community and Student Services. An intake will not be scheduled at the alternative education site until this is completed.

Student Name: _____   School: _____

Grade: _____ Parent Name: _____   Phone Number: _____

A due process meeting was held at the following date and time for the purpose of student placement in an alternative education program.

Informal Hearing Scheduled: _____   _____
                                Date   Time

Parent Contacted to attend: _____   _____
                                Date   Time

Result of the due process meeting:

☐   The student will be placed in the _____ alternative education program.

☐   The student will remain in his/her home school.

☐   Other: _____

_____   _____
       Signature   Administrator-Required

_____   _____
       Signature   Parent – Optional

_____   _____
       Signature   Student – Optional

TEAM MEMBERS – "Please Print Clearly"

4

DEAR PRINCIPAL, MY TEACHER IS A BULLY

B y the end of the 2011-2012 school year, it was evident to me that my concerns regarding my assessment that a teacher had created a "hostile work environment for staff and an unhealthy learning environment for students" would not be appropriately addressed by the district. Therefore, I made the decision to share my concerns in an op-ed letter, in an effort to inform the community and the school board.

It was my hope that shedding light on this concern, in a public forum, would move people to action in support of my students. Unfortunately, it was not enough to get the desired result. However, it did place an additional focus on me on the part of the superintendent and the teacher's union.

The following op-ed letter was published in The Morning Call on July 4, 2012:

They are teased, ridiculed, belittled and made to feel unworthy. Those tormented by bullies often feel a sense of hopelessness and despair. They are made to feel this way by their bullies – peers, acquaintances and sometimes teachers.

Over the past few years, the issue of bullying has grabbed national attention and has pushed state lawmakers to pass new legislation to protect the targets of bullies. The Massachusetts Anti-Bullying Law was passed in 2010, in response to the suicides of two young students tormented by bullies. This bill requires teachers and other school staff to report bullying to the principal, mandates annual anti-bullying training for teachers and staff, and calls for anti-bullying lessons to be included as part of the curriculum at every grade level.

In New Jersey lawmakers passed the Anti-Bullying Bill of Rights in September 2011 – one year after Tyler Clementi, an 18-year-old Rutgers University freshman committed suicide after being tormented online by his roommate.

Suicides related to bullying justifiably draw attention and deserve justice. However, most victims of bullying do not kill themselves. Instead many are chronically absent from school, turn to drugs and alcohol, injure themselves, become sad and depressed, or drop out of school.

The most recent high-profile bullying case, which involved a 10-year-old autistic boy from New jersey and his teachers, demonstrated how important it is to listen when students appear troubled by the thought of going to school. Although Akian Chaifetz could not articulate the bullying he was subjected to by some of his teachers, his father was able to give him a voice by placing a recorder in his pocket.

This case suggests that the best defense we can provide for those targeted by bullies is an opportunity to be heard. We must provide these individuals a voice – a safety outlet where they feel comfortable and confident enough to step up and expose their tormentors.

This case also exposed that the people we entrust to protect our students – teachers – sometimes violate that trust and engage in bullying behaviors directed at their students.

Unfortunately exposing these cases does little to curtail the problem.

The lack of specific legislation to address bully teachers combined with a powerful and politically influential teacher's union stacks the odds against our most vulnerable students.

As a public school administrator, this really is very frustrating. Based on what my students have told me regarding their experiences with bully teachers, I could write this letter for them:

Dear Principal,

I have been absent from school a lot lately, my grades have dropped and I feel sad and depressed. Some of my teachers may have reported that they have seen me crying in class and that I have asked to speak with my guidance counselor more frequently. Each time I spoke with someone regarding an incident where I was bullied, I was asked to complete a student statement form and report the incident. I actually completed several forms describing the bullying behaviors and I pleaded with you to do something, often shedding tears on the forms as I wrote. Unfortunately, I found that the abuse only got worse. My bully knows that I have reported the bullying to you. This teacher has made comments in class about students writing reports. The fact that the teacher can make fun of this situation only suggests that you are also powerless to stop this bully from inflicting more abuse on those of us targeted. If you cant protect us from this bully, then who can?

I'm very troubled and confused. I thought teachers became teachers because they wanted to motivate and inspire students. I know that most do. But for all the positive things that good teachers do to help students like me, it only takes one bad teacher – a bully teacher – to tear it down. One of my teachers told me that bad teachers are protected by the teacher's union and tenure. My only question is: Who is supposed to protect me? I don't think I can take this much longer!

As Pennsylvania lawmakers continue to propose new anti-bullying legislation, this may be a great opportunity for them to set the standard for other states by passing legislation with specific language intended to protect our students from bully teachers.

Special Education – We Have a "Serious Problem"
===◆===

As detailed in the Education Law Center complaint to the U.S. Department of Justice, special education students are afforded specific protections under the law. It is the professional responsibility of teachers, counselors, special education administrators, building level administrators as well as central office administrators to adhere to the laws and provide the appropriate services and protections including due process requirements. Unfortunately, this does not always happen and special education students often do not receive the more costly services and specific educational programing detailed in their I.E.P. (Individualized Education Plan).

Is this the result of limited resources, indifference or incompetence?

Rosado, Jose (Sr.)

From:	Hartman, Deborah W.
Sent:	Tuesday, June 12, 2012 8:08 AM
To:	Rosado, Jose (Sr.)
Cc:	Novak, Logan; Bronson, Matthew R; Brady, Brigid E
Subject:	IBEAM Student – ██████████

Jose
As a follow-up to our discussion – re: ██████████

The student we discussed is appropriate for the IBEAM program... He is very high adaptively (including street smarts)... Actually in a LifeSkills – this does present some challenges. He can outsmart the MR student quickly and actually take advantage of his adaptive skills. Academically his functions at a mid-elementary level, but understand concepts presented verbally or through demonstration. He is a transfer from New Jersey. **Our reevaluation confirms the MR diagnosis, but confirms his social-ability.** IBEAM is considered the LRE for him. He threatened his teacher and pushed his para. He should begin the school year there (at IBEAM) and we will reassess how responsive he is during the first quarter. Please remember the MR status prevent the suspension option.

Deborah Hartman
Director of Special Education
Allentown School District
31 South Penn Street, Box 328
Allentown, PA 18105
hartmand@allentownsd.org
484-765-4162
FAX 484-765-4188

This e-mail and any attachments are pre-decisional, for discussion purposes only, or draft working papers.

1

From: Hartman, Deborah W.
Sent: Monday, May 02, 2011 3:53 PM
To: Brodt, Rebecca
Cc: Rosado, Jose (Sr.); Brady, Brigid E
Subject: Male Student - Latino/Hispanic (Special Education)

Becky,

Please move (Student) from VISTA to IBEAM (ASAP). Notify Jeremy Warrick (probation) of this change in placement. Thank you.

PS I know he is an 8th grader, but we are close enough to the end of the year to make the move.

Debby

Deborah W. Hartman
Director of Special Education

From: Novak, Logan
Sent: Monday, September 12, 2011 3:29 PM
To: Rosado, Jose (Sr.)
Subject: Male Student - Latino/Hispanic (Special Education)

Jose,

I just wanted to touch base with you regarding (Student). He was an 8th grader at IBEAM last year, who was unsuccessful in passing the 2010-2011 school year. This makes him an 8th grader again this year. I just wanted to bring this to your attention.

Logan

From: Novak, Logan
Sent: Wednesday, October 10, 2012 10:25 AM
To: Brady, Brigid E
Cc: Rosado, Jose (Sr.); Lozada, Susan; Wentz, Nichole
Subject: MDR Request

Brigid,

We will need an MDR scheduled for Male Student - Latino/Hispanic (Special Education). He was involved in an incident in which he became physically aggressive with our security staff person. (Student) grabbed the staff member's shirt after throwing & knocking over desks in the ATS room. The student was restrained after grabbing the staff member's shirt. The information will be added to Sapphire shortly.

Thank you,

Logan
Logan Novak, M.Ed.
School Counselor
IBEAM Academy, Allentown School District

From: Martinez, Sam
Sent: Monday, March 11, 2013 9:43 AM
To: Wentz, Nichole; Novak, Logan
Subject: Male Student - Latino/Hispanic (Special Education)

Good Morning Logan and Nikki,

(Student) came into my office at 9:30, March 11 and picked up a pair of scissors off Nikki's desk and walked out into the hallway where I ended up coming after him to retrieve it. At that time he ran up stairs and Mr. Aziz (security) brought him back down and along with Mr. Blount escorted him out of the building

Sam Martinez
Fatherhood Coordinator
Communities In Schools/IBEAM Academy

From: Novak, Logan
Sent: Monday, March 11, 2013 11:58 AM
To: Brady, Brigid E
Cc: Rosado, Jose (Sr.)
Subject: FW: Student

Good morning Brigid,

Where are we at with this student and the IU? Any updates?

Thanks,

Logan

Logan Novak, M.Ed.
School Counselor
IBEAM Academy, Allentown School District

From: Szalachowski, Diane M
Sent: Friday, September 21, 2012 10:26 AM
To: Rosado, Jose (Sr.); Lozada, Susan; Hartman, Deborah W.
Cc: Nickischer, Genevieve
Subject: Problem

I just came across a meeting that was happening at Allen HS. It was for an intake for a special education student to CIS. Despite my numerous emails that stated this student was NOT eligible for CIS nor did she have the appropriate paperwork, a meeting was in process of being held at AHS.

This cannot happen.

Such back room deals are inexcusable. Do we have a process that it is to be followed or not? No meeting should be held without a special ed representative present for ANY special education student.

As per state regulations, this student would not qualify as an AEDY student to the CIS program.

We need to meet as a group and discuss this situation further.

Diane
Diane M. Szalachowski
Assistant Director of Special Education
Allentown school District

From: Nickischer, Genevieve
Sent: Friday, March 15, 2013 2:56 PM
To: Derrick, Frank
Cc: Morrow, Bob; Rosado, Jose (Sr.)
Subject: Serious Problem

Jennifer Young, facilitator at ALC, informed me that a special education student was placed in the AEDY program at ALC from SMMS. The student is (Male Student). I have notes from an earlier meeting with Sara Jane on this student. Moving him without benefit of legal documentation through his special ed paperwork is a due process nightmare. In addition, he was placed in a totally inappropriate program – more legal problems. I'm sure this was just a mistake, but we need to fix it. How would you like to handle it?

Genevieve Nickischer
Assistant Director of Special Education
Allentown School District

From: Rosado, Jose (Sr.)
Sent: Thursday, March 07, 2013 6:37 PM
To: ekelly@kingspry.com
Cc: Wildonger, David M; Lozada, Susan
Subject: Incident Report Re: M. Cunningham

Liz,

Please see the attached email below regarding an alleged comment made by Matt Cunningham.

Please consider this with the other information, which I have provided.

Thank you!!!

Jose Rosado

From: Hanna, Lynne
Sent: Wednesday, March 06, 2013 3:31 PM
To: Rosado, Jose (Sr.)
Subject: Today

A comment made today by Mr. Cunningham which I thought you might want to be aware of....

Today, during first period, Mr. Cunningham brought up (Male Student – Latino/Hispanic – Special Education) a past student, and told the class that he has "loveboy" tattooed across his chest but it's missing the "S" on the end. He said, "You know,... Love Boys...."

From: Rosado, Jose (Sr.)
Sent: Wednesday, March 13, 2013 11:05 AM
To: ekelly@kingspry.com
Cc: Wildonger, David M; Lozada, Susan
Subject: Re: Incident Report Re: M. Cunningham

Liz,

The student that Mr. Cunningham allegedly made reference to in the attached email (below) (Male Student – Latino/Hispanic – Special Education), has been re-enrolled at IBEAM today. I am very concerned that other students that allegedly heard the comment may inform the student of the alleged comments Mr. Cunningham made in reference to him (specifically the comment about the tattoo "LOVEBOY"….. "LOVEBOYS").

I will also consult with Special Education – Deb Hartman – regarding my concern.

Thank you!!!

Jose Rosado
Director of Community & Student Services
Allentown School District

From: Elizabeth Kelly < ekelly@kingspry.com >
Sent: Wednesday, March 13, 2013 11:17 AM
To: Rosado, Jose (Sr.)
Subject: Re: Incident Report Re: M. Cunningham

Jose,

Keep me informed if there are any developments that involve improper interactions between student and teacher. Thanks, - Liz

Elizabeth M. Kelly, Esquire

From: Rosado, Jose (Sr.)
Sent: Wednesday, March 13, 2013 11:25 AM
To: Hartman, Deborah W.; Nickischer, Genevieve
Subject: Re: Incident Report Re: M. Cunningham

Ladies,

Please see the attached emails (below). Urgent!!!

Thank you!!!

Jose Rosado
Director of Community & Student Services
Allentown School District

From: Nickischer, Genevieve
Sent: Thursday, March 14, 2013 10:00AM
To: Rosado, Jose (Sr.)
Subject: Male Student - Latino/Hispanic (Special Education)

(Student) will not be attending IBEAM. I hope the root cause of the issue can be addressed to the benefit of the students.

Genevieve Nickischer
Assistant Director of Special Education
Allentown School District

HARASSMENT

W orkplace harassment comes in many forms and is perpetrated by individuals at every level. However, regardless of the varying behaviors associated with the harassment or the title of the alleged offender, all forms of harassment must be taken seriously and addressed per the employer's harassment policy. When this does not happen consistently, it can lend itself to a hostile and/or unsafe work environment and potential legal issues. The issue of harassment and responding appropriately to reports and/or allegations of harassment is crucial in any work environment. Harassment in a school setting, where you have students interacting with adults, can often present unique challenges due to the age difference and status difference between the two groups. Therefore, it is paramount that concerns and/or allegations of harassment between a student and a teacher (or any adult) be afforded the proper attention regardless of the potential political challenges and/or retaliation that can result.

Failure to do so is a derelict of duty!

February 15, 2012

MEMORANDUM

TO: Susan Lozada, Executive Director

FROM: **Jose Rosado, Principal, IBEAM Academy**

SUBJECT: **Concern Regarding Ryan Miller/Student Interactions**

CC: Dr. Regina Cesario, Rita Perez, Robert Wheeler

I have cause for concern regarding Ryan Miller and his interactions with students at IBEAM Academy. Students that are removed from class due to inappropriate behaviors are asked to complete a student reaction form while they are in the "refocus room".

Several students have provided statements, which suggest that Ryan Miller's actions contributed to the disruptions. These students have characterized Ryan Miller's behaviors as "antagonizing", "annoying", "dramatic", "sarcastic", "rude", and "ignorant".

One particular student's reaction form has caused me significant concern. This form was completed by (Female Student – Latino/Hispanic)) on 2/12/12. I have attached a copy of her form along with a typed copy for clarity. I believe this student reaction form will justify my level of concern.

As the Principal of IBEAM Academy I have responsibility to investigate this matter in an effort to assure the safety of my staff and students and also to address any potential concerns regarding Ryan Miller's interactions with students.

However, my efforts to investigate this matter are impeded by Ryan Miller's refusal to meet with me without the specific representation of Deb Tretter during any meetings that I would pursue with him.

Attachments

IBEAM ACADEMY STUDENT COMMENT CARD

Student: Female Student – Latino/Hispanic

Date: 2/10/12

Student Comments:

I have an issue with Mr. Miller. He's always putting students down saying we're going to be "failures". He's very sarcastic, rude, ignorant and thinks he's better than anyone else. He's an antagonizer and pushes students buttons and then when we react we get in trouble when he's the one who instigates it. I've seen him do this with several students. I try my hardest to tolerate him but my patience can only take so much. I do what's expected of me so I could hurry and get out of here, but he always finds a way to ruin it. He's the only teacher I seem to have problems with. I'm not sure how much longer I can put up with him.

Reviewed By: Jose Rosado, IBEAM Academy Principal

Date: 2/10/12

February 15, 2012

MEMORANDUM

TO: Susan Lozada, Executive Director

FROM: **Jose Rosado, Principal, IBEAM Academy**

SUBJECT: **Proceeding with Meeting with Ryan Miller Concerns at IBEAM Academy**

CC: Dr. Regina Cesario, Rita Perez, Robert Wheeler

On Friday, February 3, 2012, I met with Ryan Miller to discuss a question regarding the IBEAM mentoring period. The meeting with Ryan was necessary because Ryan refused to answer my questions when I asked him during my walkthrough of the mentoring period.

At that time, Ryan stated to me that he would not talk with me or meet with me without union representation. I made arrangements to have Matt Cunningham (AEA Building Representative) available for a meeting with Ryan and myself. The meeting took place later that morning.

During our meeting, Ryan pulled his "union card" out of his wallet and placed it in front of me and said, "I want Deb Tretter."

Ryan made it clear that he would not meet with me for any future meetings unless Deb Tretter was specifically present to represent him. Ryan also stated that I was not to talk to him or question him regarding his teaching duties and responsibilities at IBEAM unless I scheduled a meeting with him, and Deb Tretter was available and present to represent him.

Since this meeting I have had and continue to have questions and concerns that need to be addressed with Ryan Miller.

His refusal to meet with me without the specific representation of Deb Tretter presents a concern regarding scheduling and the availability of Deb Tretter on short notice.

I trust that you appreciate my level of concern especially given that IBEAM Academy is an alternative education program and the nature of my concerns with Ryan Miller involve his interactions with students.

His refusal to meet with me without the specific representation of Deb Tretter impeded my responsibility to address the concerns in a timely manner.

I am seeking input as to how to best proceed regarding this matter in an effort to carry out my professional responsibilities as the Principal of the IBEAM Academy.

February 16, 2012

MEMORANDUM

TO: Susan Lozada, Executive Director

FROM: **Jose Rosado, Principal, IBEAM Academy**

SUBJECT: **Ryan Miller – Confrontational Behavior Directed at Principal**

CC: Dr. Regina Cesario, Rita Perez, Robert Wheeler

On Wednesday, February 15, 2012 I was scheduled to meet with Ryan Miller and Deb Tretter at 9:00 am, to discuss concerns I have regarding Ryan's interactions with students at IBEAM.

Mr. Robert Wheeler was scheduled to attend the meeting on my behalf. Just prior to the meeting I received communication from Mr. Wheeler that he would not be able to attend the meeting and that the meeting should be rescheduled.

Deb Tretter was already in the building at the time I received the communication from Mr. Wheeler. When Deb Tretter and Ryan Miller came into the Main Office, I asked Deb Tretter to meet with me in my office. While in my office, I informed Deb Tretter that we would need to reschedule the meeting because a second administrator was not available to attend on my behalf. Deb Tretter asked me to inform Ryan Miller that the meeting would be rescheduled.

At the point, I stepped out of my office and informed Ryan that the meeting would be rescheduled. Ryan asked me if he could ask Deb Tretter a question and I responded "yes". As I walked back into my office I informed Deb Tretter that Ryan wanted to ask her a question.

As Deb Tretter got up from her seat and moved towards the door, Ryan came into the doorway of my office and said to me, "If you knew we were not having the meeting why didn't you let us know." At that moment Deb Tretter placed her two hands up near Ryan's chest area and guided Ryan away from the doorway of my office and told him "Calm down Ryan, we have to reschedule." This behavior was witnessed by the secretary.

I did not respond or react to the comment that Ryan directed at me. After Ryan left the office, I asked Deb Tretter, "Was that appropriate?" Deb Tretter responded, "No it wasn't, that's just Ryan being Ryan, that's just the way he is, that's the way he has always been for thirty plus years, that's the way he's going to be, and you can't change that."

I followed by asking Deb Tretter, "Are you justifying the way he came at me? Are you suggesting that his behavior was appropriate?" Deb Tretter said, "No, it's just the way he is."

Considering the nature of my concerns regarding Ryan Miller's interactions with students and his confrontational and aggressive demeanor towards me, I believe that Ryan Miller is not appropriate to teach at the IBEAM Academy. Therefore, I respectfully ask that this matter be properly investigated and that a reassignment be considered for Ryan Miller.

From: Rosado, Jose (Sr.)
Sent: Tuesday, March 08, 2012 3:52 PM
To: Perez, Rita
Cc: Cesario, Regina; Lozada, Susan; Wheeler, Robert A
Subject: Ryan Miller
Attachments: Ryan Miller – Incident from 3-8-12.docx

Rita,

The attached email regarding Ryan Miller (Confidential Memorandum) requires your prompt attention. Please review this document and provide me your feedback regarding how we will proceed.

Thank you!!!

Jose Rosado
Director of Community & Student Services
Allentown School District
31 S. Penn Street, P.O. Box 328
Allentown, PA 18105

March 8, 2012

CONFIDENTIAL

MEMORANDUM

TO: Rita Perez, Director of Human Capital Management and Talent Development

FROM: **Jose Rosado, Principal, IBEAM Academy**

SUBJECT: **Ryan Miller – Continued concerns regarding interactions with students, Confrontational behaviors directed at Principal, Behavior detrimental to Staff and the Program, Investigation status, Schedule Change**

CC: Dr. Regina Cesario, Susan Lozada, Robert Wheeler

Please refer back to the Confidential Memorandums forwarded to you on the following dates:
- February 15, 2012 Subject:
  Proceeding with meeting with Ryan Miller/Concerns at IBEAM Academy
- February 16, 2012 Subject:
  Ryan Miller – Confrontational Behavior Directed at Principal

The concerns that I have detailed in these two documents, regarding Ryan Miller, continue to persist and escalate.

In my February 16, 2012, memorandum I requested "That this matter be properly investigated and that a reassignment be considered for Ryan Miller."

As of this date, I have not received any communication regarding my request for an investigation nor have I been made aware by you that an investigation would be conducted.

Since my prior communications, I continue to have concerns regarding Ryan Miller's interactions with students and his confrontational behavior towards me. In addition, I have been made aware of alleged "discouraging" and detrimental comments directed by Ryan Miller at other staff (teacher documentation has been provide to me).

In my opinion, Ryan Miller's conduct has created a hostile work environment for staff and an unhealthy learning environment for students.

As such, I have made the administrative decisions to change Ryan Miller's schedule in an effort to minimize his interaction with students and staff until such time that an appropriate investigation is conducted to address the nature of my concerns.

From: Rosado, Jose (Sr.)
Sent: Thursday, March 08, 2012 5:08 PM
To: Perez, Rita
Cc: Cesario, Regina; Lozada, Susan; Wheeler, Robert A
Subject: Ryan Miller – Incident Report 3/8/12
Attachments: INCIDENT REPORT.docx

Rita,

As per your request, please see the attached Incident Report.

Jose Rosado
Director of Community & Student Services
Allentown School District
31 S. Penn Street, P.O. Box 328
Allentown, PA 18105

INCIDENT REPORT

Re: Ryan Miller

Submitted to:	Rita Perez
Submitted by:	Jose Rosado
Date:	March 8, 2012

On this date at approximately 8:40 AM, I asked Mr. Cunningham (AEA Representative) to join me in my office so that he could be present when I handed Ryan Miller a memorandum regarding his schedule.

At 8:45 AM, I asked Mari Ortiz, IBEAM secretary, to call Mr. Miller in his classroom and ask him to come to the office.

NOTE: Teacher prep time is from 8:00-8:45. Students start at 9:00.

Upon Mari calling Mr. Miller, the following occurred:

- Mari asked Ryan to come to the office to see Mr. Rosado. Mr. Cunningham and I stood next to her desk.
- We were told by Mari that Mr. Miller said he was not coming to the office.
- I asked Mr. Cunningham to come along with me to see Mr. Miller in his classroom. Mr. Cunningham agreed.
- As we entered Mr. Miller's classroom he began to pace/walk throughout the classroom and stated "oh no … you know the rules…you can't be here…this is harassment…I want Deb Tretter…you can't do this…".
- I stated to Ryan that I was not there to have a meeting with him or to engage in a discussion.
- I stated to him that I needed to hand him a memorandum (attached).
- Ryan refused to take the memo from me and continued to make remarks about my presence and stated that I was harassing him.
- I told Ryan that his refusal to accept the memo from me was an act of insubordination.
- I gave the memo to Mr. Cunningham and asked him to give it to Ryan.
- Ryan refused to take the memo from Mr. Cunningham.
- Ryan walked out of the classroom and entered the boy's lavatory.
- Mr. Cunningham placed the memo on Ryan's desk. I asked Mr. Cunningham to please deliver the memo to Ryan.
- Mr. Cunningham entered the boy's lavatory and met with Ryan.
- The students arrived on busses at 9:00 am and had to be kept outside of the building until Ryan came out of the boy's lavatory and I could assess the situation.

- I made certain that no students would enter Mr. Miller's classroom and arranged for students to go into different homerooms.
- Ryan exited the boy's lavatory and went into his classroom to retrieve several items and then proceeded to go upstairs to room 201 as assigned.

INCIDENT REPORT

I was asked to call Mr. Ryan Miller by Principal Rosado to come into the office. When I called Mr. Miller's extension at 7281, I asked Ryan, "Can you please report to the office?" He asked for what reason, I told him that I did not know but Jose asked me to call you to report to the office. He said, "I refuse to go", then he asked if Deb Tretter was in the office, I stated "No, but Mr. Cunningham is here." He said, "No, if Deb is not here, I refuse to go to the office". I said okay and told Mr. Rosado that Ryan refused to come to the office.

Signed: Mari Ortiz, IBEAM Secretary

Date: March 9, 2012

From: Rosado, Jose (Sr.)
Sent: Friday, March 09, 2012 11:59 AM
To: Perez, Rita
Cc: Cesario, Regina; Lozada, Susan; Wheeler, Robert A
Subject: FW:
Attachments: MEMO 3-8-12 Ryan Miller.doc

Rita,

Per your request, I have attached a copy of the memo that I prepared for Ryan Miller yesterday. Ryan refused to accept the memo from me. The document was delivered to Ryan by Mr. Cunningham (AEA Representative) as detailed in my Incident Report to you yesterday.

Thank you!!!

Jose Rosado

MEMO

To: Ryan Miller
From: Jose Rosado, Principal
Subject: Schedule
Date: 3/8/12

Effective immediately – until further notice, your schedule is as follows:

8:00 – 8:45	Prep
8:45 – 11:30	Credit Acquisition – Science/ As Assigned (Room 201)
11:30 – 12:00	Lunch
12:00 – 3:30	Credit Acquisition – Science/ As Assigned (Room 201)
3:30	End of Contractual Day

From: Perez, Rita
Sent: Friday, March 09, 2012 12:11 PM
To: Rosado, Jose (Sr.)
Subject: RE:

Please call me or come to my office

From: Perez, Rita
Sent: Wednesday, March 14, 2012 3:47 PM
To: Miller, Ryan
Cc: Debra Tretter; Rosado, Jose (Sr.)
Subject: Teaching Assignment

Ryan:

Effective tomorrow, March 15, 2012, please report to your IBEAM science teaching assignment. Thank you.

Rita

Rita D. Perez
Director of Human Capital Management and Talent Development
Allentown School District
31 S Penn Street
Allentown, PA 18104
484-765-4231 (phone)
484-765-4239 (fax)

IBEAM ACADEMY STUDENT COMMENT CARD

Student: Male Student – Latino/Hispanic

Date: 3/7/12

Student Comments:

I was asking Mr. Miller for the page of the book multiple times and he just kept ignoring me. And I'm not the only student that has problems with that teacher. Mainly all the time I'm in Mr. Miller's class there's always someone getting sent out for dumb reasons. He slacks on being a teacher.

Reviewed by: Jose Rosado, Principal

Date: 3/7/12

IBEAM ACADEMY STUDENT COMMENT CARD

Student: Female Student – Latino/Hispanic

Date: 3/20/12

Student Comments:

Everyone is mad in class the teacher talks very loud and he is really sarcastic. I'm not in the mood I just don't really get along. He just talks annoying and I'm not taking nothing from that guy. If he would just not say a word to me, we will be ok. Mr. Miller needs to mind his business and educate us. He does everything else but that, and I'm not taking it. I want to do good and leave this school. I don't need this guy ruining everything for me. I can't deal with people like that.

He talks to me as if I'm going to be a failure. He doesn't know me. So I suggest he just mind his business.

Reviewed by: Jose Rosado, Principal

Date: 3/20/12

IBEAM ACADEMY STUDENT COMMENT CARD

Student: Male Student – Latino/Hispanic (Special Education)

Date: 4/2/12

Student Comments:

I do not want to be in Science because I feel like he is picking on me. I think that he does not like me because I can't talk. He will tell me to shut up or he would just keep talking and not listen to me. I was doing some work and he told me that he won't put a grade in for it. Today I was really mad so I told him to let me leave to a counselor and he told me to shut up so I did. Then I waited 5 minutes and he said no. I asked to go to the bathroom and got Ms. Rosario. So she pulled me out of the class and we were talking

Reviewed by: Jose Rosado, Principal

Date: 4/2/12

IBEAM ACADEMY STUDENT COMMENT CARD

Student: Female Student – Latino/Hispanic

Date: 4/2/12

Student Comments:

I asked Mr. Miller nicely a simple question about the assignment we were told to do and he replied very sarcastically "whatever you please" and I asked again and he replied sarcastically again and that's when I took a deep breath got upset and mumbled "f***" I slammed the book down and threw my pencil and just left. Everyday I always have an issue with this guy and I tried seeing if I can go to timeout or ISS (In School Suspension) and do my work there during his class so I can prevent these problems with him, but the behavior specialist said no. I talked to psychologist and he gave me advice and ways to handle certain situations but it's hard when he talks rude and sarcastic to me.

Reviewed by: Jose Rosado, Principal

Date: 4/2/12

Given the nature of the content documented by the students in the student comment cards, it would be expected that as the principal I would have intervened to address the concerns being reported by the students. Especially since I had already reported my concerns regarding the teacher creating an "Unhealthy learning environment for students." However, I could not intervene. Why not? Because I was directed by Rita Perez to "refrain" from interacting with Ryan Miller – a teacher in my building, interacting with students under my care!

From: Rita Perez
Sent: Tuesday, March 20, 2012
To: Jose Rosado
Cc: Lozada, Susan; Cesario, Regina
Subject: Miller follow-up

Importance: High

Jose:

As a follow up to our conversation just now. Please refrain from conducting walkthroughs or interacting with Ryan Miller until further notice. This request was also made to you on March 14, 2012 during a meeting with you, me, Susan Lozada and Regina Cesario.

Thank you.

Rita

Rita D. Perez
Director of Human Capital Management and Talent Development
Allentown School District

From: Rosado, Jose (Sr.)
Sent: Friday, March 23, 2012
To: Cesario, Regina; Lozada, Susan; Perez, Rita
Cc: Wheeler, Robert A.
Subject: Student Injury – Sustained After Confrontation with Mr. Miller

On Friday, March 23, 2012 at approximately 11:10 AM a (Female Student – African/American) was in the hallway during the changing of class. The student was in possession of a crutch, which belonged to another student. She admitted that she was playing with the crutch in the hallway and was confronted by Mr. Miller. The student was unable to write a statement due to her injury. She provided me with the following account of the incident:

"I was walking in the hallway playing with (another student's) crutch. Mr. Miller told me to stop and give it back to (Male Student – African/American). I was going to hand it back to (student) and Mr. Miller grabbed the crutch and tried to push my fingers off of the crutch (Injured student demonstrated how Mr. Miller made physical contact with her and tried to pry her hands and fingers off of the crutch). Mr. Miller called a behavior specialist and then snatched the crutch from my hands and walked away. I was crying so I walked to the bathroom and punched the glass to get my anger out."

NOTE: Student suffered a laceration and cuts to her right hand and forearm. The student was treated by the school nurse and referred to the hospital for medical treatment.

Student's stepfather, (Mr. —-), was called and came to the school. I met with (stepfather) and explained the incident based on the information I had. I explained that I was still investigating the incident and would provide additional information at a later time. (Stepfather) asked to meet with Mr. Miller and I explained to him that I would attempt to schedule a meeting for a later time. (Stepfather) was upset with the situation and expressed his displeasure with the teacher making physical contact with the student. (Stepfather) took his stepdaughter and left the school.

Mr. Miller provided an Incident Report to Mr. White (VISIONQUEST Program Director). However, I was unable to meet with him as part of my investigation due to his insistence on having Mrs. Tretter present for all discussions with him.

Ms. Avrich (Teacher) and Mr. Brantley (VISIONQUEST Behavior Specialist) provided Incident Reports.

Copies of the INCIDENT REPORTS will be provided with a hard copy of this electronic communication.

This incident will require additional investigation, including the questioning of the student, teacher involved and witnesses.

However, given that Mr. Miller refuses to meet with me without Mrs. Tretter present, I am requesting a consultation regarding how to proceed with the investigation.

In light of this incident, I would also like to discuss my concern regarding Mr. Miller's confrontations with students and my assessment that his confrontations have created an "unhealthy learning environment for students."

Jose Rosado
Director of Community & Student Services
Allentown School District

From: Perez, Rita
Sent: Friday, March 23, 2012
To: Rosado, Jose (Sr.)
Cc: Cesario, Regina; Lozada, Susan; Wheeler, Robert A.
Subject: Student Injury – Sustained After Confrontation with Mr. Miller

Jose:

Please give any hard copies to Kim Diehl – she will PDF them and email them to me.
I will contact you with further directions.

Rita

Sent from my iphone

SCAN Miller Incident Report
SCAN Averich Incident Report

On 3/23/12 at 11:12 ████████ was swinging a crutch
around and the hallway. I asked her to give it to me.
She refused (I called for a BS) and continued to swing
the crutch. As she got closer to me I took possession
of the crutch. (According to Mr. White) ███ then
gestured as if she was going to hit me. When I turned
around she was walking down to the bathroom. Then I
heard glass braking.

Incident 3-23-12 11:10 am

Students were walking back to classes from group. ████████████ was walking with ███████████, carrying his crutch in her hand. Student was confronted by Mr. Miller and told to give crutch back, he then grabbed the crutch out of ████████ hand, she became agitated. I told her to go in my room and relax, she started to cry and walked towards the bathroom. I announced that she needed a time out, then she punched the glass windowpane. I went into bathroom to check on student, her hand was cut and bleeding, I had her hold it under cold water, then wrapped in paper towels.

Signed: *Candice H. Ark*

Date: 3 | 23 | 12

From: Rosado, Jose (Sr.)
Sent: Tuesday, June 12, 2012
To: Taglang, Mary Theresa
Cc: Lozada, Susan; Cote, Brian L.
Subject: Ryan Miller Investigation

Mary Theresa,

Just checking back with you to see if you have the information I requested regarding the investigation of the incident between Ryan Miller and a student that resulted in a student injury.

I would like to have a copy of the findings of this investigation so that I may consider it for the summative evaluation.

Thank you!!!

Jose Rosado
Director of Community & Student Services
Allentown School District

From: Taglang, Mary Theresa
Sent: Tuesday, June 12, 2012
To: Rosado, Jose (Sr.)
Cc: Lozada, Susan; Cote, Brian L.
Subject: Re: Ryan Miller Investigation

Jose,

Susan Lozada and I interviewed the individuals involved or who were witnesses to the incident. The notes were then passed on to Rita Perez. It was conveyed to me that there would be nothing done about it. I do not have a copy or result of the investigation.

Mary Theresa

From: Rosado, Jose (Sr.)
Sent: Wednesday, June 13, 2012
To: Cote, Brian L.
Cc: Lozada, Susan; Taglang, Mary Theresa; Cesario, Regina
Subject: FW: Ryan Miller Investigation

I am very troubled and concerned with the lack of follow up/investigation regarding this incident. An IBEAM student suffered multiple cuts and a laceration requiring seven stiches after she punched through a glass window in reaction to being physically confronted by Ryan Miller.

I spoke with the parents of this student after the incident and told them that the incident would be referred to the appropriate Central Office administrators and that an appropriate investigation would be conducted. I also told them appropriate follow up would be provided to them.

Although I am the building principal, I was excluded from this investigation and was not provided any additional information until my recent inquires.

I do not know what, if any, information was provided to the parents.

Based on the email from Mary Theresa an investigation was initiated, but "there would be nothing done about it."

Please let me know what, if any, further actions are being taken to address this case.

Jose Rosado
Director of Community & Student Services
Allentown School District

MEMORANDUM   **April 13, 2012**

TO: Ryan Miller, Teacher at IBEAM Academy
FROM: Rita D. Perez
RE: Harassment Complaint

This memorandum represents a summary of my investigation into a complaint of harassment submitted on March 8, 2012 by Mr. Jose Rosado, Sr. Principal of record at IBEAM Academy, alleging that you took actions to create a hostile work environment at IBEAM Academy.

Mr. Rosado's complaint that you are creating a hostile work environment at IBEAM has not been proven on the basis of evidence uncovered in the investigation.

Nevertheless, the investigation has revealed that you admittedly do not espouse the IBEAM philosophy or approach to handling students; whish is contrary to the chosen approach that the District has directed teachers to use. Also, you were disrespectful to Mr. Rosado on occasion (e.g., the November 30, radio incident). These are matters of serious concern that will be addressed separately, as this memorandum is not intended for any purpose other than providing you with a summary report following investigation into the allegations of the Complaint.

You are reminded to maintain strict confidentiality. All communication about this complaint shall be confidential. If you are not satisfied with my decision you may appeal to the Superintendent pursuant to Board Policy 447.1

C: Deb Tretter, AEA President
            Personnel File

MEMORANDUM   **April 2, 2012**

TO: C. Russell Mayo, Ed. D
FROM: Rita D. Perez, Director of Human Capital Management and Talent Development
RE: IBEAM Harassment Complaints

On March 9, 2012, I informed you of a harassment complaint filed by Jose Rosado, Sr, Principal of Record at the IBEAM Academy against IBEAM Academy teacher Ryan Miller (RM). On March 13, 2012, I received a harassment complaint filed by IBEAM Academy teacher Ryan Miller against Jose Rosado, Sr., Principal of Record. I informed you of this complaint on March 13, 2012.

My investigation of Mr. Rosado's complaint began March 13, 2012. My investigations of Mr. Miller's complaint began March 14, 2012. The event that is the subject of both complaints occurred on March 8, 2012.

Deborah Hartman, Director of Special Education, assisted me with this investigation.

People Interviewed

Jose Rosado, Sr, Director of Community and Student Services; Principal of Record for Alternative Education:
March 13, 2012 & March 19, 2012
Matthew Cunningham, IBEAM Special Education Teacher & AEA Building Representative:
March 13, 2012 & March 14, 2012
Harold White, Program Director, VisionQuest: March 13, 2012
Ryan Miller, IBEAM Science Teacher: March 14, 2012
Debra Ninesling, IBEAM Social Studies Teacher: March 14, 2012
Candice Avrich, IBEAM English Teacher: March 14, 2012
Theresa Kemp, IBEAM Special Education Teacher: March 14, 2012
Alisha Keiser, IBEAM Math Teacher: March 21, 2012

Background

Deb Tretter, AEA President, asked if I would mediate a conflict between Ryan Miller and Jose Rosado. I agreed. Robert Wheeler, Cleveland Principal and ACT 93 President, was also present in support of Jose. The mediation occurred on January 18, 2012. Both parties recounted incidents where there was mocking, belittling and/or the perception of harassment. However, Jose initially refused to discuss prior incident/meeting because he had already responded and didn't have his notes. Ryan acknowledged belittling behavior towards Jose regarding adjusting the volume on radios ("do you want me to show you how") and also stated that he apologized twice. Jose stated that he refused the apology because he claimed it was not sincere. Ryan also claimed that his students are the only ones that receive reflection forms when they are sent to "time out". Jose denied targeting or harassing Ryan. Ryan stated that it was his perception and Jose's lunging and hand waving were intimidating. Jose's behavior during the meeting was indignant. At one point he forcibly pushed his rolling chair away from the meeting table and sat at the far end of the office with his legs crossed and used a loud voice to talk. Jose also recognized that he used his hands to talk. Ryan was at times sarcastic though calm and even toned. At the conclusion of the mediation both parties agreed:

1. Jose would schedule regular staff meetings.
2. There would be expectations for circle time.
    a. Jose indicated that a meeting was scheduled for January 25, 2012 and he would clarify expectations and provide staff with the opportunity to ask clarifying questions.
3. There would be no more one: one meetings between Ryan and Jose

Deb treated the mediation as the action requested for a Level I grievance, which Jose signed.

Facts

Both parties claim the other is creating a hostile work environment. Both claims were brought as a result of an incident that occurred on March 8, 2012. The incident began when Jose asked Ryan, via the main office secretary, to come to the office to receive a memo. Ryan refused because Deb Tretter was not present. Matt Cunningham, AEA Building Rep, and Harold White, Project Director for VisionQuest, were present.

Jose left the office and walked to and entered Ryan's room. Matt was behind Jose and Harold remained in the hall. Ryan became agitated and told Jose he didn't want to meet with him and refused to accept the memo. Jose made broad arm movements in trying to give the memo to Ryan. Matt and Ryan contend Jose was blocking the door and wouldn't let Ryan leave. Harold did not see Jose blocking the door. Ryan did leave the room and entered the bathroom door and called Deb Tretter. The memo was given to Ryan by Matt and Ryan followed the directive.

The incident occurred prior to student's arriving. Jose arranged the delivery of the memo for this time so the students would not be involved or see the incident. The contents of the memo directed Ryan to report to room 201 for a science credit recovery class. Ryan was not given advance notice, curriculum or a student roster. In fact, there is no student roster for this room. Jose stated on two occasions that the intent of re-assignment was to give Ryan a "time-out". Jose claims Ryan is guilty of insubordination for refusing to take the memo from him, though he eventually took the memo and complied with the directive.

Context

Interviews of IBEAM and VisionQuest staff found that Ryan has not invested in the IBEAM philosophy. Ryan himself claims to not agree with the philosophy and states that this philosophy of "hammer, hammer, hug" is the appropriate way to work with alternative education students. As a result, he has removed and has been stated "trigger" for students into inappropriate behavior that requires their removal from the classroom. It was reported that Ryan makes sarcastic remarks during "circle time" (staff debriefing) and in-services. Staff have reported that they have not seen the interactions between Ryan and Jose but have heard about them. Ryan also claims that Jose walks through his classroom without taking notes, giving feedback and at times "just stares at me or out the window". It has been reported that the supportive, skill building philosophy of IBEAM is rejected by Ryan and causes students to act out and resist going to Ryan's room.

Jose claims that Ryan challenges his authority and interacts inappropriately with staff and students. Jose admits that he has not approved individual classroom management plans, provided formal corrective action for Ryan's refusal to follow the IBEAM/District-endorsed policy or give feedback during walkthroughs. There are no classroom observations or summative evaluations for Ryan Miller. It has been reported that attention is focused on Ryan when others could use corrective focus. It has been reported that the academy climate has gotten worse since the new year and as a result of more frequent visits by Jose. It has also been reported that Jose frequently attends in-service, "circle time" and has frequent faculty meetings.

Findings

Ryan's refusal to follow and comply with the district alternative education philosophy contributes to discourse among staff, which is leading to the formation of "camps" within the building. In a building of about 8 ASD staff members, the division is highly detrimental to the formation of a supportive alternative education climate for students.

Jose's lack of leadership, demonstrated by lack of attendance participation in group meeting and not providing personnel and program supervision are contributing to the "I'll do it my way" mentality.

Recommendation

Both parties need to learn strategies for dealing with conflict, differences of opinion and anger.

Ryan must understand that he is being insubordinate for his continual refusal to comply with the IBEAM philosophy. If he intends to remain an alternative education and/or Allentown School District teacher he must implement the district curriculum and code of conduct and use professional and appropriate mechanisms for addressing concerns and facilitating change.

Jose must provide focused and structured leadership for alternative education programs. This includes regular staff meetings that focus on learning the IBEAM philosophy with opportunities to problem solve, plan and learn new strategies. Regular classroom supervision must include formal classroom observations, administrative walkthroughs and learning walks for teachers to see the implementation of the IBEAM philosophy.

Finally, a collaborative approach with VisionQuest and IU21 Sites Program must be initiated. While IBEAM is an ASD program our partners contribute to our success. The IBEAM philosophy has much potential and must be attended to in order to achieve success.

On April 9, 2012, Rita Perez sent a second memorandum to Dr. Mayo regarding her investigation (Harassment Complaints – IBEAM). The content of the memorandum was essentially the same as the prior memorandum of April 2, 2012. The only significant differences between the two memorandums were that the second memorandum included significant allegations made by Ryan Miller against me (Mr. Miller provided typewritten statement logging Mr. Rosado's actions). It is important to note that I was never presented with, nor provided an opportunity to respond to, the specific allegations made against me by Ryan Miller (obvious violation of Due Process). The other difference between the two memorandums was the recommendation. The recommendation made in the second memorandum included a 3-day suspension without pay for me.

Did Rita Perez change her recommendation on her own, or was she directed to include a 3-day suspension without pay by Dr. Mayo?

MEMORANDUM   April 17, 2012

TO: Jose Rosado, Sr. Principal of Record at IBEAM Academy
FROM: Rita D. Perez, Director of Human Capital Management and Talent Development
RE: Harassment Complaint

This memorandum represents a summary of the investigation into a complaint of harassment submitted by Ryan Miller, Teacher at IBEAM Academy, on March 13, 2012, alleging that you took actions to harass him.

After investigation, it was found that you engaged in numerous visits to Mr. Miller's classroom beginning in February, 2012 and continuing until the March 8 incident in which you attempted to give Mr. Miller a memorandum to place him in "time out," to use your own words. Unfortunately, Mr. Miller, who apparently did not fail to seek the advice and counsel of his union representative, filed his complaint of harassment based on all of these actions taken by you. Although I believe that you were motivated by the sincere desire to see the students best served and you wanted to end Mr. Miller's resistance to the IBEAM philosophy, which is a valid motivation, I must conclude that your actions toward Mr. Miller were ill-advised, because they did take on the character of harassment.

It appears that you did not know how to effectively deal with Mr. Miller's resistance. For this reason, a focused assistance plan will be developed for you that includes coursework in curriculum, instruction and supervision and you will be provided with a mentor who will work with you side by side to assist in your acquisition of the tools needed to effectively perform your administrative responsibilities until at least the close of the 2011-2012 school year. A determination on continuing the focused assistance plan will be made no later than June 29, 2012.

It is recommended that you learn effective strategies for dealing with conflict, differences of opinion and anger.

Because of the serious nature of harassment, even a lack of knowledge of effective management techniques cannot serve as an excuse. You are herby suspended without pay immediately for 3 days. While on suspension, you may not come on any school grounds or property of the Allentown School District for the duration of the period of suspension.

The information about the investigation and other information stated in this Memorandum are to be kept CONFIDENTIAL.

Any failure on your part to comply with the directive to cease and desist from harassing conduct toward employees you supervise will result in further disciplinary action up to and including termination.

If you disagree with any portion of this memorandum referencing our meeting, you may submit your written account, and it will be placed in the file with this memorandum.

C: Dr. C. Russell Mayo, Acting Superintendent
           Susan Lozada, Executive Director of Student and Community Services
           Robert Wheeler, Act 93 President
           Personnel File

From: Rosado, Jose (Sr.)
Sent: Thursday, April 26, 2012 11:14 AM
To: Mayo, Russ
Cc: Perez, Rita; Cesario, Regina; Lozada, Susan; Wheeler, Robert A; Fenstermaker,
            Barbara
Subject: Appeal of Suspension Without Pay

Dr. Mayo,

I am requesting to meet with you regarding my recent three-day suspension without pay. The purpose of this meeting is to appeal the suspension.

I am seeking to have the suspension rescinded and have my lost pay restored.

Please advise me as to the scheduling of this meeting.

Jose Rosado
Director of Community & Student Services
Allentown School District
31 S. Penn Street, P.O. Box 328
Allentown, PA 18105

From: Perez, Rita [ritadperez@gmail.com]
Sent: Saturday, April 28, 2012 11:40 AM
To: Mayo, Russ
Cc: Wheeler, Robert
Subject: Items requested in April 25, 2012 letter

Russ:

…You also requested a letter explaining my duress. My duress is a personal matter and I am under no obligation to discuss that with you.

Sincerely,

Rita D. Perez

On April 29, 2012, at 6:16 AM, "Mayo, Russ" mayor@allntownsd.org wrote:

Before Liz Kelly reviews your report on the Rosado investigation, I need you to put it in final form, as requested. This means the usual memorandum format you use to communicate these to me, which includes your conclusion and findings. What you have sent is a chronology of meetings, etc. I need you professional opinion of what you found for the record.

On the matter of duress, I am obligated to investigate any complaint (personal or otherwise) that is brought to my attention by an employee about working conditions. Again, I need to know specifically the duress you have suffered so we may investigate as soon as possible.

So, I still need two things from you: First, I need your final report on your investigation with findings, and second, I need to have your written explanation of the duress you feel that you have suffered.

Thanks,

Dr. C. Russell Mayo
Superintendent
Allentown School District
31 S Penn St.
Allentown, PA 18102

Memorandum

Date: May 4, 2012
To: Jose Rosado, Sr., Director of Community and Student Services and Principal
            of Record for Alternative Education
From: Susan Lozada, Executive Director of Community and Student Services
Subject: Focused Assistance Plan

This document serves as a Focused Assistance Plan. This plan covers the period from April 20, 2012, through June 29, 2012. This plan is based on the outcome of the investigation into a complaint against you by a staff member. My hope is that this plan will improve your understanding and increase your chances for success as an administrator and principal. The directives in this plan must be followed until and unless directed differently by me as your supervisor.

This Focused Assistance Plan is issued in response to your ability to complete your duties as an administrator and principal effectively. Specifically, emphasis is placed on improving your ability to supervise and lead staff and manage difficult situations with staff. This plan lists performance expectations in which you need support. Following these performance expectations, activities are listed to raise your performance levels.

You are directed to follow all items listed within this plan with particular attention to the activities intended to raise your performance. If you fail to follow any directives provided in this assistance plan, your behavior will be considered insubordinate and will result in progressive disciplinary action. Finally, if you fail to carry out your job responsibilities or tasks at satisfactory levels, disciplinary measures may be taken that may lead to termination.

As your supervisor all issues, concerns, requests, and questions, shall be directed to me for day-to-day questions. You will be informed on June 29, 2012 about the progress of your performance as it relates to this assistance plan.

The items listed below constitute the performance and activities that you must achieve and complete:

Performance Expectations

    A. You manage difficult or emotional situations judiciously.
    B. You exhibit sound and accurate judgment and react well under pressure
    C. You provide regular performance feedback to faculty and staff
    D. You develop the skills of faculty and staff and encourage growth

Activities to Address the Objectives

    1. You are to review, understand, and use appropriately the information provided in the Allentown School District Teacher Expectations, Evaluation and Development

Plan. If you are unclear after reading this information, you are to tell me, and I will arrange for a discussion with the appropriate person or persons.

2. You are to review, understand and use appropriately the Allentown School District Due Process Manual. If you are unclear after reading this information, you are to tell me, and I will arrange for a discussion with the appropriate person or persons.

3. You are to develop and implement an administrative walkthrough schedule that includes all teachers, instructional focus and feedback systems. If you are unclear after reading this information, you are to tell me, and I will arrange for a discussion with the appropriate person or persons.

4. You are to develop a professional development plan for the 2012-2013 school year, that includes staff input and focus on academic and social/emotional growth of students and includes the Wednesday early dismissal as well as district in-service days dedicated to building level information. If you are unclear after reading this information, you are to tell me, and I will arrange for a discussion with the appropriate person or persons.

5. You are to develop a plan for approving and monitoring classroom management plans. If you are unclear after reading this information, you are to tell me, and I will arrange for a discussion with the appropriate person or persons.

6. You will learn strategies for dealing with conflict and differences of opinion. If you are unclear after reading this information, you are to tell me, and I will arrange for a discussion with the appropriate person or persons.

We as educators and the district are committed to providing safe and nurturing environments for our students and staff. As such, it is my expectation that you will adhere to the requirements listed above, recognize and complete your duties as a member of a team of educators, and complete all responsibilities and tasks of your position at satisfactory levels.

Again, your performance will be observed and/or reviewed several times. A determination on continuing the focused assistance plan will be made no later than June 29, 2012.

Please sign below indicating that you have reviewed and received a copy of this assistance plan.

Sign: _____ Date: _____

Cc: Brian Cote, Executive Director of Accountability
        Robert Wheeler, Act 93 President
        Personnel File

On May 8, 2012, I met with Dr. Mayo to appeal my suspension. During our meeting I shared the following concerns regarding the investigation:

- I was never informed (by Rita Perez or anyone else) of the specific allegations I was accused of.
- I was never asked, or given an opportunity, to respond to specific allegations made against me by Ryan Miller.

Dr. Mayo told me that he had been informed "You visit his classroom 15 times a day for 20-25 minutes per visit." I told him that was not true. He then said "Don't hold me to this, I think I was told this or read this somewhere." I then stated, this is why I am troubled with the investigation and the lack of a hearing. I was not told what he had accused me of. I did not have an opportunity to hear and respond to his allegations. Dr. Mayo then acknowledged, "He's a bad teacher, I know that."

When I asked Dr. Mayo about the appeal process, he told me "Your appeal stops with me. I'll make the final decision. This can't be appealed to the board per board policy." He then went on to say "I know that you have been talking with people in the community, I hear things. What do you think that is going to do for you?"

Prior to concluding our meeting, Dr. Mayo informed me that he would "Conduct an investigation of the investigation." He told me that he would interview Susan Lozada, Deb Hartman, Regina Cesario and Bob Wheeler. When I inquired about Rita Perez, Dr. Mayo smiled and responded " Rita is not available, she left the district on less than good terms." I was very bothered by the fact that the person that led the investigation would not be interviewed as part of my appeal.

From: Rosado, Jose (Sr.)
Sent: Monday, June 11, 2012 12:50 PM
To: Wheeler, Robert
Cc: Lozada, Susan
Subject: Appeal of Suspension Without Pay

Bob,

I met with Dr. Mayo on May 8, 2012 to appeal my suspension. As of today, I have not been informed of his decision regarding my appeal.

I just met with Susan regarding a second Focused Assistance Plan that I am being put on as result of the suspension.

How can I be put on another Focused Assistance Plan while my suspension is still under review?

Please inquire with Dr. Mayo regarding the status of my appeal.

Thank you!!!

Jose Rosado
Director of Community & Student Services
Allentown School District
31 S. Penn Street, P.O. Box 328
Allentown, PA 18105

-----Original Message-----
From: Rosado, Jose (Sr.)
Sent: Thursday, October 18, 2012 10:10 PM
To: Mayo, Russ
Cc: Lozada, Susan; Wheeler, Robert A
Subject: Suspension Appeal/ Appeal to School Board

Dr. Mayo,

I have received a memorandum (Subject: Meeting Summary: Investigation of Investigation) regarding the appeal of a 3 day suspension without pay imposed on me as the result of allegations of harassment made by Ryan Miller against me.

Although the memo states that "after a thorough investigation of the investigation, it was determined that proper due process procedures were followed properly.", I still question and have not been informed of the specific allegations which were made against me. I was never provided with or presented any document which detailed the specific allegations made against me (Due Process).

I informed you of this during my appeal meeting with you prior to the investigation of the investigation. Also during this meeting you stated to me that "you (I) visited his (Ryan Miller) classroom up to 15 times a day for up to 20-25 minutes per visit.

Upon my telling you that this was not true, you stated - don't hold me to this, I think I was told this or read this somewhere. I follow up by telling you - that is exactly why I am so troubled by the suspension and the initial investigation.

At the conclusion of our meeting, you committed to investigate the investigation. However, you also noted that Rita Perez would not be interviewed or questioned as part of the investigation of the investigation.

I question how "thorough" this investigation could have been without interviewing the person that led the initial investigation.

Furthermore, during the meeting to discuss the findings of the investigation of the investigation I again questioned the specific allegations made against me. Once again, no specific allegations were provided to me. Instead, you questioned my leadership style. I was suspended because I allegedly harassed Ryan Miller, not because of my leadership style.

I am not in agreement with the decision to uphold the suspension and I want to pursue an appeal to the ASD Board of Directors.

You have stated to me that an appeal to the board is not an option afforded to me. You stated that you are the final decision maker regarding the suspension.

However, the memo from Brian Cote (10/3/12) does not note that my appeals within the district have been exhausted. Therefore, I will seek to appeal the suspension to the board unless I am informed in writing that my appeals within the district have been exhausted and that an appeal to the board is not an option afforded to me.

Thank you

Jose Rosado

Sent from my iPad

From: "Mayo, Russ" <mayor@allentownsd.org<mailto:mayor@allentownsd.org>>
Date: October 25, 2012 10:49:04 AM EDT
To: "Rosado, Jose (Sr.)" <rosadojo@allentownsd.org<mailto:rosadojo@allentownsd.org>>
Subject: RE: Suspension Appeal/ Appeal to School Board

Jose,

The last level of appeal per Board Policy #447.1 is the Superintendent.   Board Policies are on
our website.

Russ

Dr. C. Russell Mayo
Superintendent
Allentown School District
31 S. Penn Street
Allentown, PA 18102
484-765-4235 Tel
484-765-4239 Fax

"It's a Set-Up"

On October 11, 2012, I met with my supervisor Susan Lozada for an FAP meeting. Prior to discussing the components of the FAP and any specific performance areas, we talked about the basis of the FAP and the June meeting where the FAP was implemented. During our conversation Susan stated to me "I don't think you are going to be able to do it. It's an unrealistic FAP... near impossible... It's a set-up."

As you will read in the chapter titled The Depositions, Susan confirmed this conversation during her sworn deposition.

Susan shared with me that David Wildonger had said to her, the FAP for Jose "Has to be a priority."

I was not surprised to hear this, especially given what had occurred during the June 12, 2012, meeting where the FAP was imposed on me. As you will read on the following page, two versions of the FAP were ultimately presented to me during the meeting. At the time of the meeting, my suspension was still under appeal. As such, I questioned if the FAP (Version #1) would be voided if my suspension was rescinded? The FAP noted "This plan is based on the outcome of the investigation into a complaint against you by a staff member."

Upon my question, Mr. Wildonger informed me that the FAP was based on my 2011-2012, evaluation. I responded, this FAP does not state that. At that point, Mr. Wildonger requested a brief meeting with Susan and Brian Cote. Upon reentering the office, Mr. Wildonger informed me that the FAP would be changed to reflect, "This plan is based on your 2011-2012, evaluation highlighting specific performance expectations listed below" (Version #2).

As you will read in this chapter, Ryan Miller filed a second harassment charge against me. The outcome of the second claim of harassment revealed that Ryan Miller made "Falsified documented statements" against me. And although Mr. Wildonger was directly involved in the interviews during the investigation, when questioned during his sworn deposition "Now, you understand that Ryan Miller was found by the Allentown School District to be lying about Jose Rosado, do you not?" He responded, "I am not fully aware of all that, no." When asked, "Are you aware of it at all, if not fully aware of it?" He responded, "I've heard of it. I was not involved in that." Was he being indifferent? Was he incompetent? Or was he not being truthful?

Memorandum

Version #1

Date: June 12, 2012
To: Jose Rosado, Sr., Director of Community and Student Services and Principal
            of Record for Alternative Education
From: Susan Lozada, Executive Director of Community and Student Services
Subject: Focused Assistance Plan

This document serves as a Focused Assistance Plan. This plan will cover the period from the issue of this memorandum, as dated above, through the academic school year 2012-2013, ending on June 28, 2013. This plan is based on the outcome of the investigation into a complaint against you by a staff member. This plan is being designed to assist in improving your understanding and increase your chances for success as an administrator. The directives in this plan must be followed until and unless directed differently by me as your supervisor...

Memorandum

Version #2

Date: June 12, 2012
To: Jose Rosado, Sr., Director of Community and Student Services and Principal
            of Record for Alternative Education
From: Susan Lozada, Executive Director of Community and Student Services
Subject: Focused Assistance Plan

This document serves as a Focused Assistance Plan. This plan will cover the period from the issue of this memorandum, as dated above, through the academic school year 2012-2013, ending on June 28, 2013. This plan is based on your 2011-2012 evaluation highlighting the specific performance expectations listed below. This plan is being designed to assist in improving your understanding and increase your chances for success as an administrator. The directives in this plan must be followed until and unless directed differently by me as your supervisor...

Rosado, Jose (Sr.)

From:	Rosado, Jose (Sr.)
Sent:	Friday, June 22, 2012 1:04 PM
To:	Wildonger, David M
Cc:	Lozada, Susan
Subject:	IBEAM Parent (AR) Re: Science Grade - Ryan Miller
Attachments:	████████████████████████████████████

Dave,

Please see the attached message from ████████████. She is the parent that came to the board meeting last month and spoke with you regarding her son and Ryan Miller.

I was not included in the conversation so therefore, I do not know what, if any, arrangements or commitments were made in regard to the student's science grade.

Do you want to return this parents call or provide me with any information to pass on to her?

Jose Rosado
Director of Community & Student Services
Allentown School District
31 S. Penn Street, P.O. Box 328
Allentown, PA 18105
Phone: 484-765-4074
Fax: 484-765-4076
rosadojo@allentownsd.org

Community & Student Services
Contact Referral Form

Method of Contact: ☒ Phone ☐ In Person   **ASD Contact Person** <u>K. Toner</u>

Contact Information		
Name of Person Making Contact: ▓▓▓▓▓		**Date:** 6-22-12
Student's Name (if applicable): ▓▓▓▓▓		**Home Phone:** **Cell Phone:** ▓▓▓▓▓
Relationship to Student: Mother	**School:** IBEAM **Grade:** 10	**Special Ed:** ☐ Yes ☒ No

Reason			
☐ Suspension / Detention	☐ Attendance	☐ Enrollment	☐ Disenrollment
☐ Change of School	☐ Threat	☐ Abuse	☐ Bullying / Harassment
☐ Spoke with Principal / Counselor	☒ Other <u>Report Card - Final Grade Science</u>		

Details

Description of Concern:

▓▓▓▓▓ called to explain a conversation she had with Mr. Dave Wildonger at last month's School Board Meeting (May). Mom said she wanted to speak at the School Board Meeting but never did. She states Mr. Wildonger pulled her aside and stated the "incident" involving Mr. Miller and her son would not effect her son as far as failing Science and he would be pulled from Mr. Miller's Science class and would not fail the class. Mom also stated that Ms. Lozada was present during this conversation.

Mom received ▓▓▓▓▓ report card today he failed Science class and would need to make up the credit in summer school.

Mom would like a return phone call from either Mr. Rosado or Mr. Wildonger to resolve his Science grade.

Referred to: J. Rosado	**Date of Referral:** 6-22-12
Follow up:	

Referred to:	**Date of Referral:**
Follow up:	

05-04-12 P03:30 IN

EMPLOYEE COMPLAINT FORM – HARASSMENT

1. Name: _Ryan J. Miller_

2. School/Building: _I - BEAM_

3. Describe the conduct you found objectionable, including what force, if any was used; verbal statements (threats, requests, demands, etc.); what if any physical contact was involved (additional sheets may be attached):

     see attached documentation

4. The name of the person or persons alleged to be harassing you:
     Jose Rosado

5. If the alleged unlawful harassment was directed against another person identify the other person: _N/A_

6. Date of the incident described in #3: _4/20/12 to present_

7. Approximate time of the incident's occurrence, as described in #3: _see attached documentation_

8. Location of the incident described in #3:
     see attached documentation

9. Names of any witnesses to the incident described in #3:
     Deb Vinesling

10. Please briefly identify the actions you would like to be taken by the School District in correcting the matter you have identified:

I would like to be assured, by the Allentown School District that all types of harassment towards me, from Mr. Rosado, cease immediately, using whatever the district deems necessary to prevent further harassment of me in the future.

11. Date this complaint was submitted: Complainant's Signature:

_5/4/12_   _Ryan J. Miller_

RETURN YOUR COMPLAINT TO YOUR PRINCIPAL OR THE ASSISTANT SUPERINTENDENT, HUMAN RESOURCES AND OPERATIONS, OR THE SUPERINTENDENT.

After the Harassment complaint was founded:

1. On 4/20/12, at 3:00 PM, the students were unusually disruptive. One student said, "Don't worry Miller, they're just doing that to get you fired." Then, another student, (Student), began arguing with him. She said, "It was just us students and one teacher who signed it because we hate Mr. Miller. We just want to get him fired." Then, another student, (Student), said, "Our petition is going to hit the papers. And we'll get him fired."

2. On 4/24/12, at 10:15 AM, Jose came down to the gym, where I was the only staff member there, stared at me and smiled. I moved away from him. As he walked out of the gym, he stared at me again and smiled this time for over thirty seconds.

3. On 4/24/12, at 11:59 AM, Jose came in the classroom I am assigned to (room 201), stared at me when he came in the room. He spoke with Ms. Keiser, then stared at me and smiled as he walked out of the room.

4. On 4/25,12, at 11:25 AM, Jose came up to the computer lab, where I was the only staff member there. I said, "Can you cover the class? I need to go to the bathroom." Jose said, "No, you have a class." As he said this, he blocked the door by putting his arm against the doorway. I said, "Ok," and moved to the opposite side of the room. He stared and smiled at me, periodically, for the five minutes he was walking around the room.

5. On 5/2/12, at 9:05 AM, I received an email from Jose, stating the following: "Ryan, Ms. Avrich has requested that you not be present in the credit acquisition classroom during her assigned class period. As a result, you should not go into the credit acquisition classroom during your "as assigned" period as I previously directed. You should remain available during your as assigned period to provide coverage as needed." Ms. Lozada was cc'd on this email.

6. On 5/3/12, at 8:07 AM, Mr. White and Jose were in the main office. I asked Mr. White if I could talk to him in private. Mr. White and I went to another room. Jose came to the doorway of that room, as we were talking, and looked in. Jose made eye contact with me and left the doorway.

7. On 5/3/12, at 8:21 AM, I was talking to Mrs. Bennis. Jose stood nearby and stared at me. I immediately excused myself from the conversation and walked away.

8. On 5/3/12, at 9:45 AM, Chad Rutherford and Mr. White came down to my classroom, directed by Jose, to talk to me about a concern a student had about my well-being. I told them: I feel this building is not a safe place and is not helping students as best as it could. There is too much inconsistency. Some staff, in this building, get whatever they want, yet I cannot get issues of *Current Science* for $11.99 or even go to the bathroom, without worrying if I am going to get in trouble. I am dealing with the continued harassment by my administrator, as well as the thought that the students have regarding their thoughts "to get Mr. Miller fired". I told Chad and Mr. White that it saddens me that this building has become what it is…Years ago, I could do dissections, work with chemicals, and use microscopes. Now it would be unsafe to do those activities in this environment. I take pride in alternative education in

Allentown and to watch it fall apart is hard. I am completely capable of doing my job and helping the students the best that I can.

9. On 5/3/12, at 10:52 AM, I asked Chad if Jose asked him about what I said. Chad told me that Jose did ask and Chad told him that he offered services and Chad felt that I was fine.

10. On 5/3/12, at 1:40 PM, two students, (Student) and (Student), asked me to close the classroom door. They told me that two men took them upstairs, to the second floor, and asked them to write down "bad things about you." We said no, I ain't no snitch. He didn't even do anything wrong. He was trying to help us." According to the students, one of the men said, "Ok, we will check back with you later to see if you've changed your mind." (Student) also said to me that "the English teacher knew about it. She sent me up there, that's why she kept me in her room when you came to get us for rec."

5/3/12
Debra Ninesling
Social Studies Teacher
I.B.E.A.M. Academy

A student, (Male Student – Latino/Hispanic) came into my class around 10:30 AM. After (Student) began his class work, he started talking to me and another student about something that had happened earlier that day. (Student) disclosed to us that he was pulled into a room in the building and he was asked to write down stuff and sign his name to a paper about Mr. Miller. (Student) referenced a conversation he and some other students had with Mr. Miller. (Student) felt Mr. Miller did nothing wrong, so he refused to "write anything down or sign a paper." He was very adamant about his decision not to sign.

A few minutes later another student, (Male Student – Latino/Hispanic), came to class and conversation continued. (Student) stated he too was asked to write stuff about Mr. Miller, but he refused to sign as well. He also believed Mr. Miller did nothing wrong. Both seemed bothered and clearly affected by what had occurred. They told me one student wrote something but they wouldn't "snitch" and tell me who the student was. I did not ask them who the student was who signed the paper. Both students did disclose to me that the Principal, Mr. Rosado, was present for some of the time during their interview. (Student) said the Principal said they would be allowed down later during lunch to see if the boys had "changed their mind about signing and writing a statement about Mr. Miller."

During the next class period, a student (Male Student – Latino/Hispanic) approached me and quietly asked if the Science teacher (Mr. Miller) was going to be fired. I asked him where he had heard such a thing. He simply told me he heard some students said they signed a petition to get him fired. He told me he did not sign it. I began telling him about past challenging teachers that I had growing up. That those were the teachers I learned the most from.

Meeting June 25, 2012 Re: Second Harassment claim made by Ryan Miller

Attending: David Wildonger, Brian Cote, Robert Wheeler, Susan Lozada

I was questioned/interviewed regarding the second HARASSMENT claim made by Ryan Miller against me.

Prior to answering any questions I stated that my suspension letter (based on the first Harassment claim filed by Ryan Miller) stated that if I were to be found guilty of harassment of anyone I supervise I would face additional consequences including TERMINATION.

I asked if I could be terminated if I were found to be guilty of this charge. Mr. Wildonger responded "Yes."

I answered the questions and I was told I would be informed of the findings.

MEMORANDUM

Date: July 10, 2012
To: Dr. C. Russell Mayo, Superintendent
From: Brian L. Cote
Subject: Follow-up of Investigation Ryan Miller 2nd Harassment Complaint Findings and Recommendation Against Jose Rosado Sr.
Cc: David Wildonger, Chief Operations Officer
             Susan Lozada, Executive Director of Community and Student Services
             Elizabeth Kelly, Attorney King Spry Law Firm

This is a summary of an investigation regarding a second complaint of harassment against Jose Rosado Sr., Director of Community and Student Services, submitted by Ryan Miller, IBEAM science teacher. Mr. Rosado is the principal of record for alternative education in the Allentown School District; therefore, the direct supervisor to Mr. Miller. Mr. Miler submitted ten (10) statements alleging Mr. Rosado Sr. of harassing him. These statements were documented between the time periods of April 20, 2012 through May 3, 2012.

On May 30, 2012 at 10:00 AM, Brian Cote, Executive Director of Accountability, and David Wildonger, Executive Director of Secondary Education conducted an interview with Mr. Miller. AEA President Deb Tretter was also present during this interview. The May 30, 2012, meeting was stopped due to inconsistencies between what Mr. Miller documented on statement #2 and what was witnessed in video footage of the event documented on 4/24/2012 at 10:15 AM. It was suggested that Mrs. Tretter and Mr. Miller go back to verify their information for accuracy and notify Mr. Cote and Mr. Wildonger to schedule a continuance of the meeting. A continuance of the meeting occurred on June 6, 2012 at 12:23 PM.

Interviews

Ryan Miller:

On May 30, 2012 at 10:00 AM, Brian Cote, Executive Director of Accountability, and David Wildonger, Executive Director of Secondary Education conducted an interview with Mr. Miller. AEA President Deb Tretter was also present during this interview. During this interview, each statement was reviewed separately with Mr. Miller. Mr. Miller was asked the same three questions to verify each statement. The questions were as followed:
1. Is this the statement you submitted?
2. Is this statement true and accurate?
3. Is there anything you wish to change, add, or delete about this statement?

Mr. Miller responded to each question relative to his submitted statements. Mr. Miller's response to each question relative to his ten statements was consistent. The results of his response are as followed:

1. Is this the statement you submitted? Mr. Miller replied, "Yes!"
2. Is this statement true and accurate? Mr. Miller replied, "Yes!"
3. Is there anything you wish to change, add or delete about this statement? Mr. Miller replied, "No change."

After each statement was verified independently, the interview process continued to dig deeper into each of the statements submitted by Mr. Miller. Again, before digging deeper into each statement independently, Mr. Miller was asked the same three questions above to ensure the accuracy of each statement. When asked if Mr. Miller was completely sure of his statements he responded, "Yes." Specifically, when statement number two (2) was read which is noted directly below, the following questions were asked in order to clarify the statement.

Mr. Miller's Statement:

On 4/24/12, at 10:15 AM, Jose came down to the gym, where I was the only staff member there, stared at me and smiled. I moved away from him. As he walked out of the gym, he stared at me again and smiled this time for over thirty seconds.

Follow up questions for statement two (2): Mr. Miller's response(s) will follow each question:

Do you have a class in the gym at this time?
- "Yes!"

What are students doing in the gym?
- "Playing basketball."

What is your role as the teacher during this period?
- "Monitor students, maintain safety, and maintain integrity of the building."

Do you remain in the gym at all times during this period?
- "Yes, I position myself in a doorway inside the gym."

Where were you located in the gym when Mr. Rosado approached you?
- "Right there in the doorway. The doorway inside the gym."
  Can you describe how he stared and smiled at you?
- "Cocky arrogance to it." Mr. Miller demonstrated the alleged stare and smile. Mr. Miller explained that Mr. Rosado came in the doorway, shrugged his shoulders, and adjusted his own suit jacket by grabbing the lapels on his chest while adjusting his jacket as he was smiling and smirking. After adjusting his jacket and staring, Mr. Miller continued to share and demonstrate that Mr. Rosado began pacing back and forth in the proximity of about five (5) to six (6) feet away while staring and smiling at Mr. Miller.

If I smiled and stared at you, would you consider that as harassment?
- "No! There is no history. Yes, if you had a history like Jose."

Why do you believe Mr. Rosado is harassing you by smiling?
- "He continuously does it over and over since September."

What was Mr. Rosado's proximity to you while he was staring and smiling at you?
- "About five to six feet away." He stared and was shrugging at me for over 30 seconds."

30 seconds is a long time to be staring at someone. Are you sure it was 30 seconds?
- "Yes!"

This event is clear to you in your mind?
- "Yes!"

Was there any voice interaction or comments made during this time or was it all mannerisms?
- "All mannerisms, no voice."

Were you in the gym during this date and time of this occurrence?
- "Yes!"

Are you certain this is what happened and you're sure of the date and time?
- "Yes!"

At this point in the investigation it was shared that Mr. Wildonger and Mr. Cote would like to share video footage of the alleged incident Mr. Miller reported back on 4/14/12 at 10:15 AM in the gym. Mr. Miller again agreed with the date and time in the video footage was correct and accurate with the statement he submitted in writing regarding the "Second Harassment Complaint against Jose Rosado." The video footage captured started at 10:12 AM on 4/24/12 and concluded at 10:23 AM 4/24/12. The video footage showed some students leaving the gym facility to use the bathroom and to get a drink of water. This was confirmed by Mr. Miller while he was watching the video. At 10:14 AM, Mr. Miller was seen walking out of the gym area to the hallway outside the gym doors. Mr. Miller paced the hallway outside the gym door for approximately one minute. At 10:15 AM, Mr. Miller was observed as leaving the entire gym area by exiting the vicinity through the stairwell doors to the right of the gym leaving all students in the gym unsupervised while playing basketball as he noted in his interview questions above. Again, at 10:20 AM, Mr. Miller came out from the gym, this time operating his cell phone. Mr. Miller confirmed using his cell phone during this time while watching the video. Mr. Miller stated he was probably documenting something. Mr. Miller remained in the hallway operating his cell phone while pacing the hallway outside the gymnasium for over two minutes. At 10:22 AM, Mr. Rosado was observed as walking from the stairwell doors to the right of the gym moving toward the gym vicinity. As Mr. Rosado approached the stairwell door threshold, Mr. Miller again exited the gymnasium. The video footage shows Mr. Miller walking out with his head down looking toward the floor and Mr. Rosado waiting for Mr. Miller to pass him by. The two may have made a split second of eye contact with each other as they met at the thresholds of each door. Mr. Miller moved to the opposite wall of the gymnasium directly across from the gym entrance. At this time, Mr. Rosado entered the gym to observe students in the gymnasium. It appears in the video that Mr. Rosado remained in the gym for approximately twenty seconds. Upon exiting the gym, it appears that Mr. Rosado did look in the direction of Mr. Miller, who was standing with is back against the wall directly across from the gym door entrance. Mr. Rosado proceeded to leave this vicinity and never look back to Mr. Miller. As Mr. Rosado left the vicinity, Mr. Miller stepped away from the wall to the center of the hallway and stared at Mr. Rosado as Mr. Rosado left the vicinity. Mr. Miller returned to the gym area Mr. Rosado exited the hallway.

After reviewing the video footage there was a moment of silence in the room. Mr. Miller and Mrs. Tretter were asked if they would like to see the video again. Mrs. Tretter responded, "No, that would not be necessary." Mr. Miller was asked again if the date and time on the video footage was accurate with what he submitted in his complaint as statement number 2. Mr. Miller responded, "Yes!" After viewing the video footage, Mr. Miller was quick to say there must be a mistake with the facts he submitted, because he may have documented the wrong dates and times. What I wrote did not occur during this date and time." Mr. Miller was asked when he keeps logs, how long does he wait to make an entry in to his log? Mr. Miller responded, "As soon as I get a chance, usually the same day." Mr. Miller shared that he sends all documents to Mrs. Tretter. Mrs. Tretter stated that she would go back to her office and review the documentation that Mr. Miller sent her on 4/24/12/ to ensure the accuracy of the statement. The May 30, 2012 investigation meeting adjourned due to a sudden change in Mr. Miller's response to the video footage, and so Mr. Miller and Mrs. Tretter may check their email and documentation trails for accuracy.

On May 30, 2012, at 8:18 PM, Deb Tretter confirmed the only email she received regarding the date of 4.24/12, contained the same information that is in Mr. Miller's documentation. Mrs. Tretter continued to state in her email to Mr. Wildonger and Mr. Cote, "There is no explanation for the discrepancy between Ryan's testimony and the videotape, although we have explored several possibilities. It is possible that Ryan wrote the email after a period of time had passed, and that the date is incorrect. It is also possible that Ryan's perception of the event was off."

Upon receiving Mrs. Tretter's email on May 30, 2012, Mr. Miller and Mrs. Tretter were "ready to continue the interview, in an effort to complete the investigation very soon." The meeting continued on June 6, 2012, at IBEAM. Mr. Wildonger, Mr. Cote, Mr. Miller and Mrs. Tretter were in attendance for this meeting.

The same process for verifying each statement continued during and throughout this interview period by asking Mr. Miller the same three questions as mentioned above; furthermore, Mr. Miller responded the same for statements three through ten which he submitted in his alleged second harassment complaint:

1. Is this the statement you submitted? Mr. Miller replied, "Yes!"
2. Is this statement true and accurate? Mr. Miller replied, "Yes!"
3. Is there anything you wish to change, add or delete about this statement? Mr. Miller replied, "No change."

Statement three was submitted by Mr. Miller as:

On 4/24/12, at 11:59 AM, Jose came in the classroom I am assigned to (room 201), stared at me when he came in the room. He spoke with Ms. Keiser, then stared at me and smiled as he walked out of the room.

Mr. Miller could not presume Mr. Rosado's intentions for being in the classroom at this time. It was determined that Mr. Rosado said nothing to Mr. Miller during this visit. Mr. Miller did state that Mr. Rosado did come into the classroom stared and smiled with an arrogant smirk.

Follow up questions for statement three (3): Mr. Miller's response(s) will follow each question (*)

Who is Ms. Keiser?
- "Math Credit Recovery Teacher"

What was Mr. Rosado's proximity to you while he was staring and smiling at you?
- "Approximately fifteen (15) feet." There were approximately 8-10 students around the room in the proximity of Mr. Miller

Did Mr. Rosado look at you or stare at you?
- "More like a glance, not a stare."

Statements four (4) through ten (10) were all thoroughly investigated with the same consistency of verifying questions as well as follow up questions. Mr. Millers' statements remained consistent with the staring and smiling from Mr. Rosado directing him to not be present in the credit acquisition classroom due to a request from another teacher. Mr. Rosado was honoring the request and asked Mr. Miller to be available during his as assigned period to provide coverage as needed.

Mr. Miller submitted the following documentation of accounts for May 3, 2012:

On 5/3/12, at 8:07 AM, Mr. White and Jose were in the main office. I asked Mr. White if I could talk to him in private. Mr. White and I went to another room. Jose came to the doorway of that room, as we were talking, and looked in. Jose made eye contact with me and left the doorway.

Mr. Miller was asked the following questions in addition to the three verification questions:

Were you in a confidential setting?
- "To me I was."

Did you or Mr. White close the door?
- "No!"

Did Mr. Rosado know you were in this room?
- "No, not sure."

Do you believe this was harassment?
- "Yes!"

In what way?
- "He knew we wanted to meet privately." Jose was in the room when the request was made."

Did Mr. Rosado get up right away when you and Mr. White left the room to meet privately?
- "No!"

Where was the private meeting being held?
- In the faculty/planning room in the main office, directly next to Mr. Rosado's office and on the opposite side of the main office visitor counter.

Where were you and Mr. White standing in the room? (Mr. Wildonger, Mr. Cote, Mr. Miller, and Mrs. Tretter visited the room to see where the two were standing).
- When one walks in the room, the two were positioned straight back from the door about 10-12 feet from the door.

On 5/3/12, at 8:21 AM, I was talking to Mrs. Bennis. Jose stood nearby and stared at me. I immediately excused myself from the conversation and walked away.

On 5/3/12, at 9:45 AM, Chad Rutherford and Mr. White came down to my classroom, directed by Jose, to talk to me about a concern a student had about my well-being. I told them: I feel this building is not a safe place and is not helping students as best as it could. There is too much inconsistency. Some staff, in this building, get whatever they want, yet I cannot get issues of *Current Science* for $11.99 or even go to the bathroom, without worrying if I am going to get in trouble. I am dealing with the continued harassment by my administrator, as well as the thought that the students have regarding their thoughts "to get Mr. Miller fired". I told Chad and Mr. White that it saddens me that this building has become what it is...Years ago, I could do dissections, work with chemicals, and use microscopes. Now it would be unsafe to do those activities in this environment. I take pride in alternative education in Allentown and to watch it fall apart is hard. I am completely capable of doing my job and helping the students the best that I can.

On 5/3/12, at 10:52 AM, I asked Chad if Jose asked him about what I said. Chad told me that Jose did ask and Chad told him that he offered services and Chad felt that I was fine.

On 5/3/12, at 1:40 PM, two students, (Student) and (Student), asked me to close the classroom door. They told me that two men took them upstairs, to the second floor, and asked them to write down "bad things about you." We said no, I ain't no snitch. He didn't even do anything wrong. He was trying to help us." According to the students, one of the men said, "Ok, we will check back with you later to see if you've changed your mind." (Student) also said to me that "the English teacher knew about it. She sent me up there, that's why she kept me in her room when you came to get us for rec."

Alisha Keiser:

An interview was conducted with Alisha Keiser on June 11, 2012 at 12:58 PM at IBEAM, Mr. Cote and Ms. Keiser were present. Alisha Keiser was mentioned in statement number three provided by Mr. Miller.

On 4/24/12, at 11:59 AM, Jose came in the classroom I am assigned to (room 201), stared at me when he came in the room. He spoke with Ms. Keiser, then stared at me and smiled as he walked out of the room.

This interview was conducted by Mr. Cote to verify information regarding the contents of this statement. Ms. Keiser verified that she works on the same teacher team as Mr. Miller. Ms. Keiser verified that 4/24/12 was a Tuesday, and neither Mr. Miller nor Ms. Keiser would be in room 201 because their class meeting time is from 10:30 AM to 11:15 AM as their as assigned period, Ms. Keiser then stated, "At 11:59 AM, we would not have been in that room, I think Mr. Miller's time is a little off." Ms. Keiser could not verify that Mr. Rosado stared at Mr. Miller. Additionally, Ms. Keiser stated that Mr. Rosado does come in periodically to check on kids.

Ms. Keiser stated during a morning staff circle meeting, a date of the meeting could not be recalled, Mr. Miller openly said IBEAM building isn't safe. Ms. Keiser feels she is safe in the building. Additionally, Ms. Keiser stated that on different occasions Mr. Miller would use his walkie-talkie to call the behavior management specialist or administration for students acting out in his room. Ms. Keiser shared the following statement," Ryan called over the radio (walkie-talkie) because kids were yelling out the window. Ryan stated over the walkie-talkie, "I don't know what to do anymore."

Ms. Keiser shared that on a separate occasion Mr. Miller did not take all students up to the room with him after the recreational period in the gymnasium. He only took three students and not he whole class.

Ms. Keiser stated that she will work with anyone and will get along with anyone. Ms. Keiser stated that Mr. Miller is "very sarcastic" and does not like the tone he uses with her or the students. Ms. Keiser shared she is happy with her job.

Ms. Keiser stated the following, "It's hard to come into work everyday knowing you have to work with him (Mr. Miller). His demeanor is not good. He is not here for the students anymore, but says he is."

Deb Ninesling:

An interview was conducted with Debra Ninesling on June 11, 2012 at 1:35 PM at IBEAM. Mr. Cote and Matt Cunningham, AEA representative, were present during the interview. The purpose of this interview was to gather clarification on statements provided by Mr. Miller. It was also requested by Mrs. Tretter and Mr. Miller that Mr. Cote speaks with Ms. Ninesling.

Ms. Ninesling is a colleague of Mr. Miller. Mr. Miller was a mentor for Mrs. Ninesling for the 2011-2012 school year. Mrs. Ninesling confirmed all teachers have a walkie-talkie. Furthermore, it was shared by Mrs. Ninesling that all walkie-talkies are on the same frequency, unless requested to be on a different channel. Additionally, it was noted that a majority of the transmissions going across the walkie-talkies is for students leaving the room to use the restrooms, students attempting to leave the classroom, or when students are being uncooperative in the classroom or hallway and teachers need assistance.

Jose Rosado Sr.:

An interview was conducted with Jose Rosado Sr. on June 25, 2012 at 9:30 AM in Mr. Wildonger's office at the Administration Center. The following people were present: Mr. Cote, Mr. Wildonger, Bob Wheeler (Act 93 President), Susan Lozada (Executive Director of Community and Student Services), and Mr. Rosado.

Each one of the ten statements documented on Mr. Miller's second harassment complaint against Mr. Rosado was shared with Mr. Rosado. Below will show the statements provided by Mr. Miller and how Mr. Rosado responded.

Ryan Miller statement 1

On 4/20/12, at 3:00 PM, the students were unusually disruptive. One student said, "Don't worry Miller, they're just doing that to get you fired." Then, another student, (Student), began arguing with him. She said, "It was just us students and one teacher who signed it because we hate Mr. Miller. We just want to get him fired." Then, another student, (Student), said, "Our petition is going to hit the papers. And we'll get him fired."

Mr. Rosado's response:

"I have no knowledge of a petition. I had nothing to do with it. I was not aware of it."

Ryan Miller statement 2

On 4/24/12, at 10:15 AM, Jose came down to the gym, where I was the only staff member there, stared at me and smiled. I moved away from him. As he walked out of the gym, he stared at me again and smiled this time for over thirty seconds.

Mr. Rosado's response:

"I make routine rounds of the building. I walk through classrooms. Students were in the gym during rec. period; I went to monitor students. Usually when I visit, he (Mr. Miller) is in the hallway outside the gym sitting in a chair, or on the steps, he is usually on his cell phone." Mr. Rosado stated he never addressed this issue with Mr. Miller. When Mr. Rosado was asked if he saw a problem with students being in the gym and Mr. Miller being outside the gym area, Mr. Rosado replied, "He (Mr. Miller) can't maintain visual contact of students if he is sitting on the stairs, there is limited supervision."

Ryan Miller statement 3

On 4/24/12, at 11:59 AM, Jose came in the classroom I am assigned to (room 201), stared at me when he came in the room. He spoke with Ms. Keiser, then stared at me and smiled as he walked out of the room.

Mr. Rosado's response:

"This is the credit recovery room. I went there to check the room to make sure kids could log on. Kids were having technical problems logging on to the program in the past." When asked if he stared at Mr. Miller, Mr. Rosado replied. "No."

Ryan Miller statement 4

On 4/25,12, at 11:25 AM, Jose came up to the computer lab, where I was the only staff member there. I said, "Can you cover the class? I need to go to the bathroom." Jose said, "No, you have a class." As he said this, he blocked the door by putting his arm against the doorway. I said, "Ok," and moved to the opposite side of the room. He stared and smiled at me, periodically, for the five minutes he was walking around the room.

Mr. Rosado's response:

That's an outright lie. I did not block the door. Ryan walked right at me when I entered the room and he said," I got to go to the bathroom, you're covering. " Mr. Rosado said he replied with, "This is your class, I'm not covering." At this point Mr. Miller walked to the other side of the room and continued teaching his class. It was also shared that Mr. Miller did not request to use the bathroom again during this room visit. Mr. Rosado stated, "He (Mr. Miller) has a radio. If he needed coverage for the restroom, he could call for coverage. The way he (Mr. Miller) approached me was unprofessional and inappropriate."

Ryan Miller statement 5

On 5/2/12, at 9:05 AM, I received an email from Jose, stating the following: "Ryan, Ms. Avrich has requested that you not be present in the credit acquisition classroom during her assigned class period. As a result, you should not go into the credit acquisition classroom during your "as assigned" period as I previously directed. You should remain available during your as assigned period to provide coverage as needed." Ms. Lozada was cc'd on this email.

Mr. Rosado's response:

"This staff member feels intimidated by Ryan Miller. Candice Avrich requested meditation between herself and Ryan Miller. Candice Avrich did not want Ryan there. Candice sent me an email requesting Ryan Miller be reassigned." Therefore, Mr. Rosado issued an email to Mr. Miller stating Ms. Avrich requested that Mr. Miller not be present in the credit acquisition classroom during that assigned period, and as a result of this request Mr. Miller should not go into the credit acquisition classroom during his "as assigned" period. Instead, Mr. Miller should remain available during his as assigned period to provide coverage as needed.

Ryan Miller statement 6

On 5/3/12, at 8:07 AM, Mr. White and Jose were in the main office. I asked Mr. White if I could talk to him in private. Mr. White and I went to another room. Jose came to the doorway of that room, as we were talking, and looked in. Jose made eye contact with me and left the doorway.

Mr. Rosado's response:

Mr. Rosado was not sure where Mr. Miller and Mr. White went for their private meeting since he was in the office when Mr. Miller and Mr. White left.

Ryan Miller statement 7

On 5/3/12, at 8:21 AM, I was talking to Mrs. Bennis. Jose stood nearby and stared at me. I immediately excused myself from the conversation and walked away.

Mr. Rosado's response:

"Don't recall. I could have made eye contact."

Ryan Miller statement 8

On 5/3/12, at 9:45 AM, Chad Rutherford and Mr. White came down to my classroom, directed by Jose, to talk to me about a concern a student had about my well-being. I told them: I feel this building is not a safe place and is not helping students as best as it could. There is too much inconsistency. Some staff, in this building, get whatever they want, yet I cannot get issues of *Current Science* for $11.99 or even go to the bathroom, without worrying if I am going to get in trouble. I am dealing with the continued harassment by my administrator, as well as the thought that the students have regarding their thoughts "to get Mr. Miller fired". I told Chad and Mr. White that it saddens me that this building has become what it is...Years ago, I could do dissections, work with chemicals, and use microscopes. Now it would be unsafe to do those activities in this environment. I take pride in alternative education in Allentown and to watch it fall apart is hard. I am completely capable of doing my job and helping the students the best that I can.

Ryan Miller statement 9

On 5/3/12, at 10:52 AM, I asked Chad if Jose asked him about what I said. Chad told me that Jose did ask and Chad told him that he offered services and Chad felt that I was fine.

Ryan Miller statement 10

On 5/3/12, at 1:40 PM, two students, (Student) and (Student), asked me to close the classroom door. They told me that two men took them upstairs, to the second floor, and asked them to write down "bad things about you." We said no, I ain't no snitch. He didn't even do anything wrong. He was trying to help us." According to the students, one of the men said, "Ok, we will check back with you later to see if you've changed your mind." (Student) also said to me that "the English teacher knew about it. She sent me up there, that's why she kept me in her room when you came to get us for rec."

Mr. Rosado's response to statements 8 through 10:

Mr. Rosado stated he was not in the office at this time on May 3, 2012, and Mrs. Lozada confirmed his absence. Mrs. Lozada stated since Mr. Rosado was out of the office on May 3, 2012, she authorized Mr. Rutherford and Mr. White to check on the well-being of Mr. Miller. Susan stated that she followed the same procedures as she does for all employees when there is a concern and support is needed. Mr. Wheeler confirmed this is standard procedure and practice across the District, and this practice occurs in his building when needed.

Observations

After watching the video footage of Mr. Miller's statement number two, and Mr. Miller confirming on five occasions in his interview that the following did occur (see statement 2 below), Mr. Miller was quick in trying to retract this statement indicating that he must have submitted the wrong date and time with this event.

Ryan Miller statement 2:

On 4/24/12, at 10:15 AM, Jose came down to the gym, where I was the only staff member there, stared at me and smiled. I moved away from him. As he walked out of the gym, he stared at me again and smiled this time for over thirty seconds.

Mrs. Tretter submitted a copy of an email (noted below) to Mr. Cote, which she received from Mr. Miller. Its compelling that Mr. Miller documented this occurrence on 4/24/12 at 10:15 AM then documented the occurrence in an email to Mrs. Tretter at 12:10 PM on 4/24/12 the same day, one hour and fifty-five minutes after the alleged incident. Again, Mr. Miller agreed to the accuracy of this statement on five occasions before watching the video. Mr. Miller also agreed to the date and time on the video monitor for accuracy.

Based on this sudden attempt to retract his statement, additional random video footage was captured. The video footage captured on 4/26/12 in the hallway near the gymnasium from 10:00 AM to 10:25 AM shows Mr. Miller in the hallway not supervising students in the gym as well as Mr. Miller sitting on a chair opposite the gym doors across the hall having a conversation with a student. Based on the evidence of the two videos captured on two separate occasions, where Mr. Miller stated in his May 30, 2012 meeting that he remains in the gym at all times to, "Monitor students, maintain safety, and maintain integrity of the building," on 4/24/12, and 4/26/12, there is convincing evidence that Mr. Miller was not supervising students in the gym as he said he was during the May 30, 2012 meeting. Additionally, Mr. Miller state that,

On 4/24/12, at 10:15 AM, Jose came down to the gym, where I was the only staff member there, stared at me and smiled. I moved away from him. As he walked out of the gym, he stared at me again and smiled this time for over thirty seconds.

The video dated 4/24/12 from 10:12 AM to 10:23 AM, did not capture Mr. Rosado staring and smiling at Mr. Miller as he submitted in his statement. Furthermore, this video did not show Mr. Rosado staring and smiling for over thirty seconds with a "Cocky arrogance to it." Mr. Miller demonstrated the alleged stare and smile. Mr. Miller explained that Mr. Rosado came in the doorway, shrugged his shoulders, and adjusted his jacket as he was smiling and smirking. After adjusting his jacket and staring, Mr. Miller continued to share and demonstrate that Mr. Rosado began pacing back and forth in the proximity of about five (5) to six (6) feet away while staring and smiling at Mr. Miller.

In fact, when Mr. Rosado left the gymnasium on 4/24/12 at approximately 10:23 AM. He did not look back at Mr. Miller, but it was Mr. Miller who stared down at Mr. Rosado until he exited the hallway at which point Mr. Miller may have entered back into the gym area.

Furthermore, Mr. Miller documented that,

On 4/24/12, at 11:59 AM, Jose came in the classroom I am assigned to (room 201), stared at me when he came in the room. He spoke with Ms. Keiser, then stared at me and smiled as he walked out of the room.

After speaking with Ms. Keiser, she indicated that she could not have been in room 201 during this time on 4/24/12, since her class ended at 11:15 AM on this day.

It is also important to note in this observation section of the report, that Mr. Miller was afforded several opportunities to clarify and assure his statements submitted in the second harassment complaint against Mr. Rosado. Mr. Miller stated that all statements were statements that he submitted in this complaint, Mr. Miller stated that all statements were true and accurate; and Mr. Miller replied, "No change" when he was asked if there was anything he wished to change, add or delete from each statement.

Mr. Miller documented the following statement three,

On 4/24/12, at 11:59 AM, Jose came in the classroom I am assigned to (room 201), stared at me when he came in the room. He spoke with Ms. Keiser, then stared at me and smiled as he walked out of the room.

When Mr. Miller was asked, did Mr. Rosado look at you or stare at you?

Mr. Miller replied, "More like a glance, not a stare." It is important to note the investigative questions for this statement started off a new meeting on

June 6, 2012, since Mr. Miller quickly stated his documentation may be a bit inaccurate from his May 30, 2012 meeting after viewing the video footage regarding the time and date of the incident he submitted in his second harassment complaint against Mr. Rosado; which he verified again was the true and accurate statement he submitted and would not change, add or delete anything from the statement.

It is also important to note that Mr. Rosado stated he observed Mr. Miller on several occasions on his personal cell phone and pacing the hallway outside the gymnasium. It is compelling that Mr. Rosado never directed Mr. Miller to stay off his personal cell phone during work time and remain in the gym during activity time when students are engaged in activities. Mr. Rosado indirectly sent a message to Mr. Miller that this behavior of pacing the hallway and using his personal cell phone is acceptable, when in fact it is not. Students should be supervised at all times.

Findings

Based on the evidence of the interviews, documentation and video footage, it is determined that Mr. Rosado Sr. did not harass Mr. Miller. In fact, it was determined that Mr. Miller was not supervising students, as he should during his assigned period. Mr. Miller was witnessed pacing the hallway on two separate occasions of 4/24/12 and 4/26/12. Additionally, he was observed using his personal cellphone, at one point completely vacated the gymnasium area through the stairwell doors, and observed sitting opposite the gymnasium in a chair having a conversation with another student, all while students were participating in basketball recreational time in the gym with no other teacher supervising his class. Additionally, most students were out of Mr. Miller's sight while he was not directly in the gymnasium supervising students.

Mr. Rosado failed to supervise Mr. Miller when he observed Mr. Miller on several occasions using his personal cell phone during instructional time and pacing the hallway, to remain in the classroom or gym area when students are present and not to use his personal cellphone during instructional time. When students are not supervised closely during activities, it poses a great liability for the District and compromises the well being of the student or students.

It is also determined based on evidence from interviews, documentation and video footage, that Mr. Miller falsified documented statements, which on several occasions during his interview, he held a confident stand behind these statements as true and accurate as he submitted, in contrary to the video footage. Mr. Miller's credibility is now in question based on how he stood firm and demonstrated how Mr. Rosado would stand and stare at him during multiple visits. During the investigative meetings these allegations were in conflict with the video footage and comments from individuals during the investigative interviews. Based on this evidence, Mr. Rosado never acted in such a manner.

Recommendations

According to Board Policy 447.1 UNLAWFUL HARRASSMENT under the Discipline section the policy states, "If it is concluded that an employee has made false accusations, such employee shall be subject to disciplinary action. That action may include procedures to terminate employment.

It is recommend that Mr. Miller be transferred to another teaching assignment with the District if such a position exists or be terminated for falsifying multiple statements entries in his second alleged harassment complaint against Mr. Rosado.

NOTE: Although, it was recommended that Mr. Miller be transferred to another teaching position or terminated, Dr. Mayo did neither. Rather, he allowed Ryan Miller to continue working at IBEAM with me as his supervisor. Was this part of the "set-up?"

Further, when asked during his sworn deposition, "Now at some point did Ryan Miller make a complaint against Jose Rosado, which the school district determined was bogus? Dr. Mayo responded, "No. At least based on my recollection the answer is no to that."

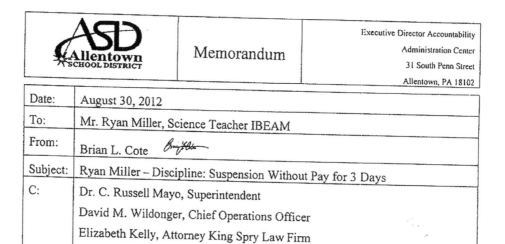

		Executive Director Accountability
	Memorandum	Administration Center
		31 South Penn Street
		Allentown, PA 18102

Date:	August 30, 2012
To:	Mr. Ryan Miller, Science Teacher IBEAM
From:	Brian L. Cote
Subject:	Ryan Miller – Discipline: Suspension Without Pay for 3 Days
C:	Dr. C. Russell Mayo, Superintendent
	David M. Wildonger, Chief Operations Officer
	Elizabeth Kelly, Attorney King Spry Law Firm
	Deb Tretter, AEA President
	Personnel File

Findings

It is determined based on evidence from interviews, documentation and video footage that you falsified documented statements which on several occasions during his interview, you held a confident stand behind these statements as true and accurate as you submitted, in contrary to the video footage. Your credibility is now in question based on how you stood firm and demonstrated how Mr. Rosado would stand and stare at you during multiple visits. During the investigative meetings these allegations were in conflict with the video footage and comments from individuals during the investigative interviews. Based on this evidence, Mr. Rosado did not act in such a manor. Based on the evidence of the interviews, documentation and video footage, it is determined that Mr. Rosado Sr. did not harass you.

Recommendations

According to Board policy 447.1 UNLAWFUL HARASSMENT under the Discipline section the policy states, "If it is concluded that an employee has made false accusations, such employee shall be subject to disciplinary action. That action may include procedures to terminate employment.

Due to the nature of inaccurate documentation regarding the accusations made against another employee by you on multiple accounts, you shall serve a three day suspension without pay. The suspension without pay will be deducted from September 13, 2012 payroll. You will serve his suspension on September 10, 11, and 12. You will have lesson plans generated for his substitute for these three days of suspension. You should not report to work on these three days or report on any school district property during the time of this suspension. You are permitted to return to work on September 13, 2012.

You may attach a rebuttal to this document which will be placed in your personnel file.

	Memorandum	Executive Director Accountability Administration Center 31 South Penn Street Allentown, PA 18102

Date:	October 3, 2012
To:	Jose Rosado Sr., Director of Community and Student Services
From:	Brian L. Cote
Subject:	Finding: 2nd Harassment Complaint
C:	David M. Wildonger, Chief Operations Officer Susan Lozada, Executive Director of Community and Student Services Bob Wheeler, Act 93 President

Findings of Investigation

It was determined based on evidence from interviews, documentation and video footage that Mr. Miller provided inaccurate documented statements which on several occasions during his interview, he held a confident stand behind these statements as true and accurate as he submitted, in contrary to the video footage. During the investigative meetings these allegations were in conflict with the video footage and comments from individuals during the investigative interviews. Based on this evidence, Mr. Rosado did not act in such a manor. Based on the evidence of the interviews, documentation and video footage, it was determined that Mr. Rosado Sr. did not harass Mr. Miller as alleged by Mr. Miller in his second complaint.

	Memorandum	Executive Director Accountability Administration Center 31 South Penn Street Allentown, PA 18102

Date:	10/3/2012
To:	Jose Rosado Sr., Director of Community and Student Services
From:	Brian L. Cote
Subject:	Meeting Summary: Investigation of Investigation
C:	Dr. C. Russell Mayo, Superintendent
	David M. Wildonger, Chief Operations Officer
	Bob Wheeler, Act 93 President

This memorandum is a summary of your appeal request meeting with Dr. Mayo regarding your administrative suspension without pay for founded allegations which determined that you harassed Mr. Ryan Miller, teacher at IBEAM.

Your request as presented in this meeting on October 2, 2012, was to have an investigation of the procedures of the first harassment complaint against you. For this investigation, you requested an investigation be thoroughly conducted to ensure that proper due process procedures were followed during the investigatory process of the first harassment complaint against you.

After a thorough investigation of the investigation, it was determined that proper due process procedures were followed properly.

-----Original Message-----
From: Rosado, Jose (Sr.)
Sent: Sunday, October 07, 2012 8:11 PM
To: Wildonger, David M
Cc: Lozada, Susan; Wheeler, Robert A; Cote, Brian L.
Subject: Focused Assistance Plan(s)

Dave,

In my review of the expectation of the F.A.P Imposed on me, I have the following concerns:

1) As we move beyond the mid-quarter point of the first marking period I continue to operate without access to my budget (alternative education budget). I brought up this concern during the Operational Planning Meeting last month and I have also included you on my emails to Dr. Belardi regarding this concern. The lack of a budget impacts curriculum alignment and Instruction.

The lack of a budget will have a detrimental impact on my Performance Expectations as detailed in the FAP (Provides Instructional Leadership).

2) On September 18, 2012, during a meeting with Ryan Miller (Brian Cote, Bob Wheeler, Deb Tretter and Cory Yencho were also present), you defined our roles and set expectations (principal, teacher). However, Ryan clearly stated "I don't feel that I can get a fair shake in that building and with Mr. Rosado. I'm concerned with Mr. Rosado's Intentions of me. I'm very nervous with Mr. Rosado evaluating me. I'm looking for an alternate evaluator. Mr. Rosado is not fair to me and other teachers close to me. I won't get a fair shake from Mr. Rosado."

Deb Tretter stated "we want to move forward with a clean slate.....Ryan is not there yet..... We are all hopeful."

Ryan Miller's blatant refusal to acknowledge and accept my role as principal and his immediate supervisor clearly demonstrates his unwillingness to establish a professional working relationship with me as his supervisor.

Furthermore, the Findings of Investigation (Completed by Brian Cote on October 3, 2012 - Harassment Allegations made against me by Ryan Miller) clearly stated that Ryan Miller made inaccurate allegations against me and provided statements contrary to the evidence.

This information troubles me and causes me great concern as it pertains to the Performance Expectations of the FAP and the impact it may have on my career.

The FAP states that failure to meet the expectations may lead to termination.

Given the finding of the Investigation, I believe Ryan Miller has discredited himself and should be impeached.

Given that the FAP's Imposed on me are founded on grievances and harassment allegations made against me by Ryan Miller and furthermore, the fact that Ryan Miller has now been found to have provided false allegations and false statements against me; the FAP's should be voided.

Jose Rosado

Rosado, Jose (Sr.)

From:	Rosado, Jose (Sr.)
Sent:	Tuesday, May 28, 2013 1:38 PM
To:	Wildonger, David M
Cc:	Lozada, Susan; ekelly@kingspry.com; Wheeler, Robert A; Mayo, Russ
Subject:	Administrative Status - Job/Title

Dave,

As you are aware, this past Thursday May 24, 2013, Nick Perez was on the board agenda for an administrative reassignment - from principal of Jefferson Elementary School to Director of Community and Student Services. During the meeting the school board approved the reassignment effective July 1, 2013.

The approval of this reassignment - Nick Perez to become the director of community and student services – prompts me to question my status with the Allentown School District given that I am currently the director of community and student services. I have been approached and contacted by numerous people from within the district as well as the community and I am uncomfortable with responding since no one from the district has spoken to me about this. The rumors and the perception created by this move are very troubling to me personally and professionally!!!

I am very concerned about my status and future with the district. Apparently Nick Perez will assume my job and title on July 1, 2013, yet I have not been officially notified of the pending change and any future plans for my role with the district.

I have spoken with my direct supervisor Susan Lozada and she informed me that she has not been provided with any information regarding my status with the district and could not provide any information regarding the reassignment of Nick Perez to my current position.

I would like to meet with you, and anyone else that may be able to provide me with information regarding my status, at your earliest convenience.

Thank you!!!

Jose Rosado
Director of Community & Student Services
Allentown School District
31 S. Penn Street, P.O. Box 328
Allentown, PA 18105
Phone: 484-765-4074
Fax: 484-765-4076
rosadojo@allentownsd.org

1

THE KELLY CONFLICT

D uring my tenure in the Allentown School District principals worked very closely with the Executive Director of Human Resources. This was particularly true in situations pertaining to investigations regarding alleged teacher misconduct and potential teacher discipline. It was the principals' responsibility to respond to any complaints and/ or incidents brought to his/her attention and then conduct an investigation, if warranted, based on the allegation(s) and evidence provided at the time. Obviously, for those matters that may rise to the level of a criminal investigation, the principal would be responsible for contacting the police. However, most cases of teacher misconduct do not rise to the level of a criminal complaint.

If it was determined that an investigation was warranted, the principal was then responsible for interviewing any potential victims and witnesses as well as gathering any other evidence which may be relevant. Upon completing an investigation the principal forwarded the findings, along with a recommendation, to the Executive Director of Human Resources for any Recommendation of Discipline beyond a verbal reprimand. The principal could not issue a Notification of Discipline to a teacher without the approval of the Executive Director of Human resources. Throughout this process, the teacher's union (Allentown Education Association) was involved and monitoring the status of the investigation and the timeline regarding potential teacher discipline. Therefore, it was crucial for the Executive Director of Human Resources to respond in a timely manner to avoid a due process grievance for a delayed reprimand.

Unfortunately, between April of 2012, and January of 2013, there was much turnover in leadership positions within the human resources office. Shortly after Rita Perez resigned in April of 2012, Mary Theresa Taglang was hired. Less than a year later, Mary Theresa Taglang also resigned from the Allentown school District.

In an effort to fill the void, the district "engaged" Elizabeth Kelly, an attorney with the district's solicitor's office, to serve as "Interim Executive Director, Human Resources." So, at that point, in addition to working closely with the superintendent on matters pertaining to the district, she was also responsible for working with principals and other administrators on matters pertaining to personnel.

Could this have presented a potential conflict of interest?

Rosado, Jose (Sr.)

From:	Elizabeth Kelly
Sent:	Thursday, January 03, 2013 12:21 PM
To:	Adams, Christin; Birts, Kim; Cole, Scott; Davis, Scott; Dellatore, Tonya; Martin, Erin; Polek, Tiffany; Price, Karen; Radcliffe, Joshua; Scipio, Kris; Seng, William; Stoltz, Mark; Cowen, Corey C; Finnerty, David; Fisher, Scott; Licausi, Joseph A; Magditch, Jason; Marcks, Michael; McAndrew, Carrie; McNulty, Patrick; Piripavel, Christine; Shafnisky, Luke; Thatcher, Joshua; Wolff, Janet; Alotta, Jacqulyn; Bodnar, Rebecca; Bodolus, Troy; Carls, Jim; Morrow, Bob; Nicholson, Andrew P; Surita, Ferdinand; Thatcher, Jeremy R; Barnes, Deb; Bennett, Heather; Boardman, Karen J; Dopera, Karen; Hahn, David; Kern, Richard W; Kornfeind, Marybeth E; Lesko, Lisa; Marcks, Melissa A; Mayes, Peter; Perez, Nicolas; Pletz, Elsie; Ramos, Jennifer M.; Schreiber, Jane A; Smith, Melissa L; Wheeler, Robert A; Bocian, Susan; Mayfield, Shannon; Rosado, Jose (Sr.); Schreiber, Jane A; Custer, Daria; Derrick, Frank; Elliott, Susan M; Rosado, Jose (Sr.); Schreiber, Jane A; Serensits, Stephen
Cc:	Mayo, Russ; Wildonger, David M; Taglang, Mary Theresa; Fenstermaker, Barbara
Subject:	INTERIM HUMAN RESOURCES - FYI

Good morning,

    The purpose of this email is to let you know that Mary Theresa Taglang has accepted a very nice position in the field of Higher Education, and will be leaving us. Her last day at ASD is January 11, 2013. I wish her well in her new position, and I am sure many of you share in the warm wishes for MT. The District is currently engaged in a search to hire a replacement for her, as well as a replacement for the position of Executive Director of Personnel and Human Capital.

    In the meantime, the District has engaged me to temporarily step in as Interim Executive Director, Human Resources, to assist all of you with your HR needs. So, after January 11, 2013, and until the replacements are hired, please contact me at this email, or at extension 4275, or at my law firm email ekelly@kingspry.com. Please note: The law firm email is by far the best way to reach me, as it is the only email I can access on my iphone.

    Thank you,

    Liz Kelly, Esquire

1

130

From: Rosado, Jose (Sr.) [mailto:rosadojo@allentownsd.org]
Sent: Monday, March 04, 2013 12:18 PM
To: Elizabeth Kelly
Cc: Wildonger, David M; Lozada, Susan
Subject: Alleged Harrassment - Teacher on staff, teacher on students

Liz,

I am looking to schedule a meeting with Mat Cunningham and his AEA representative to address the attached email from an IBEAM Staff. I will inform Mr. Cunningham that I need to schedule a meeting with him and tell him the nature of the meeting is investigatory (regarding allegations made by a staff). Please let me know when you would be available this week to attend the meeting.

Thanks!!!

Jose Rosado
Director of Community & Student Services
Allentown School District
31 S. Penn Street, P.O. Box 328
Allentown, PA 18105
Phone: 484-765-4074
Fax: 484-765-4076
rosadojo@allentownsd.org

From: Hanna, Lynne
Sent: Friday, March 01, 2013 2:21 PM
To: Rosado, Jose (Sr.)
Subject: as requested....

I don't want to cause problems because I work closely with Mr. Cunningham but felt that it needed to be brought to your attention that Mr. Cunningham can oft times make very negative, demeaning comments to individual students. His behavior has, at times, been very childish as well. Back when ▮▮▮▮▮ was here and had upset Mr. Cunningham, ▮▮▮▮ was sent out of the class and Mr. C took ▮▮▮▮ cereal, threw it on the floor and said, "Is this ▮▮▮▮? Not anymore." Then he stepped on it to crush it. He has told some students they shouldn't reproduce. He really crosses a line with some of his comments...

This negative attitude has at times also been directed toward me but I do my best to ignore his comments and tell the students to do the same.
Yesterday, 2-28-13, ▮▮▮▮▮ yawned and Mr. C stopped class, getting up and going to the door to call for a behavioral specialist to remove ▮▮▮▮ from the room for his disruption which, of course, put ▮▮▮▮ on the defensive. Soon after this incident, ▮▮▮▮ asked Mr. C if he hated his job. She is not the first student I have heard ask him this.

This morning, ▮▮▮▮ asked Mr. C if he could give his cereal to ▮▮▮▮. Mr. C said, "After the way he treated me yesterday...NO." This spurred the more mature response from the student, ▮▮▮, to say, "Today is a new day." Mr. C then made a childish sound in response.

It is clear that, for a few of our students, Mr. C is their trigger, starting in on them as soon as walk in his classroom door.

From:	Elizabeth Kelly <ekelly@kingspry.com>
Sent:	Monday, March 04, 2013 5:16 PM
To:	Rosado, Jose (Sr.)
Subject:	RE: Alleged Harrassment - Teacher on staff, teacher on students

Jose,

What Ms. Hanna reported in the email below is vague. First she says, Mr. C can often make demeaning comments, but gives no specific example. The example she does give on 2/28 is an example of a student yawning, Mr. C sending the student to call for a behavior specialist to remove him, and the student making a remark to Mr. C. This does not appear to be an example of Mr. C making a demeaning comment to a student.

The only other example in the email below is an example of a childish remark made by Mr. C to a student, but Mr. C indicates that there is more to the story — referring to "the way he treated me yesterday". This is also not an example of a demeaning comment.

Finally, these are not allegations by staff, but allegations of students reported by a staff member. This is not the kind of report we like to have when we take disciplinary action — we prefer first hand reports of what the staff member herself saw or heard.

Do you disagree with my analysis above? If so, let me know. I am open to your thoughts. —
Liz

Elizabeth M. Kelly, Esquire
King Spry Herman Freund & Faul, LLC
One West Broad Street, Suite 700
Bethlehem, PA 18018
(610) 332-0390
Fax: (610) 332-0314

Rosado, Jose (Sr.)

From:	Rosado, Jose (Sr.)
Sent:	Tuesday, March 05, 2013 2:07 PM
To:	ekelly@kingspry.com
Cc:	Lozada, Susan; Wildonger, David M
Subject:	FW: Alleged Harrassment - Teacher on staff, teacher on students

Liz,

I agree that Ms. Hanna provided some general statements regarding Mr. Cunningham's interactions with students. However, she also did provide some firsthand accounts of behaviors she witnessed directly.

General statements:

- "Mr. Cunningham can oft times make very negative, demeaning comments to individual students"
- "He really crosses a line with some of his comments"
- "It is clear that, for a few of our students, Mr. C is their trigger..........."

Direct observations:

- "Mr. C took ▓▓▓▓ cereal, threw it on the floor and said – Is this ▓▓▓▓? Not anymore. Then he stepped on it to crush it"
- "He has told some students they shouldn't reproduce"

I believe the observed behaviors are inappropriate teacher behaviors.

Ms. Hanna told me that she can provide additional information/comments regarding Mr. Cunningham's interactions with students. Students and parents have also reported concerns to me regarding Mr. Cunningham's interactions with students.

Given the nature of Ms. Hanna's concerns, I feel that further investigation regarding her concerns are warranted.

Thank you!!!

Jose Rosado
Director of Community & Student Services
Allentown School District
31 S. Penn Street, P.O. Box 328
Allentown, PA 18105
Phone: 484-765-4074
Fax: 484-765-4076
rosadojo@allentownsd.org

Rosado, Jose (Sr.)

From:	Novak, Logan
Sent:	Thursday, March 07, 2013 4:44 PM
To:	Rosado, Jose (Sr.)
Cc:	Lozada, Susan
Subject:	Concern

Jose,

As I was completing a Threat Assessment (unrelated to the following) on ███████████████ this afternoon He disclosed several things which I found very disturbing. He reported that Mr. Cunningham frequently refers to the students in his class as, "bad ass kids" and "little motherfuckers". The student reported that Mr. Cunningham is open about his negative feelings about administration at IBEAM and stated that his negative statements have caused ██ ███████ and others to ask, "Why do you work here then?" to which he will openly tell him he doesn't want to and is looking/applying for other jobs. Our students already feel rejected and question authority, this behavior on behalf of our staff only make our daily job harder. ██████████ also stated that he was uncomfortable when Mr. Cunningham took pictures of the students with his ipad when Mr. Cunningham reportedly said he, "wanted to catch them off guard." He indicated that Mr. Cunningham spends an extended amount of time on his personal cell phone.
I'm not sure what can be done about this but it's VERY upsetting to have a student tell you that an adult speaks that way to young adults.
Logan

Logan Novak, M.Ed.
School Counselor
IBEAM Academy, Allentown School District
p. 484-765-4701
f. 484-765-4727

Inspire.Believe.Educate.Advocate.Mentor
"Let us not be content to wait and see what will happen, but give us the determination to make the right things happen."
–Peter Marshall

1

134

CONFIDENTIAL MEMO

Student Interviews

Re: Allegations of Inappropriate Behaviors/Inappropriate Comments by Mr. Cunningham

Student interviews were conducted in response of allegations made by a staff member regarding Mr. Cunningham. Documentation of the allegations have been provided to Elizabeth Kelly (Interim Executive Director of Accountability).

The following student interviews took place on Friday, March 8th, 2013:

❖ ██████████████

- "I don't like the way he (Mr. Cunningham) talks with my peers. He calls them: "Little Motherfuckers" – This week "Assholes" – Recently (last week)
- He tells them:
"You can be dicks sometimes" – Recent Comment
- He takes pictures of us – Recent he says he doesn't want to be here – Recent "Last Friday (3/1/13) I talked to him about it. I told him look, you don't want to be here as much as we don't want to be here. Do us a favor and stop coming here. You're miserable. He started tearing up!
- He said "any job would be better than this job working with bad ass kids."
- Me and him (Mr. Cunningham) have personal conversations. He tells me about his family. He has told me:
  - He is going through divorce
  - He got kicked out of his house
  - He moved back in because of the kids
  - He is drinking
  - He sleeps on the couch

This conversation took place last month (February).

- ❖ ▨▨▨▨▨▨▨▨▨
  - Mr. Cunningham makes comments about not liking his job
  - Nobody likes him
  - I don't like him because of his attitude
  - I yawned and he told me to get out of his class. (Recent – last week)

- ❖ ▨▨▨▨▨▨▨▨▨
  - Mr. Cunningham talks to us like we are slow.
  - He told me I should not reproduce. I told him I take offense to that comment. I stopped coming to school for a while after that (about a month ago)
  - He called me stupid because I'm 18 in ~~1th~~ 11th grade (about 2 weeks ago)
  - He talked about ▨▨▨ tattoo. He said the tattoo says Love Boy, but it should be "Love Boys". He was probably calling ▨▨▨ gay (about 2 months ago)
  - Told ▨▨▨ Bigfoot is his relative (this happened today 3/8/13)

- ❖ ▨▨▨▨▨▨▨▨▨
  - Mr. Cunningham told me that Bigfoot is my relative (3/8/13)

- ❖ ▨▨▨▨▨▨▨▨▨
  - Mr. Cunningham said something I took offense to today. We were talking about dinosaurs and he said to me "we are going to talk about your family" (3/8/13)
  - Two weeks ago he said to the class "why is ▨▨▨▨▨▨▨▨▨ ▨▨▨▨ still running the street? Why hasn't he got shot yet?
  - When I ask for help with my work he says "Oh do you want me to hold your hand?"

Rosado, Jose (Sr.)

From:	Rosado, Jose (Sr.)
Sent:	Tuesday, April 16, 2013 11:31 AM
To:	ekelly@kingspry.com
Subject:	FW:
Attachments:	MEMO 4-15-13 M Cunningham.doc

Liz,

Please review the attached letter (draft) regarding my Investigation of Matt Cunningham.

Thanks!!!

Jose Rosado
Director of Community & Student Services
Allentown School District
31 S. Penn Street, P.O. Box 328
Allentown, PA 18105
Phone: 484-765-4074
Fax: 484-765-4076
rosadojo@allentownsd.org

Draft

Confidential Memorandum

To: Matthew Cunningham

From: Jose Rosado, Principal

To: Liz Kelly

Subject: Investigation Regarding Alleged Inappropriate Comments made by Mr. Cunningham

Date: April 11, 2013

This memorandum represents a summary of our discussion, which began at approximately 1:40 pm, March 26th, 2013 in my office. In addition to us, Elizabeth Kelly (Interim Executor Director of Accountability) and Debra Tretter (Allentown Education Association President) were present. As indicated to you in an email from me dated March 11th, 2013, the purpose of the meeting was investigatory in nature.

During the meeting, I asked you – During this school year, have you referred to students as:

- "Little motherfuckers", you replied, "No".
- "Assholes", you replied, "No".

I asked you – have you said to students:

- "You can be dicks sometimes", you replied, "No".

Have you shared your personal life with them, you replied, "No".

Next, I read an email that was sent to me by Lynne Hanna, paraprofessional dated March 1st, 2013. In her email Ms. Hanna alleges:
"Mr. Cunningham can often times make very negative, demeaning comments to individual students. His behavior has, at times, been very childish as well." Ms. Hanna also provided examples of student interactions with three students. Ms. Hanna further noted, "It is clear that for a few of our students, Mr. Cunningham is their trigger." Ms. Hanna also alleged that "He has told some students they shouldn't reproduce." You denied making the

statements or behaving in the manner alleged by Ms. Hanna (email March 1st 2013.)

Next I shared with you allegations made by students during student interviews I conducted (March 8th, 2013).

Students alleged the following:
- He calls us "Little motherfuckers, assholes, dicks"

Students also alleged:
- He takes pictures of us
- He shares personal information (divorce, drinking…)
- He tells us he doesn't like his job

You denied making the alleged statements, sharing personal information and taking pictures of students.

I shared another email sent to me by Ms. Hanna dated March 6th, 2013. In the email, Ms. Hanna alleged: "Today, during first period, Mr. Cunningham brought up ████, a past student, and told the class that he has "loveboy" tattooed across his chest but it's missing the "S" on the end. He said, you know…Loveboys…" You did not deny this allegation ("don't remember").

On March 13th, 2013, the student re-enrolled at IBEAM. As a result, I shared the alleged comment with our Special Education Department. It was determined that the student would not attend IBEAM and was placed at the I.U.

It was also alleged by Ms. Hanna (March 21st, 2013) that you shared personal information about a student ████████ with students – "When ████ told you he was moving to New York he lied. We sent his paperwork to Reading." You acknowledged sharing this information with students.

It is my responsibility to notify you that based on the evidence you have made inappropriate comments (Harrassment/Discrimination – Sexual in nature) regarding a student (Love Boy/Love Boys comment).

You also shared personal information regarding a student (moved to Reading/we sent his paperwork to Reading)

- ❖ Violation ASD Policy
- ❖ Violation (PA) School Code

As a result, you are being issued a written reprimand.

Furthermore such behaviors/actions additional consequences.

If you disagree with any portion of this letter referencing our meeting…

Approved by:
Liz Kelly

Confidential Memorandum

To: Matthew Cunningham

From: Jose Rosado, Principal

Subject: Notice of Discipline - Inappropriate Comment about a Student and Sharing of Personal Student Information

Date: June 14, 2013

This memorandum represents a summary of our discussion, which began at approximately 1:40 pm, March 26th, 2013 in my office. In addition to us, Elizabeth Kelly (Interim Executor Director of Accountability) and Debra Tretter (Allentown Education Association President) were present. As indicated to you in an email from me dated March 11th, 2013, the purpose of the meeting was investigatory in nature.

During the meeting, I asked you – During this school year, have you referred to students as:
- "Little motherfuckers", you replied, "No".
- "Assholes", you replied, "No".

I asked you – have you said to students:
- "You can be dicks sometimes", you replied, "No".

Have you shared your personal life with them, you replied, "No".

Next, I read an email that was sent to me by Lynne Hanna, paraprofessional (date March 1st, 2013). In her email Ms. Hanna alleges:
"Mr. Cunningham can often times make very negative, demeaning comments to individual students. His behavior has, at times, been very childish as well." Ms. Hanna also provided examples of student interactions with three students. Ms. Hanna further noted, "It is clear that for a few of our students, Mr. Cunningham is their trigger." Ms. Hanna also alleged that "He

has told some students they shouldn't reproduce." You denied making the statements or behaving in the manner alleged by Ms. Hanna (email March 1st 2013.)

Next I shared with you allegations made by students during student interviews I conducted (March 8th, 2013).

Students alleged the following:
- He calls us "Little motherfuckers, assholes, dicks"

Students also alleged:
- He takes pictures of us
- He shares personal information (divorce, drinking...)
- He tells us he doesn't like his job

You denied making the alleged statements, sharing personal information and taking pictures of students.

I shared another email sent to me by Ms. Hanna dated March 6th, 2013. In the email, Ms. Hanna alleged: "Today, during first period, Mr. Cunningham brought up ████, a past student, and told the class that he has "loveboy" tattooed across his chest but it's missing the "S" on the end. He said, you know...Loveboys..." You did not deny this allegation ("don't remember"). On March 13th, 2013, the student re-enrolled at IBEAM. As a result, I shared the alleged comment with our Special Education Department. It was determined that the student would not attend IBEAM and was placed at the Intermediate Unit.

It was also alleged by Ms. Hanna (March 21st, 2013) that you shared personal information about a student ████████████ with students – "When ████ told you he was moving to New York he lied. We sent his paperwork to Reading." You acknowledged sharing this information with students.

It is my responsibility to notify you that based on the evidence you have made an inappropriate comment regarding a student (Love Boy/Love Boys comment).

You also shared personal information regarding a student with other students (moved to Reading/we sent his paperwork to Reading).

This memorandum shall serve as a written reprimand to you, to direct you to refrain from making inappropriate comments about students and sharing personal student information with other students. If you engage in the same or similar misconduct in the future, you will be subject to further discipline, up to and including dismissal.

If you disagree with any portion of this letter referencing our meeting, you may submit a written statement and it will be placed in the file with this memorandum.

IBEAM Academy

Allentown School District

Draft

MEMO

To: Matthew Cunningham

From: Jose Rosado, Principal

Subject: Notification of Discipline - Incident date April 23, 2013

Date:

On April 29, 2013 we met to discuss an incident involving you and a student on April 23, 2013 at approximately 2:15 pm.

Also present at this meeting Debra Tretter, AEA President and Deborah Hartman, Executive Director of Special Education. During the meeting I read to you a completed parent "Contact Referral Form" documentaring a concern reported by the parent of student ███████████ pertaining to the incident in question. I also read a statement provided by Mrs. Kemp as well as an incident report completed by Mr. Yasenchak, Behavior Specialist and a Sapphire report completed by you. I explained to you that during my investigation of the incident I found the following: Mr. Cunningham redirected the student for disruptive behaviors and use of profanity, Mrs. Kemp and Mr. Yasenchak intervened and were actively refocusing/redirecting the student in the hallway – away from the direction of Mr. Cunningham, the student made a comment to Mr. Yasenchak – "He's lucky I didn't slap the shit out of him, Mr. Cunningham responded to the comment by saying "is that a threat". The student turned and began to move toward MR. Cunningham, the student was restrained (physically restrained) by Mr. Yasenchak and verbally redirected by Mrs. Kemp, as the student was being restrained and redirected by two staff members, Mr. Cunningham continued to face the student and walk toward him escalating the students behaviors. The incident took place in a crowded hallway and created an unsafe situation.

Upon reviewing the video of the incident, Mr. Yasenchak and I agreed that the student was being successfully refocused and redirected away from Mr. Cunningham; the comment made by the student was made to Mr. Yasenchak and Mr. Cunningham re-engaged the student triggering his reaction and requiring a student restraint.

Upon reviewing the evidence you agreed with the findings of the investigation. I provided you with an opportunity to see the video of the incident and you declined.

Based on the investigation of the incident, I find that your actions further escalated a student disruption leading to a student restraint and provoked the student while he was being restrained. Your actions contributed to an unsafe environment and placed students and staff in danger of injury. This memorandum shall serve as a written reprimand to you, to direct you to avoid making comments that may incite students and to avoid re-engaging students when they are being refocused/redirected and/or restrained by other staff. If you engage in the same or similar misconduct in the future, you will be subject to further discipline, up to and including dismissal.

If you disagree with any portion of this letter referencing our meeting, you may submit a written statement and it will be placed in the file with this memorandum.

Deborah Hartman, Executive Director of Special Education

Allentown School District
31 South Penn Street, Box 328
Allentown, PA 18105
484-765-4162
Fax – 484-765-4188
hartmand@allentownsd.org

Summary of Meetings at IBEAM
RE: Matthew Cunningham, Special Education Teacher
4-29-13

At the request of Jose Rosado, Director of Alternative Education and principal of IBEAM Academy, Deborah Hartman participated in a meeting with a teacher and their union representation, Debra Tretter. The purpose of Mrs. Hartman's participation in the meeting was to witness the event.

The meeting lasted 30 minutes. Prior to the meeting, Mr. Rosado provided a brief reflection on the events that lead to the necessity for holding the meeting. Mr. Rosado provided a video review regarding the event prior to meeting with the teacher and union representation.

The meeting was held with Matthew Cunningham, special education teacher and his union representative, Debra Tretter. The incident, under investigation, occurred on 4-23-13.

The video of the incident clearly shows a behavior specialist successfully escorting a student away from Mr. Cunningham's room. It also shows Mr. Cunningham coming closer to the student as he was being led down the hallway. As reported by Vincent, the behavior specialist, the student said something derogatory about Mr. Cunningham to (him) the behavior specialist. Mr. Cunningham shouted back, "Is that a threat?" That comment escalated the student's behavior to the point where the student required a restraint from the behavior specialist.

The point of this review was to determine if the teacher triggered the student's behavior. Mr. Rosado stated the student's behavior was under the control of the behavior specialist and did not escalate until Mr. Cunningham shouted back at the student, "Is that a threat?"

Mr. Cunningham agreed the account(s) to the incident were accurate.

Mr. Cunningham continued to show the destruction that is occurring in his classroom (on a regular basis). He showed pictures on his iPad of desks and books thrown about his room. Mr. Cunningham feels he is a target by his students.

It was pointed out to Mr. Cunningham that he needs to review his actions to determine if he is contributing to the behaviors of his students with emotional disabilities.

At the end of the meeting, Mr. Cunningham requested a letter of recommendation.

Rosado, Jose (Sr.)

From:	Rosado, Jose (Sr.)
Sent:	Thursday, May 30, 2013 9:20 AM
To:	ekelly@kingspry.com
Cc:	Lozada, Susan; Wildonger, David M; Wheeler, Robert A; Mayo, Russ
Subject:	Notice of Dicipline Letter - Matt Cunningham

Liz,

Please share with me the status of the letter I forwarded to you regarding Notice of Discipline for Matt Cunningham regarding an incident on April 23, 2013.

I completed an investigation of the incident and forwarded my findings and recommendation to you for review and approval before issuing to the teacher.

It is very important that we have a final disposition on this incident/investigation. I will need the documentation to complete my summative evaluation for matt Cunningham.

Please let me know the status of the letter and my recommendation.

Thank you!!!

Jose Rosado
Director of Community & Student Services
Allentown School District
31 S. Penn Street, P.O. Box 328
Allentown, PA 18105
Phone: 484-765-4074
Fax: 484-765-4076
rosadojo@allentownsd.org

1

Rosado, Jose (Sr.)

From:	Elizabeth Kelly <ekelly@kingspry.com>
Sent:	Wednesday, June 12, 2013 2:38 PM
To:	Rosado, Jose (Sr.)
Cc:	Wildonger, David M; Lozada, Susan
Subject:	Another nice write up
Attachments:	Cunningham - Incident date - April 232013.doc

Jose,

     You did another very nice job on the attached written reprimand, Jose. Good job. I have no changes and I think it is fine as is. Please finalize (well, the same goes for the last memo I emailed you about – you should remove the word "draft" from both, but I am sure you know that, and issue as you see fit).-Liz

Elizabeth M. Kelly, Esquire
King Spry Herman Freund & Faul, LLC
One West Broad Street, Suite 700
Bethlehem, PA 18018
(610) 332-0390
Fax: (610) 332-0314

IBEAM Academy
Allentown School District

Approved

MEMO

To: Matthew Cunningham

From: Jose Rosado, Principal

Subject: Notification of Discipline - Incident date April 23, 2013

Date: June 14, 2013

On April 29, 2013 we met to discuss an incident involving you and a student on April 23, 2013 at approximately 2:15 pm.
Also present at this meeting Debra Tretter, AEA President and Deborah Hartman, Executive Director of Special Education. During the meeting I read to you a completed parent "Contact Referral Form" documenting a concern reported by the parent of student ▉▉▉▉▉▉ pertaining to the incident in question. I also read a statement provided by Mrs. Kemp as well as an incident report completed by Mr. Yasenchak, Behavior Specialist and a Sapphire report completed by you. I explained to you that during my investigation of the incident I found the following: Mr. Cunningham redirected the student for disruptive behaviors and use of profanity, Mrs. Kemp and Mr. Yasenchak intervened and were actively refocusing/redirecting the student in the hallway – away from the direction of Mr. Cunningham, the student made a comment to Mr. Yasenchak – "He's lucky I didn't slap the shit out of him, Mr. Cunningham responded to the comment by saying "is that a threat". The student turned and began to move toward Mr. Cunningham, the student was restrained (physically restrained) by Mr. Yasenchak and verbally redirected by Mrs. Kemp, as the student was

being restrained and redirected by two staff members, Mr. Cunningham continued to face the student and walk toward him escalating the students behaviors. The incident took place in a crowded hallway and created an unsafe situation.

Upon reviewing the video of the incident, Mr. Yasenchak and I agreed that the student was being successfully refocused and redirected away from Mr. Cunningham; the comment made by the student was made to Mr. Yasenchak and Mr. Cunningham re-engaged the student triggering his reaction and requiring a student restraint.

Upon reviewing the evidence you agreed with the findings of the investigation. I provided you with an opportunity to see the video of the incident and you declined.

Based on the investigation of the incident, I find that your actions further escalated a student disruption leading to a student restraint and provoked the student while he was being restrained. Your actions contributed to an unsafe environment and placed students and staff in danger of injury. This memorandum shall serve as a written reprimand to you, to direct you to avoid making comments that may incite students and to avoid re-engaging students when they are being refocused/redirected and/or restrained by other staff. If you engage in the same or similar misconduct in the future, you will be subject to further discipline, up to and including dismissal.

If you disagree with any portion of this letter referencing our meeting, you may submit a written statement and it will be placed in the file with this memorandum.

ASD Allentown
SCHOOL DISTRICT

31 South Penn Street ■ P.O. Box 328 ■ Allentown, PA 18105
Administration Center ■ 484-765-4231 ■ Fax: 484-765-4140

CHRISTINA MAZZELLA

Executive Director of Human Resources
mazzellac@allentownsd.org

August 8, 2013

Mr. Matthew Cunningham

RE: 2012-13-028 – "Just Cause-Delayed Reprimands

The written reprimand dated June 14, 2013 concerning the incident dates of March 1, 2013 and March 8, 2013 are hereby rescinded. It will be removed from your personnel file and shredded. If you have any other questions, please feel free to contact me.

Sincerely,

Christina Mazzella

Cc: Debra Tretter, AEA President

Rosado, Jose (Sr.)

From:	Rosado, Jose (Sr.)
Sent:	Monday, February 11, 2013 4:59 PM
To:	ekelly@kingspry.com
Cc:	Lozada, Susan
Subject:	Ryan Miller - Confrontation with Student/safety Plan
Attachments:	MEMO 2-11-13 Ryan Miller.doc

Liz,

I need to meet with you here at IBEAM so that you may view video from our security camera regarding an incident involving Ryan Miller and a student.

I am still investigating the incident and I have created a safety plan. Part of the safety plan includes limiting contact between the student and Ryan Miller.

I have drafted a memo to Ryan Miller (Administrative Directive). Please review the attached memo. I would like to meet with you tomorrow to discuss the safety plan and the attached memo.

Thank you!!!

Jose Rosado
Director of Community & Student Services
Allentown School District
31 S. Penn Street, P.O. Box 328
Allentown, PA 18105
Phone: 484-765-4074
Fax: 484-765-4076
rosadojo@allentownsd.org

1

From:	Elizabeth Kelly <ekelly@kingspry.com>
Sent:	Tuesday, March 05, 2013 2:29 PM
To:	Rosado, Jose (Sr.)
Subject:	Action re R.M.

Jose,

     I recall that you gave me a statement from Nicky Wentz that she gave you after you and I met with Ryan Miller and Debbie Tretter. I cannot now find my copy of that statement. Do you have a copy? If so, can you please send it to me? Also, I know you investigated to find out if there were studnets in Mr. Miller's homeroom on the morning of Feb 6. I can't recall the answer – were there any students in his homeroom at that time?

I just want to have a complete file.

     Also, and more important? Do you have a recommendation? I am wondering if you want to issue Ryan Miller a disciplinary notice for leaving his homeroom to go off on a mission for which he was not needed and the others were handling (Al Blount and Ms. Averich) or do you want to issue him a written directive to avoid leaving his homeroom, avoid entering the ATS room and avoid collecting science homework in the morning. Let me know your thoughts when you can. Thanks, -Liz

Elizabeth M. Kelly, Esquire

King Spry Herman Freund & Faul, LLC
One West Broad Street, Suite 700
Bethlehem, PA 18018
(610) 332-0390
Fax: (610) 332-0314

Nichole Wentz *[signature]* 2/6/13

Site Director

Communities In schools LV

IBEAM Academy

I was working at my desk on 2/6/13 around 9:00am. Mr. Miller came to me about an issue with ██████████ in Ms. Avrich's class. I immediately came with Mr. Miller to the Ms. Avrich's classroom. Ms. Avrich (Homeroom Teacher) and Al Blount (Behavioral Specialist) were already in the classroom. Upon entering the room to address █████, Al Blount reported to me that he had refocused █████ about the incident prior to returning to class. Al Blount reported that the student was fine. I checked with █████ and he reported the same. As I was speaking to █████, Mr. Miller came into the room asking for homework. Al Blount redirected Mr. Miller that it was not a good time to ask anything of █████. Mr. Miller walked away and said "somebody needs to do something". Al Blount and I had conference in the hallway to support the plan to assist and monitor the situation.

CONFIDENTIAL MEMO

Nikki Wentz Interview (Telephone Conference) Regarding Ryan Miller
Incident February 6, 2013

This interview was a follow up to written statement that Ms. Wentz provided
on 2/6/13.
Interview Date: 2/27/13
Present in my office during the interview: Logan Novak, Alvin Blount, Jose
Rosado

During the telephone conference I told Ms. Wentz I was following up on
statements/evidence regarding an incident between Ryan Miller and a
student (██████).
I asked Ms. Wentz about any specific comment she may have made during
morning circle regarding the student. Ms. Wentz stated that she did not
recall making any specific statement regarding the student.
I told Ms. Wentz that Mr. Miller claims she stated "If ██████ does one more
thing he is out." Ms. Wentz told me that "I would not have made an absolute
statement such as that." Ms. Wentz stated that she made a general statement
about student behaviors ("Issue of the week").
Ms. Wentz stated "If there is a major issue with a student come see me." The
statement was not specific to any student.
I asked Ms. Wentz what happened when Mr. Miller came to her office
regarding an incident with ██████. Ms. Wentz stated the following "he (Mr.
Miller) came to my office regarding an incident with ██████, he had a write
up and told me ██████ was in Ms. Avrich's room. He took me (walked me)
to Ms. Avrich's room to get ██████."
Ms. Wentz stated she would not have known where ██████ was unless Mr.
Miller told her.

_____
Ms. Wentz

_____
Mr. Blount

_____
Ms. Novak

_____
Mr. Rosado

CONFIDENTIAL

Draft w/ recommendation (suspension) To: Liz Kelly

To: Ryan Miller, Teacher

From: Jose Rosado, Principal

Subject: Investigation Regarding Incident with Student ▓▓▓▓▓▓

Date: March 11, 2013

This memorandum represents a summary of our discussion, which began at approximately 11:15 am, February 27, 2013 in my office. In addition to us, Elizabeth Kelly (Interim Executive Director of Accountability) and Debra Tretter (Allentown Education Association President) were present.
As indicated to you in an email from me dated February 22nd, 2013, the purpose of the meeting was investigatory in nature.
At the onset of the meeting, I again stated the nature of the meeting. Upon request, I also provided the specific nature of the concerns.
During the meeting I presented statements from staff, a student statement and notes from a meeting with▓▓▓▓▓▓▓ (student) and his mother. We also reviewed a Sapphire discipline referral you submitted and a video of the incident that took place between you and the student on February 6th, 2013.
During the interview you acknowledged a confrontation with the student at approximately 9:02 am where the student directed profanity toward you. The evidence shows that after this confrontation the student was referred to a behavior specialist (Mr. Alvin Blount) for an intervention. The evidence shows that at approximately 9:07 am, the student left his homeroom (Ms. Avrich's homeroom) to speak with Mr. Blount. The evidence shows that you and the student had a verbal exchange as he was walking down the hall toward Mr. Blount. At approximately 9:17 am, the evidence shows that Mr. Blount escorted the student back to his homeroom (Ms. Avrich's homeroom) and entered the classroom with him. Video evidence shows you

standing at the door of your classroom facing in the direction of Mr. Blount and the student as they walked toward Ms. Avrich's classroom. During questioning, you claimed not to see Mr. Blount escorting the student and entering the classroom. Upon Mr. Blount entering the classroom with the student, you immediately went to Ms. Wentz's office. Shortly, thereafter you walked Ms. Wentz to Ms. Avrich's classroom.

According to your statement during questioning, you acknowledge that you saw the student leave his homeroom and go with Mr. Blount for a refocus. You also stated that "I had no idea that Mr. Blount had escorted (student) back to homeroom (Ms. Avrich's classroom.)

However, the evidence shows that you sought out Ms. Wentz after Mr. Blount escorted the student to Ms. Avrich's classroom. According to the evidence, you went to Ms. Wentz's office with a copy of a discipline referral regarding the student. Further, you told Ms. Wentz that the student was in Ms. Avrichs's classroom and then proceed to "walk " Ms. Wentz to Ms. Avrich's classroom.

Based on your response during questioning, you last made visual contact with the student when he was walking toward the refocus room for an intervention with Mr. Blount. However, when you sought Ms. Wentz to intervene with the student you told her that the student was in Ms. Avrich's classroom and walked her to the classroom.

This evidence suggests that were not truthful during the questioning.

Further, your actions caused for staff to be placed in very compromising situations.

It is my responsibility to notify you that based on the evidence you are being suspended for (one-three days) without pay and you will be reassigned out of the alternative education program for the 2013-2014 school year.

If you disagree with any portion of this letter referencing our meeting, you may submit your written account, and it will be placed in the file with this letter.

Mr. Jose Rosado
Director of Community & Student Services
31 S. Penn Street, P. O. Box 328
Allentown, PA 18105
Phone: 484-765-4074

CONFIDENTIAL

Approved
(written reprimand)

TO: Ryan Miller

FROM: Jose Rosado, Principal

RE: Notice of Discipline – incident of Feb 6, 2013

DATE: April 29, 2013

On February 27, 2013, we met to discuss your conduct on February 6, 2013, involving a student, ███. Also present at this meeting were Debra Tretter, AEA President, and Elizabeth Kelly, Interim Executive Director of Accountability.

On the occasion of the incident, you wrote an entry in Sapphire, referring ███ for discipline, because he stated "fuck you" and "shut the fuck up" to you. Your Sapphire referral is dated February 6, 2013, at 9:02 a.m. After entering the referral, you stood outside your classroom and, as Ms. Averich and ███ walked out of their classroom, you gestured with your arms and hands, moving your arms up and down before going back inside your classroom. Ms. Averich accompanied ███ down the hallway toward the refocus room, and shortly afterward, she returned to her classroom alone.

Approximately ten minutes later, you stood outside your homeroom as Al Blount, Behavior Management Specialist, walked back to Ms. Averich's homeroom from the refocus room with ███; where both Mr. Blount and ███ entered the classroom. At this time you were standing in the hallway outside your classroom. Mr. Blount remained in the classroom, and you walked down the hall in the direction of the refocus room and returned shortly thereafter with Nicole Wentz of CIS. Near the door of Ms. Averich's classroom, Ms. Wentz opened the door to enter and you continued walking toward your classroom. Next, Ms. Wentz and Mr. Blount stood outside the classroom, apparently having a conversation. You were walking away from your classroom and passed them in the hallway to take a piece of paper, identified as science homework, from a student farther down the hallway.

At the investigatory interview on February 27, we reviewed video captured from the school's hallway cameras on the first floor, west wing, which depicted the above described events. You answered my questions except as advised by your Association representative, and you were given the opportunity to make any statement on your own behalf. On this occasion you stated that you did not see Mr. Blount and ███ return to Ms. Averich's classroom from the direction of the refocus room, although you were standing in the hallway in view of them when this occurred. I am unable to accept this statement as truthful, because you were standing and able to look in plain view of both Mr. Blount and ███ I note that you also informed me at the meeting that you were interested in seeing that "something was done" in response to ████ misconduct. After Mr. Blount returned to the classroom with ███, you immediately left the vicinity of your homeroom and went down the hallway to find Ms. Wentz. You returned with her to the classroom less than 1.5 minutes later, where ███ and Mr. Blount remained. I must conclude that you were less than fully truthful when responding that you did not know ███ and Mr. Blount were in the classroom.

When asked if there were students in your homeroom at the time you left it to find Ms. Wentz, you initially hesitated and then later replied no. However, there was no need for you to leave your homeroom at this time. You left the classroom to pursue a personal goal of your own, which you identified as making sure Ms. Wentz was aware of your referral regarding ███ in sapphire and you also indicated that you wanted to "see something done about ███" There was no valid reason for this other than your own desire that Ms. Wentz intervene, which was unnecessary at the time. The student was no longer actively engaged in misconduct when he returned the classroom with Mr. Blount.

This memo shall serve as a written reprimand to you, to direct you to avoid leaving your classroom to pursue matters relating to student discipline being handled without the need for your assistance and to avoid providing untruthful answers in investigatory interviews conducted by District administration. Your obligation in such interviews is always to tell the truth. If you engage in the same or similar misconduct in the future, you will be subject to further discipline, up to and including dismissal.

If you disagree with any portion of this letter referencing our meeting, you may submit a written statement and it will be placed in the file with this memorandum.

Date of issuance of this Memorandum to Mr. Miller: _____May 9_____, 2013

Rosado, Jose (Sr.)

From:	Rosado, Jose (Sr.)
Sent:	Friday, March 22, 2013 4:15 PM
To:	'Elizabeth Kelly'
Cc:	Wildonger, David M; Lozada, Susan
Subject:	RE: Investigatory Meeting

Liz,

Ryan responded to my email and stated that he wants Deb Tretter present to represent him. The nature of my concern is an allegation made by two students and confirmed by a third that Ryan Miller told two female students to "Shut the fuck up". Only three students were in the classroom at the time. All three provided written statements alleging that Ryan Miller made the alleged statement.

I have spoken with the mother of one of the female students and she confirmed that her daughter informed her of the incident ("Teacher refused to help my daughter with her assignment" and "Teacher cursed at my daughter"). I told the parent that I am investigating the incident and the allegations her daughter has made against the teacher (Ryan Miller).

However –again - I am not able to address the concern in a timely manner due the teachers insistence on having Deb Tretter present as opposed to the building representative.

Due to the nature of this alleged incident and the parents concern, I believe we should address this matter as expediently as possible.

During our phone conversation earlier, you indicated that you would have your secretary contact the AEA office to check Deb Tretter's availability for this meeting.

Please let me know when this meeting could be scheduled.

Thank you!!!

Jose Rosado
Director of Community & Student Services
Allentown School District
31 S. Penn Street, P.O. Box 328
Allentown, PA 18105
Phone: 484-765-4074
Fax: 484-765-4076
rosadojo@allentownsd.org

Community & Student Services
Contact Referral Form

Method of Contact: ☒ Phone ☐ In Person **ASD Contact Person** K. Toner

Contact Information		
Name of Person Making Contact: ▓▓▓▓▓		**Date:** 3-25-13
Student's Name (if applicable): ▓▓▓		**Home Phone:** **Cell Phone:** ▓▓▓▓
Relationship to Student: Mother	**School:** IBEAM	**Grade:** 9	**Special Ed:** ☐ Yes ☒ No

Reason			
☐ Suspension / Detention	☐ Attendance	☐ Enrollment	☐ Disenrollment
☐ Change of School	☐ Threat	☐ Abuse	☐ Bullying / Harassment
☒ Spoke with Principal / Counselor	☒ Other Teacher Complaint		

Details

Description of Concern:

Mom called stating ▓▓ has been having trouble in class with her one teacher - Ryan Miller. She is in the process of being tested for Spec Education this week. Mom stated ▓▓ came home and told her about Mr. Miller and a comment he made to her. She stated ▓▓ has been trying to get extra help in his class and has gone to Mr. Miller several times and he tells her "NO". Mom stated either on Wednesday or Thursday of last week (3-21 or 3-22) she asked for help again and he stated, "Do it your fucking self" and was then sent to the reflection room. Mom stated other student also heard this comment made by Mr. Miller. She said she spoke with Mr. Rosado and he has been helpful and stated he would investigate it, but she should also contact the Administration Building to make a formal concern. I explained our process to mom and let her know someone would be getting in contact with her.

3/26/13 - Mom called to let us know Mr. Miller just called her about ▓▓ behavior, mom stated she told Mr. Miller she was aware of his type of behavior in the last couple of days and he told her she should take it up with Administration and hung up on mom. Moms said she called then and spoke with Mr. Rosado and expressed her concerns of having ▓▓ remain in his classroom. Mr. Rosado stated he would remove her out of his class for today. Mom would like ▓▓ permanently removed from Mr. Miller classroom. She would also not like Mr. Miller calling the house anymore, to have Mr. Rosado call her to let her aware of anything regarding ▓▓.

Mom stated when she was in the office on 3-13-13 while in the Main Office mom overheard another student speaking about Mr. Miller and the way she was treated by him on this day in class. Mom stated she believes everything her daughter is telling her about Mr. Miller.

Referred to: J. Rosado	**Date of Referral:** 3-25-13

Rosado, Jose (Sr.)

From:	Rosado, Jose (Sr.)
Sent:	Wednesday, April 10, 2013 1:49 PM
To:	ekelly@kingspry.com
Cc:	Wildonger, David M; Lozada, Susan
Subject:	FW: Parent Concern - IBEAM
Attachments:	~~████████████ IBEAM ████████~~

Liz,

Please see attached parent contact referral form regarding Ryan Miller.

This is the mother of one of the girls that alleged Ryan told her to "Shut the fuck up."

I have completed my investigation regarding the alleged incident and have forwarded my findings and recommendation to you for review. Please let me know when I can proceed with a follow up meeting with Ryan regarding this incident and my recommendation.

Thank you!!!

Jose Rosado
Director of Community & Student Services
Allentown School District
31 S. Penn Street, P.O. Box 328
Allentown, PA 18105
Phone: 484-765-4074
Fax: 484-765-4076
rosadojo@allentownsd.org

Community & Student Services
Contact Referral Form

Method of Contact: ☐ Phone ☒ In Person   **ASD Contact Person** K. Toner

Contact Information			
Name of Person Making Contact: ▓▓▓▓		**Date:** 4-10-13	
Student's Name (if applicable): ▓▓▓▓		**Home Phone:** **Cell Phone:** ▓▓▓▓	
Relationship to Student: Mother	**School:** IBEAM	**Grade:** 9	**Special Ed:** ☐ Yes ☒ No

Reason			
☐ Suspension / Detention	☐ Attendance	☐ Enrollment	☐ Disenrollment
☐ Change of School	☐ Threat	☐ Abuse	☐ Bullying / Harassment
☐ Spoke with Principal / Counselor	☒ Other Teacher		

Details

Description of Concern:

Mom stated ▓▓▓ is having trouble with Ryan Miller a teacher; he has been giving ▓▓▓ a hard time. Mom said she understands that they should be giving them a hard time since it is IBEAM, but Mr. Miller stated to ▓▓▓, "Shut the fuck up". Mom stated this happen about two weeks ago and she is still having trouble in his class. Mom stated another time ▓▓▓ was going to his class and he has told the students if the door is closed you don't come in. Mom stated ▓▓▓ tried going to class and the door was closed so she went to the refocus room and then tried to return to his class a little later. When she arrived the door was open and she entered and he said with an attitude, "You're later". Mom said he did make another comment, but she didn't know what it was.

Mom said she has spoken with the Principal, Mr. Rosado and he told her she should come to file an official report at the Adm. Building. Mom also mentioned ▓▓▓ isn't the only student having trouble with Mr. Miller. I explained our procedures to mom and let her know someone would be calling her.

Referred to: J. Rosado	**Date of Referral:** 4-10-13
Follow up:	
Referred to:	**Date of Referral:**

Confidential Memorandum

Draft
TO: Liz Kelly

To: Ryan Miller, Teacher

From: Jose Rosado, Principal

Subject: Investigation Regarding Incident with Student ████████
████████) Incident Date - March 21, 2013

Date: April 9, 2013

This memorandum represents a summary of our discussion, which began at approximately 2:25 pm, March 26, 2013 in my office. In addition to us, Elizabeth Kelly (Interim Executive Director of Accountability) and Debra Tretter (Allentown Education Association President) were present. As indicated to you in an email form me dated March 22, 2013. The purpose of the meeting was investigatory in nature.

During the meeting I presented student statements completed by ████████ and ████████ . Both of these students reported trust during your Science class on March 21, 2013, you engaged in a verbal interaction with the students and allege that you said to them "shut the fuck up". Both of these students left your classroom and went to the "refocus room". One student from that class remained in your classroom. While the tow students were in the refocus room, they each completed a student reaction form alleging that you made the inappropriate comment (using profanity directed at students). While the tow students alleging you made the inappropriate the third student about the incident. This student ████████ provided me a statement and completed a student reaction form which supported the statements provided by the two students that made the allegation ("Mr. Miller told both of them to shut the fuck up"). This student had no contact with the other two that made the allegation. Further, this student received all 2's (maximum rating) from you during the class period in question. You also commented "great job" on the students point sheet.

During the meeting we also discussed the Sapphire discipline reports you completed for the students ████████ and ███████). On the date in question, you noted that both students left your classroom due to their disruptive behaviors. During our meeting you denied making the alleged comment ("shut the fuck up"). However, the evidence supports the student statements. Specifically the statement provided by ████████ which corroborated the statements of the two students that made the allegation. This student was interviewed prior to having any contact with the students that made the allegation. This evidence suggests you were not truthful during the questioning.

During our meeting I also shared with you a telephone call that I received from the mother of ████████

Mrs. ████ told me she had received a call from you at approximately 9:45 am. She made the following comments regarding your conversation:

- "I don't want him calling me anymore"
- "I'm very concerned with my daughter with him"
- "Mr. Miller cursed at my daughter and refused to help her"
- "I don't want my daughter in his classroom"
- "I'm calling the administration building to report this"

During our meeting you did acknowledge that you called Mrs. ████, upon my directive, to discuss the incident in question. You also acknowledged that the conversation did not go well and the call was abruptly terminated. It is my responsibility to notify you that based on the evidence you are being issued a written reprimand. If you disagree with any portion of this letter referencing our meeting, you may submit your written account and it will be placed in the file with this letter.

From: Wildonger, David M
Sent: Monday, April 15, 2013 3:32 PM
To: Rosado, Jose (Sr.)
Subject: Re: Meeting Request

Jose
Please continue to work with Susan as your supervisor and Liz Kelly in H.R.

Sent from my iPhone

On Apr 15, 2013, at 10:41 AM, "Rosado, Jose (Sr.)" <rosadojo@allentownsd.org> wrote:

Dave,
I have completed my interview/Investigation with Ryan Miller regarding two Incidents (Possible Acts Of Insubordination). I am requesting a meeting with you to review video evidence (Liz Kelly has seen the video) which supports my findings and the recommendation I will make. I spoke with Nidia on Friday and requested a meeting for Tuesday or Wednesday (if you were available). Please let me know when we could meet.

Thanks!!!

Jose Rosado
Director of Community & Student Services
Allentown School District
31 S. Penn Street, P.O. Box 328
Allentown, PA 18105
Phone: 484-765-4074
Fax: 484-765-4076
rosadojo@allentownsd.org

Confidential Memo

Draft
To: Liz Kelly
Recommendation:
1 day suspension
w/out pay

To: Ryan Miller, Teacher

From: Jose Rosado, Principal

Subject: Investigation Regarding Possible Acts of Insubordination
           (March 26, 2013 & April 2, 2013)

Date: May 1, 2013

This memorandum represents a summary of our meeting, which began at approximately 12:10 pm, April 11th, 2013 in my office. In addition to us, Elizabeth Kelly (Interim Executive Director of Accountability), Susan Lozado (Executive Director of Community and Student Services), Deb Tretter (Allentown Education Association President) and Cori Fetcho (PSEA Uniserver Rep.) were present. You and your representatives acknowledged that I provided you appropriate notification of the nature of the meeting (Possible Acts of Insubordination – March 26th, 2013, April 2nd, 2013) via email and agreed to have both incidents discussed during this meeting. During the meeting we also reviewed and discussed a meeting which took place on September 18th, 2012 with Mr. David Wildonger, Chief Operations Officer. The purpose of that meeting was to clarify roles and expectations between us as teacher/principal and my responsibilities regarding observations/evaluations. The expectations (regarding my role as the administrators) were clear and no documentation was provided to contest the expectations established by Mr. Wildonger during the September 18th, 2012 meeting.

The first incident discussed was the March 26th, 2013 incident. I explained that I spoke with and reviewed a 'student reaction form" completed by a student (   ), in the refocus room, regarding an incident in your classroom. After meeting with the student I went to your classroom to monitor students and any other potential disruptions. Upon arriving at your classroom, I found another teacher in the classroom, Mrs. Ninesling, and no students. You acknowledged this during the meeting. Upon informing you of the purpose of my visit you noted that there were no students in the classroom. I followed by inquiring about the student that was in the refocus room. You responded by stating that you were not comfortable speaking with me in the classroom and you stepped out into the hallway where we can be on the video. You acknowledged this as accurate. Since two other teachers were in the hallway at that time, I asked you to re-enter the room to continue the conversation. At that point you pulled your Weingarten card from your wallet and invoked your Weingarten rights. I informed you that the nature of the conversation is not disciplinary in nature and that I wanted to discuss the incident with the student. At that point you read the Weingarten rights to me and held the card up to the video camera. I repeated the nature of the discussion is not disciplinary, to which you responded "I'm not refusing to talk with you or meet with you. I just won't do it without my union rep." You then walked away from me and went back into your classroom. I attempted to review the video footage of the incident with you and your representatives and you refused to watch it. Your refusal to speak with me regarding my inquiries of the incident with the student contradicted the expectations established by Mr. Wildonger. Although you invoked your Weingarten rights, those rights were not applicable in this situation and your actions are deemed an act of insubordination.

The second incident discussed was the April 2nd, 2013 incident. I explained that I was visiting teachers as a follow up to an email I sent regarding the restorative assembly (I visited every homeroom – three homerooms prior to coming to your homeroom). You acknowledged that you knew the purpose of my visit because I was holding copies of the restorative assembly email in my hand. When you opened the door I stated that I wanted to speak with you about the assembly (plan to address disruptive students/students not wanting to attend the assembly). You stated "I don't feel comfortable speaking with you in my classroom; I'm going out into the hallway where we have video." You walked into the hallway and left the students unattended.

In the hallway you pulled out the Weingarten card, held it up to the video camera and told me you were invoking your Weingarten rights. I told you I wanted to speak about the assembly and that you did not have to read the card to me – you understood the nature of my desire to speak with you. At that point I told you that if you wanted, you could give me the card to read. At that point, you walked passed me, turned, and handed me the card and said "keep it".

As I began to read the card, you started to pull your classroom door shut. I said "wait" and I reached for the door (placing my fingertips on the door) as you continued to pull the door and slam it closed. Your explanation for the door slamming was that it was caused by a "vacuum". This explanation was found to be unrealistic. Although you invoked your Weingarten rights, it has been determined that "Weingarten" was not applicable given that you clearly understood the nature of my request to meet with you and that it was not disciplinary in nature. I attempted to play the video of the incident but you and your representative declined to view it.

Your actions have been determined to be an act of insubordination and extreme disrespect toward your immediate supervisor and principal.

It is my responsibility to inform that your actions constitute an act of insubordination and thus, you are hereby notified that you will be suspended without pay for one day.

If you disagree with any portion of this letter referencing our meeting, you may submit a written statement and it will be placed in the file with this memorandum.

IBEAM Academy

Allentown School District

Draft

To: Liz Kelly

MEMO

To: Ryan Miller, Teacher

From: Jose Rosado, Principal

Subject: Notification of Discipline – Incident of April 22nd, 2013

Date:

On April 29th, 2013, we met to discuss your conduct on April 22, 2013 at approximately 2:25 pm in the hallway outside of your classroom. Also present at the meeting were Debra Tretter, AEA President and Deborah Hartman, Executive Director of Special Education.

During the meeting I presented my observations of the incident: I came into the hallway to monitor change of class, I saw you standing outside of your classroom, I heard you yell – Fight, Fight we have students fighting and no behavior specialists or security. I did not observe a fight, as I walked down the hallway you entered your classroom, I observed no fight. I also read statements provided by Sam Martinez, CIS Staff and Alisha Keiser, Teacher. The statements provided by these staff members was consistent with my own observations – specifically, they heard you yell, "Fight Fight..." and witnessed no fight. I explained to you that I requested statements from Mr. Martinez and Mrs. Keiser because they were the only other staff visibly present in the hallway at the time of the incident as seen on the video (security camera).

Upon questioning, you acknowledged being in the hallway at the time in question. You also acknowledged yelling several statements including "fight" ("the third time I yelled for help, I yelled fight").

When I asked you if a fight took place, you responded there was a "potential for a fight, two students raised their hands and squared off – yes."

I stated to you that based on the observations and statements provided by staff, the student's behaviors were prompted/escalated by your actions (students reacted to Mr. Miller yelling "fight" by "cursing at him and mocking what he was yelling down the hallway").

Although you characterized the student's behaviors as "extremely dangerous", you did not submit any Sapphire Discipline Reports for the incident. When presented with this fact, you stated that you would complete and submit the referrals (one week after the incident).

Based on my observation of the incident, as well as the statements provided by two staff members that witnessed the incident, I find that your actions prompted/escalated a student disruption, created an unsafe/potentially dangerous environment for students and staff and was generally irresponsible and reckless in nature.

This memo shall serve as a written reprimand to you, to direct you to avoid yelling out irresponsible/reckless comments which can serve to incite student disruptions and endanger the safety of students and staff. If you engage in the same or similar misconduct in the future, you will be subject to further discipline, up to and including dismissal.

If you disagree with any portion of this letter referencing our meeting, you may submit a written statement and it will be placed in the file with this memorandum.

Deborah Hartman, Executive Director of Special Education

Allentown School District
31 South Penn Street, Box 328
Allentown, PA 18105
484-765-4162
Fax – 484-765-4188
hartmand@allentownsd.org

Summary of Meetings at IBEAM
RE: Ryan Miller, Alternative Education Teacher
4-29-13

At the request of Jose Rosado, Director of Alternative Education and principal of IBEAM Academy, Deborah Hartman participated in a meeting with an IBEAM teacher and their union representation, Debra Tretter. The purpose of Mrs. Hartman's participation in the meeting was to witness the event.

The meeting lasted 30 to 45 minutes. Prior to the meeting, Mr. Rosado provided a brief reflection on the events that lead to the necessity for holding the meeting.

The meeting was held with Mr. Ryan Miller and Mrs. Tretter. This meeting was in regard to a hallway incident that occurred on April 22, 2013. Mr. Rosado prepared all documents and questions to ask of Mr. Miller in advance. Mr. Rosado began the process by discussing the evidence he had collected. This evidence included the written testimonies of three individuals who witnessed the incident. They included; Jose Rosado's observations, Sam Martinez's written account, and Alisha Keiser's written account. Mr. Rosado stated that he selected the named witnesses via their visibility on the video camera. Mr. Rosado stated the selected witnesses were postured to both see and hear the events. Mrs. Tretter stated that the video information is inadmissible evidence in disciplinary actions. The video was not shown during the meeting. The video was not seen by Mrs. Hartman either.

All three accounts were similar in that each stated that students were returning from an activity from the lower level. The school schedule was changed due to staff preparing for an audit. Mr. Miller was heard, as far away as the office, yelling, "fight, fight." After the yelling of "fight" students held up their fists to mock a fight. Mr. Rosado was physically on the scene shortly after hearing "fight, fight," but at that point students were in their respective rooms. Mr. Rosado stated that he checked with each teacher (Mr. Miller and Ms. Niseling) to make sure that there were no problems in the room. One student was asked to step out to speak with Mr. Rosado. It is Mr. Rosado's impression that the student behaviors escalated as a direct result of shouting-out of "fight, fight" by Mr. Miller. Additionally, through this meeting, it was discovered that there was no fight, but the teacher, Mr. Miller interpreted students at the water fountain as a "potentially dangerous" situation.

The point Mr. Rosado was trying to make was that yelling "fight, fight" escalated an unnecessary situation. It is believed by Mr. Rosado that the student interpreted the request to step to the hallway as a direct connection to the shout-out of "fight, fight." Mr. Rosado believes the student, Mark, thought he was being called out to address a fight that never happened. The student escalated in behaviors which required the student to be restrained and then the student was later suspended. Mr. Rosado maintains Mr. Miller's unnecessary shouting incited the student's behaviors.

Mr. Rosado prepared the artifacts for the meeting. He prepared a set of questions for direct responses from Mr. Miller. Responses from Mr. Miller were generally not specific to the questions asked. There was hostility expressed to Mr. Rosado with many salacious remarks made to Mr. Rosado commenting on his organization and operation of the alternative school.

Mr. Miller did not appear to see any connection between his yelling of "fight, fight" as a precipitating antecedent to the behaviors exhibited by the student.

Now, 7-days after the incident, uncharacteristically, Mr. Miller has not enter the incident into Sapphire. However he indicated he sent a write-up to Mrs. Tretter. Additionally, he mentioned he would enter the incident into Sapphire subsequent to the meeting.

When asked of Mr. Miller, "Would there have been any other way to handle the non-incident?" No viable response was offered.

The meeting did not appear to result in a clearer understanding of maladaptive student behaviors or how to defuse or deescalate student behaviors.

Rosado, Jose (Sr.)

From:	Rosado, Jose (Sr.)
Sent:	Thursday, May 30, 2013 9:11 AM
To:	ekelly@kingspry.com
Cc:	Lozada, Susan; Wildonger, David M; Mayo, Russ; Wheeler, Robert A
Subject:	Notice of Dicipline Letters - Ryan Miller

Liz,

Please share with me the status of the three letters I forwarded to you regarding Notice of Discipline for Ryan Miller regarding incidents on the following dates:

Incident date – March 21, 2013 (Incident with two female students – alleged profanity toward students)
Incident date – March 26, 2013 & April 2, 2013 (Possible Acts of Insubordination)
Incident date – April 22, 2013 (Comment Creating an unsafe Environment)

I completed investigations on all of these incidents and forwarded my findings and recommendations to you for review and approval before issuing to the teacher.

It is very important that we have a final disposition on these incidents/Investigations. I will need the documentation to complete my Summative Evaluation for Ryan Miller.

Please let me know the status of the letters and my recommendations.

Thank you!!!

Jose Rosado
Director of Community & Student Services
Allentown School District
31 S. Penn Street, P.O. Box 328
Allentown, PA 18105
Phone: 484-765-4074
Fax: 484-765-4076
rosadojo@allentownsd.org

1

On June 4, 2013, at 11:48 AM, "Rosado, Jose (Sr.)" rosadojo@allentownsd.org wrote:

Dave,

I have spoken with Liz regarding the status of the Notification of Discipline Letter referenced below. As you are aware, Summative Evaluations for teachers are due next week – June 12, 2013. I need the documentation to include as part of my summative evaluation for Ryan Miller.

If Liz is unable to review and approve the letters this week, is there someone else available/able to review and approve the letters that I have already written?

Would I be able to use the incidents (my investigation, findings and recommendation) if the Notification of Discipline Letters are not issued?

Thank you!!!

Jose Rosado
Director of Community & Student Services

From:	Elizabeth Kelly ekelly@kingspry.com
Sent:	Wednesday, June 5, 2013 12:26 PM
To:	Rosado, Jose (Sr.)
Cc:	Wildonger, David M
Subject:	Re: Notification of Discipline Letters – Ryan Miller

Jose,

Right now, I am afraid there is no one else to review the notices. You can put the incidents as matters of concern on the evaluations, but you should not "double dip" by sending both a notice of discipline and giving them a lowered rating for the same underlying incident. If you want to, we can speak about this tomorrow.

Sent from my iphone

Confidential Memorandum

Approved

To: Ryan Miller, Teacher

From: Jose Rosado, Principal

Subject: ~~Notice of Discipline~~ - Incident Date - March 21, 2013

Date: June 14, 2013

This memorandum represents a summary of our discussion, which began at approximately 2:25 pm, March 26, 2013 in my office. In addition to us, Elizabeth Kelly (Interim Executive Director of Accountability) and Debra Tretter (Allentown Education Association President) were present. As indicated to you in an email form me dated March 22, 2013. The purpose of the meeting was investigatory in nature.

During the meeting I presented student statements completed by ███████ ██████ and ██████████. Both of these students reported that during your science class on March 21, 2013, you engaged in a verbal interaction with the students and allege that you said to them "shut the fuck up". Both of these students left your classroom and went to the "refocus room". One student from that class remained in your classroom. While the two students were in the refocus room, they each completed a student reaction form alleging that you made the inappropriate comment (using profanity directed at students). While the two students alleging you made the inappropriate comment were in the refocus room, I interviewed the third student about the incident. This student ██████████, provided me a statement and completed a student reaction form which supported the statements provided by the two students that made the allegation ("Mr. Miller told both of them to shut the fuck up"). This student had no contact with the other two that made the allegation. Further, this student received all 2's (maximum rating) from you during the class period in question. You also commented "great job" on the students point sheet.

During the meeting we also discussed the Sapphire discipline reports you completed for the students ████████ and ████████). On the date in question, you noted that both students left your classroom due to their disruptive behaviors. During our meeting you denied making the alleged comment ("shut the fuck up"). However, the evidence supports the student statements. Specifically the statement provided by ████████ which corroborated the statements of the two students that made the allegation. This student was interviewed prior to having any contact with the students that made the allegation. This evidence suggests you were not truthful during the questioning.

During our meeting I also shared with you a telephone call that I received from the mother of ████████.

Mrs. ████ told me she had received a call from you at approximately 9:45 am. She made the following comments regarding your conversation:

- "I don't want him calling me anymore"
- "I'm very concerned with my daughter with him"
- "Mr. Miller cursed at my daughter and refused to help her"
- "I don't want my daughter in his classroom"
- "I'm calling the administration building to report this"

During our meeting you did acknowledge that you called Mrs. ████, upon my directive, to discuss the incident in question. You also acknowledged that the conversation did not go well and the call was abruptly terminated. It is my responsibility to notify you that based on the evidence you are being issued a written reprimand. If you disagree with any portion of this letter referencing our meeting, you may submit your written account and it will be placed in the file with this letter.

Confidential Memor *Approved*
By: Liz Kelly
- No Suspension

To: Ryan Miller, Teacher

From: Jose Rosado, Principal

Subject: Memorandum of direction
            (March 26, 2013 & April 2, 2013)

Date: June 14, 2013

This memorandum represents a summary of our meeting, which began at approximately 12:10 pm, April 11th, 2013 in my office.

On April 11, 2013, we met to discuss two incidents, which occurred on March 26, 2013 and April 2, 2013. Also present were Elizabeth Kelly, Interim Executive Director of Accountability, Susan Lozada, Executive Director of Community and Student Services, and your Association President, Debra Tretter. Cori Fetcho, PSEA Uniserv Representative, was also present. I indicated that you were given advance notice of the meeting and the two incidents that were subjects of discussion, and you acknowledged receipt of the notice.

We reviewed a prior meeting that occurred on September 18th, 2012, with David Wildonger, Chief Operations Officer. On that occasion, we met to clarify each other's roles as teacher and principal and to review expectations. We discussed that it is necessary for principal and teacher to communicate with each other concerning various matters in the workplace on an ongoing basis.

Next, we discussed an incident that occurred on March 26th, 2013. I explained that I spoke with and reviewed a 'student reaction form" completed by a student ██████████, in the refocus room, regarding an incident in your classroom. After meeting with the student, I went to your classroom to monitor students and other potential disruptions. Upon arriving at your classroom, I found another teacher, Mrs. Ninesling, and no students. Upon informing you of the purpose of my visit you noted that there were no students in the classroom. I asked you about the student who was then in the refocus room. You responded that you were not comfortable speaking with me in the classroom and you stepped out into the hallway to be in the line of sight of the school's video cameras. Because two other teachers were in the hallway at that time, and I did not wish to discuss the student matter in their presence out of respect for you, I asked you to re-enter the room to continue the conversation.

You responded by presenting me with a "Weingarten Rights" card from your wallet and you invoked your Weingarten rights. I immediately informed you that the nature of my conversation was not disciplinary and that I wanted to discuss the incident with the student. You read the card to me and held it up to the video camera. I repeated that the nature of the discussion was not disciplinary, to which you responded "I'm not refusing to talk with you or meet with you. I just won't do it without my union rep." You then walked away from me and went back into your classroom. At our meeting with the union representatives, I offered to review the video footage of the incident with you and your representatives refused to watch it. You also denied that I informed you that the nature of the conversation was not disciplinary.

Your refusal to speak with me regarding my inquiries of the incident with the student contradicted the expectations established by Mr. Wildonger. Although you invoked your Weingarten rights, it is important to remember that Weingarten rights are not intended for use as a shield to avoid conversation with a supervisor on all occasions. Rather, the purpose behind Weingarten rights is to enable you to have the support of a union representative to help you formulate an appropriate response when questioned in an investigation from which there is a reasonable expectation that discipline could be imposed on you. When I told you that my questions were not accusatory or disciplinary, that should have made you aware that you could answer my questions without fear of disciplinary consequences. In other words, you should have answered my questions.

We next discussed the second incident, of April 2nd, 2013. I explained that I was visiting teachers as a follow up to an email I sent regarding the restorative assembly. On that occasion, I visited three homerooms prior to coming to your homeroom. You acknowledged that you knew the purpose of my visit because I was holding copies of the restorative assembly email in my hand. When you opened the door I stated that I wanted to speak with you about the assembly, at which I planned to address disruptive students/students not wanting to attend the assembly. You stated "I don't feel comfortable speaking with you in my classroom; I'm going out into the hallway where we have video." You walked into the hallway and left the students in your classroom unattended.

In the hallway you presented your Weingarten Rights card, held it up to the video camera and told me you were invoking your Weingarten rights. I told you I wanted to speak about the assembly and that you did not have to read the card to me. At that point I told you that if you wanted, you could give me the card to read. At that point, you walked past me, turned, and handed me the card and said "keep it."

As I began to read the card, you started to pull your classroom door shut. I said "wait" and I reached for the door, placing my fingertips on the door, as you continued to pull the door and slam it closed. Your explanation for the door slamming was that it was caused by a "vacuum". I find this explanation not credible, however.

Although you invoked your Weingarten rights, this was also a situation in which my questions were about a routine matter, and not investigatory in nature. In order to move forward in a positive way, and to facilitate communication between us as principal and teacher, I am hereby asking that, if you have doubt as to whether you can be subject to discipline as a result of any question you ask me, you first ask me if the nature of the question is investigatory and could lead to discipline. I will answer the question honestly. I am hoping this simple step will help clarify whether there will be questioning that could reasonably lead to disciplinary consequences for you for both of us, and will lead to better communication between us about matters that may arise in the building for which I may need input from you.

I will keep a copy of this memorandum, and I will make a copy available for you to keep.

Subject **FW: Nice job!**
From Rosado, Jose (Sr.) <rosadojo@allentownsd.org>
To jose@joserosado.org <jose@joserosado.org>
Date 2013-06-12 15:13

- Miller Incident 4 22.06 11 2013.doc (494 KB)

From: Elizabeth Kelly [mailto:ekelly@kingspry.com]
Sent: Wednesday, June 12, 2013 2:22 PM
To: Rosado, Jose (Sr.)
Cc: Wildonger, David M; Lozada, Susan
Subject: Nice job!

Jose,
     The attached written reprimand looks good to me. I have no changes or suggestions. Please issue as you see fit. --Liz

Elizabeth M. Kelly, Esquire
King Spry Herman Freund & Faul, LLC
One West Broad Street, Suite 700
Bethlehem, PA 18018
(610) 332-0390
Fax: (610) 332-0314

IBEAM Academy
Allentown School District

MEMO

Approved

To: Ryan Miller, Teacher

From: Jose Rosado, Principal

Subject: Notification of Discipline – Incident of April 22nd, 2013

Date: June 14, 2013

On April 29th, 2013, we met to discuss your conduct on April 22, 2013 at approximately 2:25 pm in the hallway outside of your classroom. Also present at the meeting were Debra Tretter, AEA President and Deborah Hartman, Executive Director of Special Education.

During the meeting I presented my observations of the incident: I came into the hallway to monitor change of class, I saw you standing outside of your classroom, I heard you yell – Fight, Fight we have students fighting and no behavior specialists or security. I did not observe a fight, as I walked down the hallway you entered your classroom, I observed no fight. I also read statements provided by Sam Martinez, CIS Staff and Alisha Keiser, Teacher. The statements provided by these staff members was consistent with my own observations – specifically, they heard you yell, "Fight Fight…" and witnessed no fight. I explained to you that I requested statements from Mr. Martinez and Mrs. Keiser because they were the only other staff visibly present in the hallway at the time of the incident as seen on the video (security camera).

Upon questioning, you acknowledged being in the hallway at the time in question. You also acknowledged yelling several statements including "fight" ("the third time I yelled for help, I yelled fight").

When I asked you if a fight took place, you responded there was a "potential for a fight, two students raised their hands and squared off – yes."

I stated to you that based on the observations and statements provided by staff, the student's behaviors were prompted/escalated by your actions (students reacted to Mr. Miller yelling "fight" by "cursing at him and mocking what he was yelling down the hallway").

Although you characterized the student's behaviors as "extremely dangerous", you did not submit any Sapphire Discipline Reports for the incident. When presented with this fact, you stated that you would complete and submit the referrals (one week after the incident).

Based on my observation of the incident, as well as the statements provided by two staff members that witnessed the incident, I find that your actions prompted/escalated a student disruption, created an unsafe/potentially dangerous environment for students and staff and was generally irresponsible and reckless in nature.

This memo shall serve as a written reprimand to you, to direct you to avoid yelling out irresponsible/reckless comments which can serve to incite student disruptions and endanger the safety of students and staff. If you engage in the same or similar misconduct in the future, you will be subject to further discipline, up to and including dismissal.

If you disagree with any portion of this letter referencing our meeting, you may submit a written statement and it will be placed in the file with this memorandum.

Subject **FW: Copies of Rescinded letters**
From   Rosado, Jose (Sr.) <rosadojo@allentownsd.org>
To   · jose@joserosado.org <jose@joserosado.org>
Date   2013-08-08 11:06

- 20130808070052015.pdf (54 KB)

-----Original Message-----
From: Mazzella, Christina
Sent: Thursday, August 08, 2013 10:52 AM
To: Rosado, Jose (Sr.)
Cc: Wildonger, David M; ekelly@kingspry.com
Subject: Copies of Rescinded letters

Jose, attached are letters I sent to Ryan Miller and Matthew Cunningham. These are based on Dr. Mayo's decision to rescind the two written reprimands that were issued against the advice of HR and/or Legal.

I wanted you to have them for your files so if you have a copy of them you will not be able to reference them in any disciplinary actions for these individuals, if they should arise.

Thanks much,

Christina

Just cause – Delayed Reprimands

The district is in violation of Article 10 of the collective bargaining agreement and any other applicable articles, laws, and policies.

On June 14, 2013, two IBEAM teachers, Matt Cunningham and Ryan Miller, received written reprimands following investigatory meetings conducted in March and April, 2013.

Matt Cunningham received two written reprimands on June 14: For an alleged incident on 4/23, following a meeting on 4/29; and, for an alleged incident on no specific date, following a meeting held on 3/26. In addition, Mr. Cunningham was not informed prior to the June 14 meeting that the reprimand following the March 26 meeting would be discussed at the June 14 meeting.

Ryan Miller received two written reprimands on June 14: For an alleged incident on 3/21, following a meeting on 3/26; For an alleged incident on 4/22, following a meeting on 4/29; and, a "Memorandum of Direction," for incidents which allegedly occurred on 3/26 and 4/2, following a meeting on 4/11.

In addition, Mr. Miller received a written reprimand dated April 29, which was issued to Mr. Miller on May 9, following an investigatory meeting held on February 27, for an incident which allegedly occurred on February 6.

It is the position of this Association that Mr. Rosado's delayed response to allegations against Mr. Cunningham and Mr. Miller has impeded their ability to self-correct, per Mr. Rosado's perceived concerns, prior to the conclusion of the student school year, and is a violation of their due process rights.

Remedies:
1. Removal of all written reprimands and memorandum from personnel files of the affected teachers, Mr. Cunningham and Mr. Miller, received on June 14, 2013.
2. Provide timely feedback to all professionals following investigatory or disciplinary meetings;
3. Mr. Rosado will attempt to prevent disciplinary action against professionals by conducting 1:1 meetings, for the purpose of acting in the role of mentor, prior to imposing discipline.
4. Any other award any other awards deemed appropriate by the arbitrator.

CHRISTINA MAZZELLA

Executive Director of Human Resources
mazzellac@allentownsd.org

31 South Penn Street ■ P.O. Box 328 ■ Allentown, PA 18105
Administration Center ■ 484-765-4231 ■ Fax: 484-765-4140

August 8, 2013

Mr. Ryan Miller

RE: 2012-13-028 -- "Just Cause-Delayed Reprimands

The written reprimand dated June 14, 2013 concerning the incident of March 21, 2013, is hereby rescinded. It will be removed from your personnel file and shredded.
If you have any other questions, please feel free to contact me.

Sincerely,

Christina Mazzella

Cc: Debra Tretter, AEA President

Rosado, Jose (Sr.)

From:	Rosado, Jose (Sr.)
Sent:	Wednesday, May 01, 2013 3:39 PM
To:	ekelly@kingspry.com
Cc:	Lozada, Susan; Wildonger, David M
Subject:	Ryan Miller - Harassment Complaint (Document #1of 3)
Attachments:	20130501134118053.tif

Liz,

As the principal of the IBEAM Academy, I have been made aware by students, staff and parents of an ongoing pattern of harassment being perpetuated against them by Ryan Miller.

As you know, I have been addressing the concerns as I have become aware of them. At this point, I believe it is my responsibility to forward to you a formal Harassment Complaint on behalf of the students, staff and parents that have reported concerns of harassment to me.

The attached document (1 of 3) includes statements from students staff and parents. The student statements are copies of the original hand written statements provided by the students. I will have the statements typed to provide clarity and readability.

I am requesting that the Allentown School District conduct a full investigation - Including interviewing the students, staff and parents regarding the reported concerns (possible pattern of harassment) being perpetuated against them by Ryan Miller - IBEAM Teacher.

I will provide you with a hard copy of the complaint (Employee Complaint Form - Harassment).

Thank you!!!

Jose Rosado
Director of Community & Student Services Allentown School District
31 S. Penn Street, P.O. Box 328
Allentown, PA 18105
Phone: 484-765-4074
Fax: 484-765-4076
rosadojo@allentownsd.org

1

From: Elizabeth Kelly [mailto:ekelly@kingspry.com]
Sent: Monday, May 06, 2013 8:49 AM
To: Rosado, Jose (Sr.)
Cc: Diehl, Kimberly; Toner, Kelly
Subject: Meeting today at 11 - I need to reschedule

Jose,

    I apologize, but I am going to need to reschedule our meeting for today. I, or Kim Diehl, will contact you in the near future to reschedule something, but it won't be able to be today. –Liz

Elizabeth M. Kelly, Esquire
King Spry Herman Freund & Faul, LLC
One West Broad Street, Suite 700
Bethlehem, PA 18018
(610) 332-0390
Fax: (610) 332-0314

From: Elizabeth Kelly [mailto:ekelly@kingspry.com]
Sent: Wednesday, May 08, 2013 12:21 PM
To: Rosado, Jose (Sr.)
Subject: RE: Harassment Complaint against Ryan Miller - Meeting

Jose,

    Since we last spoke, I had an idea about how to address the situation with Ryan Miller. I have to get Dave's input before we can implement anything, however. I also read the file you gave me, and I believe I have enough info to begin with. Is there anything else that is not in the file that you believe needs to be reported?

Elizabeth M. Kelly, Esquire
King Spry Herman Freund & Faul, LLC
One West Broad Street, Suite 700
Bethlehem, PA 18018
(610) 332-0390
Fax: (610) 332-0314

Rosado, Jose (Sr.)

From:	Rosado, Jose (Sr.)
Sent:	Wednesday, May 08, 2013 12:32 PM
To:	'Elizabeth Kelly'
Subject:	RE: Harassment Complaint against Ryan Miller - Meeting

Liz,

I have additional student reaction forms, staff complaints and parent complaints.

Thanks!!!

Jose Rosado
Director of Community & Student Services
Allentown School District

From: Rosado, Jose (Sr.) [mailto:rosadojo@allentownsd.org]
Sent: Thursday, May 09, 2013 2:26 PM
To: Elizabeth Kelly
Cc: Lozada, Susan; Wildonger, David M; Mayo, Russ
Subject: FW: ████████████████████ 5-9-13

Liz,

I met with this parent on Monday (5/6/13). She shared the following concerns/complaints with me regarding Ryan Miller:

- Her son claimed that Mr. Miller does not help him with the assignments – "If the student asks for help, the teachers job is to help the student"
- "if my son is going to continue to have problems with that teacher, I want him removed from that class"
- Just because you are a teacher, don't give him the right to make students feel embarrassed or stupid"
- "I don't feel that he is helping my son"
- "████ feels that he is being targeted"
- ████ stated that Mr. Miller told him that he is intimidated by his looks – "My sons appearance should not be intimidating to a teacher...I teach my son to look people in the face when he speaks to them"
- "Not proper for the teacher to tell my son – "Shut your mouth".

Parent said she would call administration Building to file a complaint regarding Ryan Miller.

Please add this email to the Harassment Complaint I filed with you on May 1, 2013.

From: Elizabeth Kelly <ekelly@kingspry.com>
Sent: Thursday, May 09, 2013 6:11 PM
To: Rosado, Jose (Sr.)
Subject: RE: ████████████████████ 5-9-13

Jose,

I will add this, but you mentioned in another email that you have some time tomorrow afternoon to discuss this matter. I cannot go to IBEAM, and I do not want to take you away from there, so why don't we do a telephone conference, just to get this started? Can you block out some time tomorrow afternoon at about 2 pm? If so, please let me know what telephone number I can reach you at. Thanks, -Liz

Elizabeth M. Kelly, Esquire
King Spry Herman Freund & Faul, LLC
One West Broad Street, Suite 700
Bethlehem, PA 18018
(610) 332-0390
Fax: (610) 332-0314

Rosado, Jose (Sr.)

From:	Rosado, Jose (Sr.)
Sent:	Friday, May 24, 2013 2:22 PM
To:	ekelly@kingspry.com
Cc:	Lozada, Susan; Wildonger, David M; Mayo, Russ
Subject:	RE: Ryan Miller - Harassment Complaint (Document #1of 3)

Liz,

I filed this Harassment Complaint Form with you on May 1, 2013. Other than you questioning me last week, I am not aware of the status of this complaint.
This concern is ongoing and I would appreciate an update on the status of the complaint/Investigation.

Thank you!!!

Jose Rosado
Director of Community & Student Services Allentown School District
31 S. Penn Street, P.O. Box 328
Allentown, PA 18105
Phone: 484-765-4074
Fax: 484-765-4076
rosadojo@allentownsd.org

Rosado, Jose (Sr.)

From:	Rosado, Jose (Sr.)
Sent:	Thursday, May 30, 2013 8:45 AM
To:	ekelly@kingspry.com
Cc:	Lozada, Susan; Wildonger, David M; Mayo, Russ
Subject:	RE: Ryan Miller - Harassment Complaint (Document #1of 3)

Liz,

Please provide me with an update/status of this Harassment Complaint.

Thank you!!!

Jose Rosado
Director of Community & Student Services Allentown School District
31 S. Penn Street, P.O. Box 328
Allentown, PA 18105
Phone: 484-765-4074
Fax: 484-765-4076
rosadojo@allentownsd.org

Rosado, Jose (Sr.)

From:	Elizabeth Kelly <ekelly@kingspry.com>
Sent:	Thursday, May 30, 2013 11:41 AM
To:	Rosado, Jose (Sr.)
Subject:	RE: Ryan Miller - Harassment Complaint (Document #1of 3)

The complaint is still open and investigation is pending.

Elizabeth M. Kelly, Esquire
King Spry Herman Freund & Faul, LLC
One West Broad Street, Suite 700
Bethlehem, PA 18018
(610) 332-0390
Fax: (610) 332-0314

Rosado, Jose (Sr.)

To: Elcock, David
Cc: Mayo, Russ; Wildonger, David M; Wheeler, Robert A
Subject: Status of Employee Complaint Form - Harassment (Ryan Miller - May 1, 2013)

Dave,

On May 1, 2013, I completed and forwarded (electronic and hard copy) an "Employee Complaint Form - Harassment" to Elizabeth Kelly (Interim Executive Director of Accountability).

The complaint was in regards to allegations (harassing behaviors) brought to my attention by IBEAM students, staff and parents. The alleged harassing behaviors were being perpetuated by Ryan Miller (IBEAM teacher).

As per the ASD Secondary & Elementary Schools Communication Procedures for Critical Events or Documents (Unlawful Harassment Form) I contacted Elizabeth Kelly and forwarded a copy of the report to her (requesting a full investigation including interviewing students, staff and parents identified in the report). I also kept a copy of the report for my file (principals file).

Due to past experiences with Ryan Miller (false allegations made by him against me and prior investigations I conducted regarding his behaviors) I would not have been viewed as an impartial party had I conducted this investigation. Elizabeth Kelly was aware of my past experiences with Ryan Miller and understood that I would not be viewed as an impartial party (documentation).

As the attached email (below) shows, Elizabeth Kelly initiated an investigation by interviewing me (telephone interview May 10, 2013).

The email also shows a communication from Elizabeth Kelly on May 30, 2013, stating " The complaint is still open and investigation pending." Other than interviewing me, I am not aware that any of the individuals identified in the complaint were interviewed.

Recently, two staff members identified in the complaint have approached me and questioned the status of the complaint/investigation.

As you may be aware, Ryan Miller has been reassigned to South Mountain Middle School. However, an investigation was not completed regarding the complaint I filed on May 1, 2013.

I am bringing this to your attention as the D.E.C. for resolution.

I will provide you with a hard copy of the complaint by this afternoon.

Thank you!!!

Jose Rosado
Director of Alternative Education
Allentown School District
31 S. Penn Street, P.O. Box 328
Allentown, PA 18105
Phone: 484-765-4074

1

<u>EMPLOYEE COMPLAINT FORM – HARASSMENT</u>

1. Name: _José Rosado – On behalf of IBEAM students, staff, parents_

2. School/Building: _I. B. E. A. M. Academy_

3. Describe the conduct you found objectionable, including what force, if any was used; verbal statements (threats, requests, demands, etc.); what if any physical contact was involved (additional sheets may be attached):

   Pattern of harassment (by Ryan Miller) toward students, staff, parents.

4. The name of the person or persons alleged to be harassing you: _Ryan Miller_

5. If the alleged unlawful harassment was directed against another person identify the other person: _Students, staff, parents – Documentation attached_

6. Date of the incident described in #3: _Noted in documents (2012-2013 SY)_

7. Approximate time of the incident's occurrence, as described in #3: _Noted in documents_

8. Location of the incident described in #3: _I. B. E. A. M. Academy_

9. Names of any witnesses to the incident described in #3: _Information noted in attached documents_

10. Please briefly identify the actions you would like to be taken by the School District in correcting the matter you have identified: _Conduct a full investigation Including interviewing students, staff and parents regarding the reported concerns (pattern of harassment)._

11. Date this complaint was submitted: _May 1, 2013_

    Complainant's Signature:

<u>RETURN YOUR COMPLAINT TO YOUR PRINCIPAL OR THE ASSISTANT SUPERINTENDENT, HUMAN RESOURCES AND OPERATIONS, OR THE SUPERINTENDENT.</u>

My name is Al Blount. I am the Behavior Specialist 1st floor at IBEAM Academy. I am writing to inform you that it has become intolerable to work with Mr. Miller. As a Behavior Specialist it is important to maintain a positive relationship with teachers as well as students. My function is to help facilitate cohesion between teacher/student during times of stress. My relationship with student is paramount in the de-escalation process. Due to Mr. Miller's constant provoking, badgering, talking down to, sabotaging as well as the writing up of students into sapphire, lying about certain incidents, yelling down the hallway... "This building is unsafe". Telling students... "Due to the climate of this building I cannot help you." On 4/22/13 while covering the ATS/Refocus room I heard Mr. Miller yelling... "Fight, Fight, We need a behavior specialist and security. I had the kids who were ATS/Refocus come out and wait in the hallway. I ran down to the fight area only to find that there was no fight.

Mr. Miller has shown himself to be increasingly angry and un-inviting toward the students. His constant negative comments during staff meetings/ in-service meetings are wearing on me as well as other staff persons in the building. He is a drain on moral and has been threatening toward other teachers.

It is my wish to meet with you to discuss this matter.

Behavior Specialist and Security Meeting   **4/24/13**

Staff in attendance:

Ashley Flores

Al Blount

Brit Riddick

Taariq Aziz

Vince Yasenchak

Concerns regarding Mr. Miller

It is becoming increasingly difficult to manage student behavior when we have witnessed rude, provoking, badgering, talking down to, sarcastic. Also restorative practices are not being used as a tool in Mr. Miller's classroom. Mr. Miller feels that he is not being supported by Behavior Specialists; we find it difficult to support Mr. Miller when we witness on a daily basis his disdain for the student's culture. He has been observed speaking to Hispanic students in a way that you would speak to a two year old…"This is on your level," "You should be able to understand this." When he responds to students in this fashion they become angry and either walk out of his class or become belligerent with him. Once the student has been refocused after the incident, they are returned to Mr. Miller's class. At this time a hallway conference has to take place prior to entering. Rather than to proceed in a restorative fashion, Mr. Miller chooses to again speak to them in a way that is not age appropriate. There by sabotaging the reentry process.

Mr. Miller has been heard yelling down the hallway: "This place is unsafe," "There needs to be some substitutes in this building," "Somebody needs to do something," Lastly, he yelled "Fight, Fight there are no behavioral specialist or security in the hall way," He then proceeded to retreat into his classroom and slam the door.

During morning circle his facial expression, posture, as well as his verbal innuendo, has a negative mental and emotional affect on all person/people in the room. The afore mentioned, has even had an impact on the instructor for Restorative Practice. At the end of the in-service when he was exiting the room, the instructor stopped him to ask if he was okay. His response was "there is not enough time to explain it all to you, this is a dangerous building and someone is going to get seriously hurt."

He has also been observed confronting other teachers about being backstabbers as well as yelling at them for not writing behaviors in Sapphire. To the point where one teacher broke down and cried, then later on said she felt threatened. This teacher commented that whenever she is in the faculty lounge she cringes at the thought of him coming in.

We would like to meet with Mr. Rosado, Nikki, and Logan to discuss how we are to proceed while maintaining a professional relationship with Mr. Miller as well as keeping the trust of the students. Trust is a must in regards of the relationship between student, behavioral specialist, and security. To support Mr. Miller, will be a death sentence to our relationship with the students. We look forward to hearing back from someone ASAP.

Rosado, Jose (Sr.)

From:	Rosado, Jose (Sr.)
Sent:	Tuesday, March 26, 2013 8:13 AM
To:	ekelly@kingspry.com
Cc:	Wildonger, David M; Lozada, Susan
Subject:	Parent Concern/Ryan Miller
Attachments:	▓▓▓▓▓▓▓▓▓▓▓▓▓▓▓▓ 3-25-13.doc

Liz,

Please see the attached document (parent concern) regarding an incident with her daughter and Ryan Miller. The parent is alleging that Ryan Miller used profanity directed at her daughter. I have brought this concern to your attention and scheduled a meeting with Ryan Miller. However, I believe we were waiting for Deb Tretter to be available. I would prefer to address this concern with Ryan Miller as soon as possible.

Thank you!!!

Jose Rosado
Director of Community & Student Services
Allentown School District
31 S. Penn Street, P.O. Box 328
Allentown, PA 18105
Phone: 484-765-4074
Fax: 484-765-4076
rosadojo@allentownsd.org

1

Community & Student Services
Contact Referral Form

Method of Contact: ☒ Phone ☐ In Person **ASD Contact Person** K. Toner

Contact Information	
Name of Person Making Contact: ▉▉▉▉	**Date:** 3-25-13
Student's Name (if applicable): ▉▉▉	**Home Phone:** **Cell Phone:** ▉▉▉
Relationship to Student: Mother **School:** IBEAM **Grade:** 9	**Special Ed:** ☐ Yes ☒ No

Reason			
☐ Suspension / Detention	☐ Attendance	☐ Enrollment	☐ Disenrollment
☐ Change of School	☐ Threat	☐ Abuse	☐ Bullying / Harassment
☒ Spoke with Principal / Counselor	☒ Other Teacher Complaint		

Details

Description of Concern:

Mom called stating ▉ has been having trouble in class with her one teacher - Ryan Miller. She is in the process of being tested for Spec Education this week. Mom stated ▉ came home and told her about Mr. Miller and a comment he made to her. She stated ▉ has been trying to get extra help in his class and has gone to Mr. Miller several times and he tells her "NO". Mom stated either on Wednesday or Thursday of last week (3-21 or 3-22) she asked for help again and he stated, "Do it your fucking self" and was then sent to the reflection room. Mom stated other student also heard this comment made by Mr. Miller. She said she spoke with Mr. Rosado and he has been helpful and stated he would investigate it, but she should also contact the Administration Building to make a formal concern. I explained our process to mom and let her know someone would be getting in contact with her.

3/26/13 - Mom called to let us know Mr. Miller just called her about ▉ behavior, mom stated she told Mr. Miller she was aware of his type of behavior in the last couple of days and he told her she should take it up with Administration and hung up on mom. Moms said she called then and spoke with Mr. Rosado and expressed her concerns of having ▉ remain in his classroom. Mr. Rosado stated he would remove her out of his class for today. Mom would like ▉ permanently removed from Mr. Miller classroom. She would also not like Mr. Miller calling the house anymore, to have Mr. Rosado call her to let her aware of anything regarding ▉

Mom stated when she was in the office on 3-13-13 while in the Main Office mom overheard another student speaking about Mr. Miller and the way she was treated by him on this day in class. Mom stated she believes everything her daughter is telling her about Mr. Miller.

Referred to: J. Rosado	**Date of Referral:** 3-25-13

During the phone call RM was sarcastic and repeated the same statements over and over, he felt unsafe and that the building was unsafe. I simply told him I would make note of his concerns. He indicated he was sharing them so it was, "dually documented" because he makes notes of everything.

4/10/2013

I asked RM for the binder of point sheets. He reported he had them and went into his classroom to get it. I told him it was needed for the class he was covering in the computer lab. He then ranted that, "it's a shame we have to cover classes. It's a shame we don't have sub's to do it". I replied, "during your as-assigned?" to which he continued to go on about how, "it's a shame teachers have to cover classes when we sent subs home." He then said flippantly, "oh, you don't want the point sheets?" I said, "they are needed in the classroom you are covering. Can you bring them with you?" I turned to walk down the hall. He said, "Oh, I guess you don't want them". I turned around and took the binder from RM and walked it down the hall, giving it to Mr. Cunningham. RM continued talking while walking down the hall making comments about the school and lack of support. He said, "Good thing this is all on camera since we love camera at IBEAM." Before walking away I told RM, "I try and support you as much as I can" and walked away.

3:35pm

Ryan was walking down the hall after being informed by Custodian Harvey that a student had jumped from the hallway window. He laughed and said, "Oh IBEAM, staff are gonna start jumping out" followed by laughter.

Brian Kennedy (Novak)

Community & Student Services
Contact Referral Form

Method of Contact: ☐ Phone ☒ In Person **ASD Contact Person** K. Toner

Contact Information		
Name of Person Making Contact: ▆▆▆▆▆		**Date:** 4-10-13
Student's Name (if applicable): ▆▆▆▆		**Home Phone:** **Cell Phone:** ▆▆▆▆
Relationship to Student: Mother	**School:** IBEAM **Grade:** 9	**Special Ed:** ☐ Yes ☒ No

Reason			
☐ Suspension / Detention	☐ Attendance	☐ Enrollment	☐ Disenrollment
☐ Change of School	☐ Threat	☐ Abuse	☐ Bullying / Harassment
☐ Spoke with Principal / Counselor	☒ Other _Teacher_		

Details

Description of Concern:

Mom stated ▆▆▆ is having trouble with Ryan Miller a teacher; he has been giving ▆▆▆ a hard time. Mom said she understands that they should be giving them a hard time since it is IBEAM, but Mr. Miller stated to ▆▆▆, "Shut the fuck up". Mom stated this happen about two weeks ago and she is still having trouble in his class. Mom stated another time ▆▆▆ was going to his class and he has told the students if the door is closed you don't come in. Mom stated ▆▆▆ tried going to class and the door was closed so she went to the refocus room and then tried to return to his class a little later. When she arrived the door was open and she entered and he said with an attitude, "You're later". Mom said he did make another comment, but she didn't know what it was.

Mom said she has spoken with the Principal, Mr. Rosado and he told her she should come to file an official report at the Adm. Building. Mom also mentioned ▆▆▆ isn't the only student having trouble with Mr. Miller. I explained our procedures to mom and let her know someone would be calling her.

Referred to: J. Rosado	**Date of Referral:** 4-10-13
Follow up:	
Referred to:	**Date of Referral:**

Rosado, Jose (Sr.)

From: Keiser, Alisha
Sent: Monday, April 29, 2013 11:51 AM
To: Rosado, Jose (Sr.)
Subject: statement

Monday, April 22, 2013 2:10-2:15 PM

Miller's and Ninesling' classes came up from the gym. I was outside in the hallway to wait for my homeroom to arrive. We were running on a Friday schedule and my homeroom was coming back to work on our decorations for diversity week. A line of students (Miller's and Ninesling's students) formed at the water fountain because they wanted to get a drink before going to class. Two students (███████████████████) began arguing in line. Miller yelled down the hallway "Fight! Fight! Fight! I need a behavior specialist. Can we get a behavior specialist down here?" Then he went into his room and slammed the door, leaving most of his students in the hallway unattended. The behaviors that I saw from ███ and ███ was just arguing and then when Mr. Miller yelled down the hall that is when the students put the fists up like they were actually going to fight, but never hit each other. I would describe the students' behavior as horse playing.

1

April 22, 2013

While I was in the hallway speaking with students Monday afternoon around 2:30 pm, the students were transitioning to their next class, being loud and just fooling around as they were switching classrooms, Mr. Miller came out of his class screaming in a loud voice, *May I get a behavior specialist, to break up this fight* being only a few feet away, I immediately looked at the students who were just fooling around and not fighting and they immediately began mocking him repeating what he just screamed out. I began to assist the student's in helping them get into their classrooms as soon as possible but shortly after he screamed the first time he did it again, *Yelling- Fight, Fight, we have a fight and no security officer or behavior specialist,* at that moment I felt he was putting the staff and the students at risk of provoking or stirring the kids up, and they actually began cursing at him and mocking what he was yelling down the hall way, when he could of calmly spoken to the kids and respectfully given them direction to just stop horse playing and get to class.

Sam Martinez

Rosado, Jose (Sr.)

From:	Rosado, Jose (Sr.)
Sent:	Wednesday, April 24, 2013 11:29 AM
To:	ekelly@kingspry.com; Wildonger, David M
Cc:	Lozada, Susan
Subject:	FW: CIS Meeting (Concern)

Please see the attached email below.

Thank you!!!

Jose Rosado
Director of Community & Student Services
Allentown School District
31 S. Penn Street, P.O. Box 328
Allentown, PA 18105
Phone: 484-765-4074
Fax: 484-765-4076
rosadojo@allentownsd.org

From: Rosado, Jose (Sr.)
Sent: Wednesday, April 17, 2013 3:55 PM
To: Lozada, Susan
Cc: Timothy Mulligan (mulligant@cislv.org); Wentz, Nichole
Subject: CIS Meeting (Concern)

Susan,

I had Nikki Wentz, CIS Program Director join the meeting with Tim today. I asked Nikki to join us to share comments she made to me over the past few days regarding Ryan Miller: "He makes bazar comments, erratic behavior, provoking students, going postal."

I was concerned that CIS (Tim) was not aware of the safety concerns regarding Ryan and the potential liability (with CIS Staff at IBEAM) if something were to happen. I asked Nikki to share her thoughts and experiences regarding Ryan so that it could not be said that I shared confidential information with non-district staff.

Nikki shared her concern for safety and gave examples of his comments and bazar/erratic behaviors.

Tim said that he would consult with his staff and follow up with the ASD.

Thank you!!!

Jose Rosado
Director of Community & Student Services
Allentown School District
31 S. Penn Street, P.O. Box 328
Allentown, PA 18105
Phone: 484-765-4074
Fax: 484-765-4076

1

Rosado, Jose (Sr.)

From:	Avrich, Candice
Sent:	Thursday, April 25, 2013 8:05 AM
To:	Rosado, Jose (Sr.)
Subject:	Incident 4/24

On April 24th at approximately 8:30AM I gave a card in a folder to Ryan Miller to get him and Deb Ninesling to sign for the intern who is leaving. Mr. Miller came back to me about 5 minutes later and said," We want nothing to do with this, You are a backstabber and you can't trust anyone in this building." This statement was heard by other staff members.

Candice Avrich
English Teacher
IBEAM Academy, Allentown School District
p.(484)765-7280
f.(484)765-4727
avrichc@allentownsd.org

Inspire. Believe. Educate. Advocate. Mentor

1

Rosado, Jose (Sr.)

From:	Avrich, Candice
Sent:	Wednesday, May 01, 2013 9:28 AM
To:	Rosado, Jose (Sr.)
Subject:	Students Refusing to Go to Science Class With Mr. Miller

Mr. Rosado,

My homeroom students' are refusing to go to Science class with Mr. Miller, they will either go straight to ATS, or leave the building instead. The following students:

███████: Already can't go to Science at parents request.
███████: Stated every time he goes in to Science class the teacher freaks out on him, and kicks him out anyway for no reason.
███████ He keeps "bitching" about every little thing I do.
███████: He tries to get me hype so he can kick me out.
███████: Kicked out too many times.

I have told them repeatedly they must go to Science class, it's not an option not to go, but they are still refusing. They were also told they do not get to choose which classes they go to or not. I have tried to convince them repeatedly to do the right thing. Please Advise.

Candice Avrich

English Teacher

IBEAM Academy, Allentown School District

p.(484)765-7280

f.(484)765-4727

avrichc@allentownsd.org

Inspire. Believe. Educate. Advocate. Mentor

1

Rosado, Jose (Sr.)

From:	Keiser, Alisha
Sent:	Wednesday, May 01, 2013 11:06 AM
To:	Rosado, Jose (Sr.)
Subject:	statement

Monday, April 29, 2013 855-910 AM

I was standing in my doorway greeting students like I do every morning. Every time Mr. Miller would open his door for a student, he would say to the students "There are lurkers in the hallway". I was the only teacher who was in the hallway when he said this. He again opened the door for another student and said the same statement "There are lurkers in the hallway". I went back into my classroom for a few minutes. Then I went back into the hallway to get one of my students (███████████) and he was standing in his doorway. He said to Mrs. Ninesling (who was in her doorway)' "Watch out here comes a lurker" and again I was the only teacher in the hallway at the time of the comment. They both quickly went back into their classrooms and slammed their doors.

1

Miller
@ 11·08

STUDENT RESPONSE FORM

Date: 5/8/13

Student: ████████████████

Grade: 9   Mentor: _____

✓ I understand that I have been referred for a possible Code of Conduct Infraction and I choose to make a statement to provide my version of the incident.

_____ I understand that I have been referred for a possible Code of Conduct Infraction and I chose not to provide a statement.

Student Explanation:

1. Explain exactly what happened. Be specific and include as much information as possible (including people names, locations and time of event).

2. Write as clearly as possible.

he called me a bum and I said that I was gone get all a's today and he said thats impossible and he just start comeing at all of us

Student Signature: ████████████████

(Office use only)

Reviewed by: _____

Date: 5/8/13

Disposition: _____

206

Miller
@ 11:08

STUDENT RESPONSE FORM

Date: May 8, 2013

Student: ██████████ Grade: 09 Mentor: _____

__√__ I understand that I have been referred for a possible Code of Conduct Infraction and
I choose to make a statement to provide my version of the incident.

_____ I understand that I have been referred for a possible Code of Conduct Infraction and
I chose not to provide a statement.

Student Explanation:

1. Explain exactly what happened. Be specific and include as much information as
possible (including people names, locations and time of event).

2. Write as clearly as possible.

he called ██████ a bum + kicked me
out for sharpening my pencil, he acts so
sweet in the hallway + gets in class
and he acts like an asshole. —.

Student Signature: ██████████

(Office use only)

Reviewed by: _____ Date: 5/8/13

Disposition: _____

Miller
@ 11:08

STUDENT RESPONSE FORM

Date: 5/8/13

Student: ▮▮▮▮▮▮▮▮ Grade: 9th Mentor: _____

__X__ I understand that I have been referred for a possible Code of Conduct Infraction and I choose to make a statement to provide my version of the incident.

_____ I understand that I have been referred for a possible Code of Conduct Infraction and I chose not to provide a statement.

Student Explanation:

1. Explain exactly what happened. Be specific and include as much information as possible (including people names, locations and time of event).

2. Write as clearly as possible.

I stopped doing my work and Mr. Miller kicked me out.

Student Signature: ▮▮▮▮▮▮▮▮

(Office use only)

Reviewed by: _____

Disposition: _____

Date: 5/8/13

Rosado, Jose (Sr.)

From: Rosado, Jose (Sr.)
Sent: Thursday, May 09, 2013 2:26 PM
To: ekelly@kingspry.com
Cc: Lozada, Susan; Wildonger, David M; Mayo, Russ
Subject: FW: ███████████████████████
Attachments: ████████████████████ 5-9-13.doc

Liz,

I met with this parent on Monday (5/6/13). She shared the following concerns/complaints with me regarding Ryan Miller:

- Her son claimed that Mr. Miller does not help him with the assignments – "If the student asks for help, the teachers job is to help the student"
- "if my son is going to continue to have problems with that teacher, I want him removed from that class"
- Just because you are a teacher, don't give him the right to make students feel embarrassed or stupid"
- "I don't feel that he is helping my son"
- "████ feels that he is being targeted"
- ████ stated that Mr. Miller told him that he is intimidated by his looks – "My sons appearance should not be intimidating to a teacher...I teach my son to look people in the face when he speaks to them"
- "Not proper for the teacher to tell my son – "Shut your mouth".

Parent said she would call administration Building to file a complaint regarding Ryan Miller.

Please add this email to the Harassment Complaint I filed with you on May 1, 2013.

Thank you!!!

Jose Rosado
Director of Community & Student Services
Allentown School District
31 S. Penn Street, P.O. Box 328
Allentown, PA 18105
Phone: 484-765-4074
Fax: 484-765-4076
rosadojo@allentownsd.org

From: Zdinak, Elizabeth
Sent: Thursday, May 09, 2013 12:08 PM
To: Rosado, Jose (Sr.)
Cc: Lozada, Susan
Subject: ███████████████████████

1

209

Mother phoned to report her son is having issues with Ryan Miller on a daily basis. Mother states that she feels her son, along with others, are being racially profiled. Mother stated paperwork was sent down to the office (c/o Kelly) regarding these issues. Mother stated other parents are becoming involved, including the NAACP.

2

The Termination Pathway

lthough I was aware of the intentions, I expected the termination procedures to follow proper due process. However, It became apparent to me that this would not happen. Although I was prepared to challenge and rebut any allegations and/or charges made against me, and I did when presented, it was unclear to me what the District was alleging I did or did not do.

On May 6, 2014, I was placed on "Administrative Suspension with Pay." When I asked to be informed of a reason for the suspension, I was told, "The decision to place you in this status follows upon the District's discovery of information indicating that you may have engaged in willful neglect of your duties as Director of Alternative Education and/or persistent negligence in the performance of same, for which your employment with the District can be terminated."

When I asked, what does that mean… what specifically did I do, or not do, to warrant being suspended? Neither Christina Mazzella, Executive Director of Human Resources, nor David Wildonger could provide me an answer.

I was further confused on May 19, 2014, when I received a certified letter from David Wildonger serving as my "Loudermill Hearing" notice. The letter stated, "Previously, at our meeting on May 6, 2014, you inquired about information relating to School Code charges brought against you by the Allentown school District. At this time, no such charges have been brought against you. However the District may consider such charges in the near future. Therefore, by this letter, I am inviting you to attend a meeting with me and Ms. Christina Mazzella, Executive Director of Human Resources, which shall serve as a Loudermill hearing. This meeting is intended to allow you the opportunity to provide us with any input you would like the District to take into consideration before a decision is made to recommend that your employment be terminated for cause as provided under School Code Section 1122."

So by this letter (Loudermill Hearing), I was being invited to attend a hearing for the purpose of responding and providing input I would like the District to consider before a decision is made to terminate for cause. However, as noted in the letter, "No such charges have been brought against you." What was I expected to respond to?

Apparently, Mr. Wildonger did not understand the purpose of a Loudermill Hearing.

Loudermill Rights

The term "Loudermill Rights" refers to those employee rights, which state that most public employees have a property right in their jobs. Pursuant to such rights, an employee cannot be dismissed without due process. It also gives the employee a right to a pre-termination hearing that gives them the opportunity to present their part.

The term "Loudermill Rights" comes from the case Cleveland Bd. Of Educ. v. Loudermill, 470 U.S. 532 (U.S. 1985), decided by the U.S. Supreme Court in 1985. The decision laid out that most public employees have property interests in their jobs, and are therefore allowed due process rights if they are fired. Loudermill rights include a written or oral notice regarding why they are being fired. Specific evidence to any charges against them must be given to them and a pre-termination hearing is also to be given where the employee can respond to the charges made against him or her. [12]

During the course of this process, I submitted a rebuttal for my 2012-2013, final evaluation, which was completed by David Wildonger. The rebuttal is included in this chapter. However, the "Exhibits" submitted with the rebuttal are too lengthy (over 80 pages) for this book. The "Exhibits" can be viewed on my website: jose@joserosado.org

I also submitted a rebuttal to my 2013-2014, Focused Assistance Plan Mid-year Evaluation. The rebuttal is likewise included in this chapter. However, again the "Appendices" are too lengthy (over 200 pages) for this book and can be found on my website.

Rosado, Jose (Sr.)

From:	Lozada, Susan
Sent:	Monday, June 03, 2013 12:26 PM
To:	Rosado, Jose (Sr.)
Cc:	Elizabeth Kelly; Wildonger, David M; Wheeler, Robert A
Subject:	FAP & Evaluation

Hi Jose,

As per our discussion on Thursday, I am following up with this email. When I submitted my letter of resignation from the ASD, effective June 28, 2013, I informed you that I would complete you 2012-2013 evaluation and complete the Focused Assistance Plan as I would be closing out the school year.

Although as your direct supervisor I personally met with you on a regular basis throughout the school year and monitored your progress and compliance, I was informed on Thursday by Mr. Wildonger that I will not be completing your final evaluation for the 2012-2013 SY. He informed me that he will assume the responsibility of completing your evaluation and monitoring of the Focused Assistance Plan (FAP).

I informed Mr. Wildonger that my overall evaluation was that satisfactory progress was made as I have noted at our FAP meetings. I have compiled a detailed binder of documents specific to your performance under the highlighted FAP items. I mentioned the concerns that persist due to outside factors – assigned teachers antagonistic to student support, assigned teachers seeking greater adjudication for students, outside agencies involvement with alternative education parents, and the persistence of what appear to be capricious and arbitrary grievances. The latest of which I shared with you on Thursday.

As I stated prior I fully expected to complete your final evaluation and the FAP but that will not be the case. Please let me know if you have any questions or concerns. Thanks,
Sue

1

Rosado, Jose (Sr.)

From:	Rosado, Jose (Sr.)
Sent:	Tuesday, June 04, 2013 12:53 PM
To:	Wildonger, David M
Cc:	Lozada, Susan; ekelly@kingspry.com; Wheeler, Robert A
Subject:	FW: FAP & Evaluation

Dave,

I am very troubled and concerned by the notification I have received from Susan regarding the completion of my evaluation for the 2012-2013, school year and the supervision of my FAP (See attached email below).

As Susan states in her email, as my direct supervisor she has supervised me all year and has met with me on a regular basis to review and monitor my progress and compliance with the FAP and my responsibilities as an administrator. Susan and I have worked very closely to assure that I am meeting all of the expectations set in the FAP in a Satisfactory manner.

Although you have sat in on a few of our meetings, you have not directly supervised me or shared any feedback with me regarding my progress and compliance.

Although Susan has submitted her resignation from the ASD – effective June 28, 2013 - as my supervisor, Susan stated to me that she would complete my evaluation for the 2012-2013, school year and complete the supervision of the FAP. This is clearly noted in her email below.

When I asked Susan if you had provided any explanation for this, she told me that you said the decision was made for the purpose of "continuity." This suggest to me that - although I have been rated as "satisfactory" by my direct supervisor – the FAP may be extended beyond the 2012-2013, school year (speculation).

I believe Susan Lozada is the "most informed " person regarding my performance during the 2012-2013 school year, and thus the most qualified to complete my evaluation and the supervision of the FAP. I believe this should be given consideration.

I remain troubled and very anxious about this situation and hope that my concerns are addressed.

Thank you!!!

Jose Rosado
Director of Community & Student Services
Allentown School District
31 S. Penn Street, P.O. Box 328
Allentown, PA 18105
Phone: 484-765-4074
Fax: 484-765-4076
rosadojo@allentownsd.org

1

214

Rosado, Jose (Sr.)

To:	Wildonger, David M
Cc:	Mayo, Russ; Mazzella, Christina; Wheeler, Robert A
Subject:	2012-2013 Evaluation

Dave,

I have thoroughly reviewed my 2012-2013 evaluation and the accompanying Anecdotal Records (Attachments to Performance Evaluation).

Upon my review, I have found that several documents (anecdotal records) are incomplete, inaccurate or missing. The multiple documents in question are too significant to be addressed in a rebuttal letter.

Therefore, I am requesting a follow up meeting with you to discuss the documents in question as they pertain to my evaluation and the Focused Assistance Plan.

Thank you!!!

Jose Rosado
Director of Alternative Education
Allentown School District
31 S. Penn Street, P.O. Box 328
Allentown, PA 18105
Phone: 484-765-4074
Fax: 484-765-4076
rosadojo@allentownsd.org

1

MEMORANDUM

To: David M. Wildonger, Chief Operations Officer

From: Jose Rosado, Sr., Director of Alternative Education

Subject: Rebuttal - **Discrimination and Retaliation in Refusal to Clarify 2012-2013 Annual Performance Evaluation Report**

Date: November 15, 2013

As per your letter of October 28, 2013, you have requested that I provide my rebuttal letter on or before November 15, 2013. This is that letter.

First of all, I incorporate by reference my second Charge with the EEOC, filed on October 23, 2013, a true and correct copy which is attached hereto as Exhibit A.

I point out that you undertook responsibility for an evaluation without doing due diligence. In addition, you failed to acknowledge that it was another supervisor (and not me) who did not provide correct information and/or that your failure to properly communicate with said prior supervisor caused the false write-up.

In addition, the problem (of you not being properly informed to conduct my evaluation) would not have occurred if you had not been involved in doing same, as is proper. I question your motivation in doing this evaluation, unprepared, and in a shoddy fashion and I deem same to be retaliation. By this letter, I also wish to expressly confirm that, despite being presented with clear evidence of your error, you have intentionally chosen to act in a retaliatory and discriminatory fashion.

You have also asked for me to address other objections to your evaluation as part of my rebuttal. I have repeatedly asked, and ask again, that you remove all negative references, inferences and reviews that arise and/or that are related to, protected ADA and/or FMLA leave days. In addition, once again, I demand that you remove or heavily discount any adverse statement, review or discipline that arises directly or indirectly out of reports made by Mr. Miller and/or Mr. Cunningham, *inter alia*, given that their credibility has been admitted to be compromised or they have retaliatory motivation.

Please be guided accordingly. I reserve all my rights in this matter.

A more specific and detailed rebuttal follows (and is inclusive) to this memorandum.

Rebuttal

This rebuttal is in reference to my final evaluation which was completed by you on August 16, 2013. The response/rebuttal will correspond to the document you titled "Attachment to Performance Evaluation" (a two page document). Each response/rebuttal will be specific to a Competency and Anecdotal Record:

Competency 1 B (April 26, 2013 Letter from Schuckman) - As I stated to you during our meeting on October 9, 2013, the letter from Mr. Schuckman stated "A determination has been made to remove the district from Corrective Action." I acknowledged to you that the district was placed on "Corrective Action" due to non-compliance with PDE (AEDY). The district was cited for 8 non-compliance violations. I stated to you that students were assigned to the AEDY program in violation of due process. I also stated to you that I placed the students into the AEDY program because that is what I was directed to do (even upon my objection). Upon you asking me who directed me to place the students in the AEDY Program (in violation of due process), I informed you that I was directed to do so by "the superintendent" (Russ Mayo).
PLEASE SEE EXHIBIT B.

Competency 1 A,B, and C (IBEAM Visit Schedule and Walkthrough Data) – Contrary to your records, complete and detailed Observation and Walkthrough Schedules were developed with my supervisor Susan Lozada in October of 2012. The Observation Schedules were documented in my daily calendar (this documentation was provided to you prior to you completing my evaluation). The Walkthrough Schedule (Supervisor of Instruction Rotation Schedule) was also completed in October of 2012, and presented to Susan Lozada. The schedule was reviewed and approved by my supervisor Susan Lozada. Both the Observation Schedule and Walkthrough Schedule were discussed throughout the school year during FAP reviews with Susan Lozada. Although you assumed the responsibility of completing my evaluation, you have acknowledged that you were unaware of the Observation Schedules when you completed my evaluation. Further, upon providing you a copy of the Supervisor of Instruction Rotation Schedule during our meeting on October 9, 2013, you refused to revise my evaluation.
PLEASE SEE EXHIBIT C.

Competency 1 C (No anecdotal records were provided to support the following statement and corresponding rating/evaluation) - "Mr. Rosado demonstrates good skills in communicating with students in a respectful manner, shows genuine interest and concern for students, but he does not demonstrate the same skills in his communication with staff and administrators.

Competency 2 D - Specific to your comment - "Mr. Rosado did not address teacher's referrals of students for discipline in the Sapphire online system in a timely manner." – As you are aware, the two teachers you noted in your comments (R.M. and M.C.) have been found to have provided false statements and false discipline referrals regarding student behaviors. Both teachers were written up for said false reports. Further, R.M. was found by the district to have filed a false grievance and false allegation of harassment against me. Regarding the timeliness of closing discipline referrals, I followed due process procedures and conducted appropriate investigations.
PLEASE SEE EXHIBIT D.

Competency 2 F (Conversation with J. Rosado (Verbal)) – You stated in the evaluation (2F), "Mr. Rosado improved his visibility at both locations after I directed him in the first semester to divide his time between the two locations of the Alt. Ed. programs as evenly as possible." As you are aware, I was out on FMLA for 38 days during the first semester. My visibility (lack of) was not due to a lack of "good supervision and management." My visibility (lack of) was due to an illness. Penalizing me (low performance evaluation) for getting sick is discriminatory.

Competency 3 A (Docs of Assessment Office Data (NHQT)) – As I stated to you during our meeting on October 9, 2013, these documents (Anecdotal Records – 10 pages) were never provided to me (PDE Form 425 – NHQT 2011-2012, 2012-2013 school years). As you know, the PRINCIPAL is REQUIRED TO SIGN (acknowledging receipt of said documents) from the assessment office. Your "Anecdotal Records (10 pages) do not include my signature because the documents were never provided to me.

Competency 3 B (April 30, 2013 memo of Wildonger to Rosado) – Mr. Wildonger failed to include my response to his memo in his Anecdotal Records.
PLEASE SEE Memo to Wildonger May 14, 2013 EXHIBIT E.

Competency 3 D (June 12, 2012 Focused Assistance Plan) – Professional Development Plans, monitoring of teacher classroom management and observation/evaluation schedules were completed and reviewed/discussed with my supervisor Susan Lozada during our regular meetings. Mr. Wildonger was not present during these regularly held meetings.
PLEASE SEE EXHIBIT F.

Competency 3 A,B,E, and G (Performance Evaluation of Professional Staff) – As you acknowledged, "Mr. Rosado provided his teaching staff evaluations to the Human Resources Office on a timely manner in both semesters." However, you questioned the observations done at the end of the semesters. I acknowledged that most of the Formal Observations for the first semester were completed toward the end of the semester. This was due to my absence due to FMLA earlier in the semester. Formal Observations for the second semester were more equitably completed throughout the semester. Summative Evaluations by definition are completed at the end of each semester. In reference to the evaluation of teacher D.N., teacher waived said "one day notice" and preferred to meet at the time I informed her that her evaluation was completed.

Competency 4 A and D (Message Note Call of Janelle Harvey) – This Anecdotal Record is a photo copy of a message/note (call from a parent). As I stated to you during our meeting on October 9, 2013, the parent requested school district data "Arrest Records for minority students for district as a whole (as stated in the note). I referred Ms. Harvey to my supervisor's office (Office of Community and Student Services). In your evaluation you stated "Mr. Rosado should have addressed the parents concern himself." As you should know, I do not gather, maintain and/or otherwise complete reports regarding the information Ms. Harvey was requesting. Thus, I could not have "addressed the parents concern (myself) himself" as you noted.

Competency 4 A (Emails to Wildonger from Principals) – Two middle school principals expressed concerns about student intakes into alternative education programs. The referrals were made during or just prior to the start of the PSSA testing period. PSSA testing took place between March 11, 2013 and May 3, 2013. Moving students from one school to another during the PSSA testing period would have caused a disruption for students during the PSSA testing period. This concern was communicated with principals prior to the PSSA Testing period. It is also important to note – with the exception of the emails from these two principals (both made on the same day) no other documentation was provided that expressed concerns about student intakes into alternative education.

Competency 5 A (No Anecdotal Records/Evidence provided to support the evaluation/rating)

Competency 5 B (No Anecdotal Records/Evidence provided to support the evaluation/rating)
PLEASE REFER TO EXHIBIT D.

Competency 5 C and E (No Anecdotal Records provided to support the evaluation/rating) – This
evaluation/rating is totally Subjective ("Displayed detachment", "this action suggested to me").

Competency 5 D (No Anecdotal Records provided to support the evaluation/rating) – As you
acknowledged in your comments "staff (Matt Cunningham) called the police to IBEAM, without
first following the DISTRICT'S SAFETY PROTOCOL (Emergency Operating Procedures).
Matt Cunningham did not comply with established and school board approved procedures.
PLEASE SEE EXHIBIT D (regarding Matt Cunningham).

On Nov 26, 2013, at 3:01 PM, "Rosado, Jose (Sr.)" <rosadojo@allentownsd.org> wrote:

Dave,

I am uncomfortable with the course of action we discussed this afternoon regarding a plan to address the NHQT at IBEAM. Although we discussed multiple options to address the concern, the option supported was to move the special education students into regular education classrooms and have the special education teachers co-teach with the regular education teachers (Highly Qualified Teachers). Although this option satisfies the concern regarding NHQT, it is in violation of the ASD Corrective Action Plan I submitted to PDE (AEDY) regarding non-compliance practices.

As you are aware, the district was removed from Corrective Action Status at the end of the 2012-2013, school year. I believe that taking action that contradicts the Corrective Action Plan and is not in compliance with our current application, could lead to further sanctions from the state.

I have contacted PDE (AEDY) and left a message indicating that the district is seeking a "waiver" or permission to "revise" the district's current AEDY application to allow for special education students to be served in the AEDY program. I have not received any contact from PDE (AEDY).

I understand that the NHQT concern is important. However, taking action that contradicts the districts AEDY application and violates the corrective action plan is also a concern. I cannot anticipate the response from PDE regarding a request for a waiver or revision of the application. Moving forward without the approval of PDE (AEDY) could lead to the district being placed on "Corrective Action Status" again.

I am uncomfortable with this course of action. However, I will proceed if that is what you direct me to do. Please advise me accordingly.

Thank you!!!

Jose Rosado
Director of Alternative Education
Allentown School District
31 S. Penn Street, P.O. Box 328
Allentown, PA 18105
Phone: 484-765-4074
Fax: 484-765-4076
rosadojo@allentownsd.org

From:	Wildonger, David M
Sent:	Tuesday, November 26, 2013 3:29 PM
To:	Rosado, Jose (Sr.)
Subject:	Re: AEDY/Special Education - Compliance Concerns

Please follow through with what was agreed upon in the meeting

Sent from my iPhone

Rosado, Jose (Sr.)

From:	Rosado, Jose (Sr.)
Sent:	Wednesday, November 27, 2013 8:25 AM
To:	Wildonger, David M
Subject:	FW: AEDY/Special Education - Compliance Concerns

Dave,

I have considered your directive -- to move the ALC and IBEAM self-contained special education students from their current placement (special education/self-contained) to the AEDY program. As I clearly stated in the attached email below, this action would be a violation of PDE (AEDY). Further, it would be a violation of the due process rights of the special education students.

As I stated to you during a meeting on October 9, 2013, I followed a similar directive (against my objections) given to me by Dr. Mayo in November of 2011 (move students into the AEDY program in violation of due process).

As you are aware, the district was monitored by PDE (AEDY) in December of 2011, and found to be in violation of AEDY. As a result, the district cited for 8 non-compliance violations. Of the eight areas of non-compliance, one particular area of non-compliance was specific to the placement of special education students into the AEDY program in violation of due process.

By complying with your directive, I would be knowingly placing special education students into the AEDY program contrary to PDE (AEDY) and due process.

I believe that this action would be illegal and unethical.

As such, I cannot comply with your directive to move the special education students into the AEDY program.

Please consider one of the other options I proposed during our meeting yesterday regarding concerns with NHQT.

Thank you!!!

Jose Rosado
Director of Alternative Education
Allentown School District
31 S. Penn Street, P.O. Box 328
Allentown, PA 18105
Phone: 484-765-4074
Fax: 484-765-4076
rosadojo@allentownsd.org

Rosado, Jose (Sr.)

From:	Rosado, Jose (Sr.)
Sent:	Friday, December 13, 2013 3:36 PM
To:	Wildonger, David M
Cc:	Mayo, Russ; Wheeler, Robert A; Boardman, Karen J
Subject:	District Non-Compliance (NHQT-Staffing & Special Education Students Assigned to Alternative Education) Unfair Evaluation/FAP

Dave,

As you are aware, meetings were held on Tuesday, November 26, 2013, to address concerns regarding NHQT (special education teachers) and the process/practice of placing special education students to alternative education.

As you are aware, three of the four special education teacher at IBEAM and the special education teacher assigned to the ALC program were all assigned to alternative education by Human Resources (prior to Christina Mazzella). None of these teachers were certified in a content area (HQT). I recommended the fourth special education teacher at IBEAM, Edward Williams, for hire based on his agreement/plan to become Highly Qualified (Mr. Williams recently took the Praxis Exam).

During the discussion regarding a plan to address the NHQT concern, several options were discussed in regards to providing instruction (HQT) for the special education students.

Also, during the discussion, several revelations/observations were made regarding the assignment/referral process for placing special education students into alternative education programs.

During the morning meeting (10:00), attended by Dr. Belardi, Christina Mazzella, Richard Joseph, Belinda Miller and myself, it was noted that the district engaged in the practice of changing special education student's IEP's so that they could be "NOREP'ed" into alternative education.

This practice was categorized/assessed as follows:

- Belinda Miller – " What Deb Hartman did is backwards...NOREP changed to place students into special education"
- Dr. Belardi – "So wrong on so many levels"
- Richard Joseph – "The process followed was not right"
- Dr. Belardi – "We have a dilemma...This is a nightmare"
- Belinda Miller – "Dumping ground for E.S. students...We need to shut it down completely...Backwards with an expletive in front of it"
- Dr. Belardi – "It's a dumping ground...Unfair, Illegal"
- Belinda Miller – "Civil Rights Violation...Shut it down"
- Belinda Miller – "Deb (Hartman) trying to keep students out of the I.U. Program"
- Jose Rosado – "I have been calling attention to this problem for three years"
- Belinda Miller – "Now you have support"

In regards to addressing the NHQT concern (special education teachers) several options were discussed:

- Moving special education students into regular education (AEDY) classrooms and have regular education teachers and special education teachers co-teach with the regular education teacher as the "teacher of record" (HQT). This was to be done (changed in Sapphire) effective November 27, 2013 (prior to Thanksgiving break) and

1

reflected in Sapphire December 1, 2013. I explained that this would violate the District's AEDY Application and Corrective Action Plan (Corrective Action for Non-Compliance) with PDE. I was asked to contact PDE and request a "waiver" or permission to revise the application.

- Change the Master schedule to allow for IBEAM regular education teachers (HQT) to co-teach 50% of the special education classes and assign additional staff (HQT) from the "home schools" on a part-time (itinerate) schedule to co-teach 50% of the special education classes.
- "Shut down" the special education classrooms and move students into appropriate programs at the home schools and/or I.U.

After the morning meeting, I contacted PDE regarding a request for a "waiver" (allowing the district to move special education students into the AEDY program) or permission to revise the AEDY application to do the same. I contacted Drew Schuckman's office (left a message for the person that has replaced him) and I also left the same message for Alfredo Gonzalez (Compliance Monitor).

During the afternoon meeting, which you and Nick Perez were brought into, we reviewed the conversation/concerns regarding NHQT and the practice of placing special education students in alternative education. We also reviewed and discussed the options/concerns which were discussed during the morning meeting. I also provided an update regarding my contacts (messages left) to PDE.

After the discussion/review, you pointed to me and stated "you didn't make a mistake, the process was incorrect." You also directed me to move the special education students at IBEAM into the regular education classrooms (AEDY) to be reflected in Sapphire December 1, 2013, and to follow up with PDE regarding a "waiver" or permission to revise the AEDY application.

I responded to your directive with an email on November 26, 2013. Upon your response to me, I followed up with another email (November 27, 2013) stating that "I cannot comply with your directive to move the special education students into the AEDY program."

Based on the revelations made during the meetings on November 26, 2013, It is apparent that the District did not comply with HQT when the special education teachers were assigned to alternative education.

Further, it is apparent that the process the District engaged in regarding the placement of special education students into alternative education programs was not proper and in violation of due process and other students rights.

These factors (NHQT and the same NHQT assigned to teach special education students improperly placed into alternative education) had an adverse impact on my evaluation.

Given the revelations made, including your own ("You didn't make a mistake, the process was incorrect"), I believe that the evaluation you completed on me for the 2012-2013 school year is an UNFAIR EVALUATION. I am requesting a meeting with you to discuss my concerns and request that my 2012-2013 evaluation and FAP be voided.

Thank you!!!

Jose Rosado
Director of Community & Student Services
Allentown School District
31 S. Penn Street, P.O. Box 328
Allentown, PA 18105
Phone: 484-765-4074
Fax: 484-765-4076

2

SCHOOL DISTRICT

31 South Penn Street ■ P.O. Box 328 ■ Allentown, PA 18105
Administration Center ■ 484-765-4231 ■ Fax: 484-765-4140

CHRISTINA MAZZELLA
Executive Director of Human Resources
mazzellac@allentownsd.org

May 6, 2014

Mr. José Rosado, Sr.
917 Delaware Avenue
Fountain Hill, PA 18015

Re: Administrative Suspension with Pay

Dear Mr. Rosado,

This letter shall serve as notice that you are hereby assigned to administrative suspension status with pay, effective upon your receipt of this letter and continuing until such time as you receive further notice, which shall be in the form of a letter from me. The decision to place you in this status follows upon the District's discovery of information indicating that you may have engaged in willful neglect of your duties as Director of Alternative Education and/or persistent negligence in the performance of same, for which your employment with the District can be terminated.

While your administrative suspension with pay status continues, you are hereby directed not to report to work at Allentown School District. You are also directed to remain away from all Allentown School District property and events, including extra-curricular and District sponsored social events, while your administrative suspension with pay continues.

In the event that you need to attend to any work duties while you remain in this status, you must first contact your supervisor and secure authorization to attend to such work duties. Please call Mr. Wildonger at (484) 765-4154, Email: WildongerD@allentownsd.org. All other communication and contact you have with the Allentown School District and any of its schools, offices or employees while you remain in this status must be initiated by you by contacting me at Telephone: (484) 765-4231. Email: Mazzellac@allentownsd.org.

Page 2
Rosado – Administrative Leave

If you fail to comply with any of the directives in this letter, this failure may constitute separate grounds for which you may be subject to charges of willful neglect of duty under the School Code.

Sincerely,

Christina Mazzella, Executive Director of Human Resources

Your signature below indicates that you have seen this Memorandum.

Signature: _____   Date:_____

C: C. Russell Mayo, Superintendent
       David M. Wildonger, Chief Operations Officer
       Personnel File

To: Jose Rosado Sr.

From: David M. Wildonger, Chief Operations Officer

Date: May 6, 2014

Subject: List of Documentation to be provided by Mr. Rosado within 10 days (May 16, 2014)

Competency 2

1. Competency 2, No. 2: Copies of all written support plans for each teacher you identified as needing support for improvement.

2. Competency 2, No. 3: On January 30, John Monahan, Supervisor of Instruction, reported to Alt. Ed. to conduct walkthroughs scheduled on that day. Mr. Monahan sat and waited in the office for 30 minutes, but you did not return to him to conduct walkthroughs with him. As a result, no walkthroughs were conducted as scheduled that day. Please provide me with an explanation as to why this occurred, in writing.

3. Competency 2, No. 3: Provide an explanation in writing as to whether Mr. Troxell obtained the books he needed in September 2013, and why Mr. Troxell needed additional books as of February 20, 2014.

4. Competency 2, No. 3: Provide an explanation in writing as to when and where you performed walkthroughs with an SOI in 2013-14, and enclose copies of the walkthrough forms completed for each teacher on those occasions.

5. Competency 2, No. 4: Provide a report to me in writing as to how you have recognized staff success for each quarter of 2013-14.

6. Competency 2, No. 5a: Provide me with a report of the training for staff on how to decrease the number of errors in Sapphire reports that were scheduled and completed to date, along with sign in sheets showing staff attendance at same.

7. Competency 2, No. 5a: Provide print outs from Sapphire showing me what the four errors in the September 2013 VISTA Sapphire records were. These four errors were the subject of six separate emails sent to you by Robin Powlus of the Assessment Office between September 16, 2013 and January 8, 2014. In addition, provide an explanation in writing describing what was needed to correct them and what was done, if anything, to correct these errors.

8. Competency 2, No. 6: Provide in writing your most recent two quarterly reports as to how you recognized staff success in improving the accuracy of entries made in Sapphire.

226

Competency 3

9. <u>Competency 3, No. 7</u>: Provide all records you kept of your follow through with staff following walkthroughs and evaluations you completed in 2013-14.

Competency 4

10. <u>Competency 4, No. 1</u>: Provide all records you kept of student transitions into and out of the Alt. Ed. programs in 2013-14.

11. <u>Competency 4, No. 3</u>: Provide all records of the short narratives you were directed in the FAP to keep.

12. <u>Competency 4, No. 4</u>: Provide all records you were directed to keep of staff attendance at training or PD on how to complete a report in Sapphire, including how to classify various offenses under the Code of Conduct.

13. <u>Competency 4, No. 5</u>: Provide all records you kept of training you provided for staff on how Communities in Schools (CIS) staff may intervene in student behavioral or disciplinary issues and when ASD staff should intervene in such issues, and also provide the attendance records you kept for same.

Competency 5

14. <u>Competency 5, No. 1</u>: Provide a written list of the topics and trainers you identified by working with your staff to identify areas in which staff felt a need for diversity or sensitivity training.

15. <u>Competency 5, No. 4</u>: Provide copies of any and all written reports regarding any mistakes and accompanying corrections you made in 2013-14.

To: David Wildonger, Chief Operations Officer

From: Jose Rosado, Director of Alternative Education

Date: May, 16, 2014

Subject: 2013-2014 FAP – Review of Supervision Provided /

Documentation Required by May 16, 2014

Attached you will find the items noted in the "Subject" of this memorandum (Above), including the "List of Documentation to be provided by Mr. Rosado within 10 days (May 16, 2014).

FAP Meeting – **August 19, 2013** – I met with Mr. Wildonger and was given a copy of the first version of my 2013-2014 FAP. Mr. Wildonger reviewed the document with me.

FAP Meeting – August 21, 2013 – I met with Mr. Wildonger and was given a copy of a second version (revised) of my 2013-2014 FAP. Mr. Wildonger reviewed the document with me.

FAP Meeting – August 23, 2013 – I met with Mr. Wildonger again to discuss the 2013-2014 FAP and the due dates for specific performance competencies.

FAP Meeting – September 11, 2013 – I met with Mr. Wildonger to review my plans/documents for the six FAP performance competencies that were due and I had submitted to Mr. Wildonger via email.

The FAP performance competencies – plans and documents – and the discussion pertaining to each were as follows:

- FAP competency 2 (2), submitted – 8/23/13. NO DISCUSSION (Copy of email attached – Appendix A)

- FAP competency 1 (3), submitted – 9/6/13. NO DISCUSSION (Copy of email attached – Appendix A)

- FAP competency 1 (3), submitted – 9/6/13. NO DISCUSSION (Copy of email attached – Appendix A)

- FAP competency 2 (1), submitted – 9/6/13. NO DISCUSSION (Copy of email attached – Appendix A)

- FAP competency 3 (3), submitted – 9/6/13. NO DISCUSSION (Copy of email attached – Appendix A)

- FAP competency 5 (1), submitted – 9/4/13. Mr. Wildonger noted that the plan was submitted late. Due 8/30/13. (Copy of email attached – Appendix A)

During the September 11, 2013 FAP Meeting, Mr. Wildonger acknowledged receiving the FAP plans/documents I had submitted to him. Mr. Wildonger did not ask any questions or offer any feedback. No discussion regarding my plans/documents. No suggestions for consideration.

FAP competency 3 (1), was due on 9/30/13. Complying with the due date was not possible Re: Human Resources Office did not provide NHQT (PA Form #425). Please see my email to Mr. Wildonger 9/27/13, with email from Christina Mazzella (9/16/13) attached. (Copy of emails attached – Appendix A)

No other FAP Meetings were scheduled by Mr. Wildonger between September 12, 2013 and February 18, 2014.

Please note: During the supervision of my 2012-2013 FAP, my supervisor Susan Lozada met with me for 21 FAP Meetings during the same time period (Susan Lozada/Jose Rosado FAP Meetings 2012-2013 attached – Appendix B)

On the following dates: November 21, 2013, December 6, 2013 and December 13, 2013, I email Mr. Wildonger (as my direct supervisor) regarding specific concerns and requested to meet with him regarding my concerns. The Subject of my emails and request for meetings is as follows:

- November 21, 2013 – Subject: FAP Competency 1 (2). I requested a meeting with Mr. Wildonger – Mr. Wildonger DID NOT RESPOND TO MY EMAIL. (Copy of email attached – Appendix C)

- December 6, 2013 – Subject: Restructuring of Alternative Education (IBEAM) – Need for Additional Resources/Support. I requested a meeting with Mr. Wildonger – Mr. Wildonger DID NOT RESPOND TO MY EMAIL. (Copy of email attached – Appendix C)

- December 13, 2013 – Subject: District Non-Compliance (NHQT – Staffing & Special Education Students Assigned to Alternative Education) Unfair Evaluation/FAP. I requested a meeting with Mr. Wildonger – Mr. Wildonger DID NOT RESPOND TO MY EMAIL. (Copy of email attached – Appendix C).

On November 27, 2013, I emailed Mr. Wildonger (Subject: AEDY/Special Education – Compliance Concerns) regarding a directive he issued to me during a meeting on November 26, 2013. In the email I informed Mr. Wildonger that "I cannot comply with your directive to move the special education students into the AEDY program." "I believe that this action would be illegal and unethical." "Please consider one of the other options I proposed during our meeting yesterday…." Mr. Wildonger did not respond to my email with a response email. Instead, during a meeting later that day, which I was called into, I was asked to review the options I had proposed and an appropriate option was agreed upon. (Copy of email attached – Appendix D).

FAP competency 3 (1), was due on 9/30/13. Complying with the due date was not possible Re: Human Resources Office did not provide NHQT (PA Form #425). Please see my email to Mr. Wildonger 9/27/13, with email from Christina Mazzella (9/16/13) attached. (Copy of emails attached – Appendix A)

No other FAP Meetings were scheduled by Mr. Wildonger between September 12, 2013 and February 18, 2014.

Please note: During the supervision of my 2012-2013 FAP, my supervisor Susan Lozada met with me for 21 FAP Meetings during the same time period (Susan Lozada/Jose Rosado FAP Meetings 2012-2013 attached – Appendix B)

On the following dates: November 21, 2013, December 6, 2013 and December 13, 2013, I email Mr. Wildonger (as my direct supervisor) regarding specific concerns and requested to meet with him regarding my concerns. The Subject of my emails and request for meetings is as follows:

- November 21, 2013 – Subject: FAP Competency 1 (2). I requested a meeting with Mr. Wildonger – Mr. Wildonger DID NOT RESPOND TO MY EMAIL. (Copy of email attached – Appendix C)

- December 6, 2013 – Subject: Restructuring of Alternative Education (IBEAM) – Need for Additional Resources/Support. I requested a meeting with Mr. Wildonger – Mr. Wildonger DID NOT RESPOND TO MY EMAIL. (Copy of email attached – Appendix C)

- December 13, 2013 – Subject: District Non-Compliance (NHQT – Staffing & Special Education Students Assigned to Alternative Education) Unfair Evaluation/FAP. I requested a meeting with Mr. Wildonger – Mr. Wildonger DID NOT RESPOND TO MY EMAIL. (Copy of email attached – Appendix C).

On November 27, 2013, I emailed Mr. Wildonger (Subject: AEDY/Special Education – Compliance Concerns) regarding a directive he issued to me during a meeting on November 26, 2013. In the email I informed Mr. Wildonger that "I cannot comply with your directive to move the special education students into the AEDY program." "I believe that this action would be illegal and unethical." "Please consider one of the other options I proposed during our meeting yesterday…." Mr. Wildonger did not respond to my email with a response email. Instead, during a meeting later that day, which I was called into, I was asked to review the options I had proposed and an appropriate option was agreed upon. (Copy of email attached – Appendix D).

On May 6, 2014, I met with Mr. Wildonger to review my Mid-Year FAP Evaluation. The meeting was also attended by Christina Mazzella and Robert Wheeler. I acknowledged receiving a copy via email prior to the meeting. Mr. Wildonger asked if I needed for him to read the 18 page document to me, I said that would not be necessary.

Mr. Wildonger then proceeded to give me a document (memorandum) regarding a list of documents I was to provide to him in 10 days (May 16, 2014). (Copy of memorandum attached – Appendix E).

Immediately after receiving the memorandum (noting the list of documents Mr. Wildonger required me to provide), Christina Mazzella gave me a letter placing me on Administrative Suspension with pay.

Although I was placed on Administrative Suspension with pay, I was required to complete the task assigned by Mr. Wildonger.

Please see the attached emails – (Appendix F) - regarding my efforts to gain access to the files and documents required to complete the assigned task.

On Thursday, May 15, 2014, I reported to the Administration Center at 12:00 noon – as directed – to review the files and documents I had requested and to complete the assigned task.

Upon reviewing the files and documents which were retrieved and brought to Christina Mazzella's office, I found that several of the files and documents I requested were not included with the files and documents that had been retrieved and provided to me. I also found an email addressed to Jacqulyn Alotta (not from me) and a file belonging to Jacqulyn Alotta along with my files and documents. I also found an email addressed to Candice Avrich (not from me) included in my files and documents. I gave these files and documents to Christina Mazzella and asked that she note that those documents were included with my files and documents.

List of Documentation to be provided by Mr. Rosado within 10 days (May 16, 2014)

1. Competency 2, No. 2: The required file/documentation was not retrieved and provided for me at the Administration Center as stated by Mr. Wildonger. Specifically a file on Sarah Lucci – a teacher at the 4th and Allen Building.

2.   Competency 2, No. 3: On Wednesday, January 29, 2014, I received an email from Susan Elliott, Raub Middle School principal. The subject of the email was: video (Copy of email attached – Appendix G). In the email Mrs. Elliott states "the video is sexual in nature." She also indicated that student #103276 was in possession of the video. This student is a PM VISTA student. On Thursday, January 30, 2014, I confirmed that the student was in attendance at 4th and Allen. I was also made aware that the video in question could be on her cell phone. Beginning at 12:00 noon – 4:30 PM, I was actively involved in a potential Sexual Harassment Investigation. I do not recall whether I saw or spoke with John Monahan while he waited in the office. During the course of the investigation I consulted with Mr. Wildonger and Mr. Makhoul. Mr. Makhoul visited the building and was present when the student and parent met with an officer from the Allentown Police Department.

3.   Competency 2, No. 3: During the Alternative Education Opening of School – Faculty Meeting (Monday, August 26, 2013) I specifically spoke about Purchase Requisitions (Books and Resources). I asked teachers to complete an inventory and forward purchase orders to me for any requests regarding books and instructional resources. Mr. Troxell was in attendance during the faculty meeting (Agenda and Acknowledgement Form attached – Appendix H). On September 10, 2013, during the Lehigh Street Campus Faculty Meeting, I again spoke about Purchase Requisitions and gave teachers copies of the purchase requisition form. I asked if teachers had completed their inventories (books/Instructional resources) and if they needed books and/or instructional resources they should see me regarding purchase requisitions. Mr. Troxell was in attendance during the faculty meeting (Agenda and Sign-In Sheet attached – Appendix H).

4.   Competency 2, No.3: Consistent walkthroughs with the SOI's was not possible due to the constant turnover (resignations/reassignments) of the SOI'S. Multiple Supervisor of Instruction Rotation Schedules were put out by Dr. Murray (Copies of the multiple schedules are attached – Appendix I). Dr. Murray and I worked closely to provide as much support as possible for the alternative education teachers. Scheduling conflicts – on the part of the SOI's - often caused the SOI's to miss a scheduled visit. Conflicts on my part due to attending to other administrative duties (code of conduct, parent conference, incident investigations and other duties) also presented a challenge. Completed walkthroughs /communications between Dr. Murray, the SOI's and myself / revised SOI Rotation Schedules and other documents pertaining to walkthroughs are attached in Appendix I).

5.   Competency 2, No. 4: I recognized staff success during "morning circle" (IBEAM), In-Service Announcements, Faculty Meeting Announcements, individual contacts with staff and the creation of a staff appreciation bulletin

board located in the main office at IBEAM (I contributed staff appreciation notes on the bulletin board).

6.   Competency 2, No. 5a: Strategies/training on how to reduce incidents of student discipline and reduce errors in Sapphire reporting was provided on the following dates: 8/26/13 (all staff), 9/9/13 (IBEAM staff), 9/10/13 (Lehigh Street Campus staff), 9/25/13 (Lehigh Street Campus – ALC staff). (Copies of Agendas, notes and Sign-In Sheets are attached – Appendix J).

7.   Competency 2, No. 5a: The issue regarding Sapphire errors was compounded by the fact that all of the alternative education programs located at the Lehigh Street Campus were moved to the 4th and Allen Building one month after the school year. On 9/23/13 course Maintenance was completed for all alternative education program located at the Lehigh Street Campus. On 10/21/13, new homerooms were added (Upon move to the 4th and Allen Building). The counselors (Jen Carter and Damaris Soto) communicated with Robin Powlus and Nancy Conway regarding adding homerooms, classrooms and student schedules. Most of the errors were corrected in a timely manner. The counselors experienced some problems with the system (could not delete courses and save changes). I worked with the counselors and Robin Powlus to address the concerns. (Copies of relevant documents are attached – Appendix K).

8.   Competency 2, No. 6: Staff recognition regarding successes in improving accuracy of entries made in Sapphire over the first two quarters was accomplished by making announcements and having discussions during "Morning Circle" (IBEAM), individual contacts with staff, team meetings, role-call meetings and faculty meetings.

9.   Competency 3, No. 7: Please see response to Competency 2, No.3 and Appendix I

10. Competency 4, No. 1: Files and documents (Rosters) pertaining to this Competency were not retrieved from my office and made available to me for the purpose of this report as requested.

11. Competency 4, No.3: Records pertaining to my contacts with parents regarding concerns they have reported (Copies of my communications with parents are attached – Appendix L).

12. Competency 4, No. 4: Please refer to Appendix J for Professional Development/Training (Agenda, Dates, Sign-In Sheets) where directions were provided regarding completing a Sapphire Discipline referral (Documentation

of Interventions, Behavior Specialist Intervention, Refocus Room, Classroom Management Plan, Describe Behaviors – do not define)

13.   Competency 4, No. 5: The roles of CIS staff (at IBEAM and The Lehigh Street Campus) were discussed and reviewed during the Opening of school Faculty Meeting (8/26/13). Agenda and Sign-In Sheets can be found in Appendix J). Specifically we discussed CIS staff interventions in support of the Behavior Specialists and in the Refocus/ATS Room. Also Ms. Grim, LSW completing Threat Assessments at IBEAM. A CIS SITE PLAN was also created. This SITE PLAN clearly identifies CIS staff and roles at IBEAM (Copy of CIS SITE PLAN is attached – Appendix M). The two CIS staff at the Lehigh Street Campus/4th and Allen, facilitate student groups.

14.   Competency 5, No. 1: This information was included in the FAP Competency 5, #1, submitted on September 4, 2013 (Copy attached – Appendix N).

15.   Competency 5, No. 4: Please see my emails of 1/9/14, (1/2 day vacation, Rescinding   ½ day vacation Request). I acknowledged that I did not make a proper request to you as my supervisor. However, I still remain very troubled by your reaction towards me in Mr. Perez's office later that morning. (Copies of emails and Harassment Complaint Narrative are attached – Appendix O).

DAVID M. WILDONGER
Chief Operations Officer
wildongerd@allentownsd.org

31 South Penn Street ▪ P.O. Box 328 ▪ Allentown, PA 18105
Administration Center ▪ 484-765-4154 ▪ Fax: 484-765-4239

May 19, 2014

Jose Rosado, Sr.
918 N. Bergen St.
Fountain Hill, PA 18015

RE: Loudermill Hearing

Dear Mr. Rosado:

Previously, at our meeting on May 6, 2014, you inquired about information relating to School Code charges brought against you by the Allentown School District. At this time, no such charges have been brought against you. However the District may consider such charges in the near future. Therefore, by this letter, I am inviting you to attend a meeting with me and Ms. Christina Mazzella, Executive Director of Human Resources, which shall serve as a Loudermill hearing.

This meeting is intended to allow you the opportunity to provide us with any input you would like the District to take into consideration before a decision is made to recommend that your employment be terminated for cause as provided under School Code Section 1122. The meeting is scheduled on Friday, June 6, 2014 at 10:00 am in the Administration Building.

You may bring a representative from the Act 93 Employees' group or an attorney to this meeting. Please respond to let us know your choice of representative to Christina Mazzella at (484) 765-4231 or Mazzellac@allentownsd.org, on or before May 29, 2014, no later than noon.

Sincerely,

David Wildonger

C: Christina Mazzella

An Equal Opportunity Employer

To: David Wildonger, Chief Operations Officer

From: Jose Rosado, Director of Alternative Education

Date: May 28, 2014

Subject: Rebuttal – 2013-2014 Focused Assistance Plan Mid-Year
           Evaluation

Please find attached to this memorandum my rebuttal regarding the
Mid-Year Evaluation you completed for my 2013-2014 Focused
Assistance Plan.

Please attach my rebuttal to my 2013-2014, Mid-Year Evaluation.

REBUTTAL – 2013-2014, Focused Assistance Plan Mid-Year Evaluation

Review of supervision/lack of provided by Mr. Wildonger:

FAP Meeting – August 19, 2013 – I met with Mr. Wildonger and was given a copy of the first version of my 2013-2014 FAP. Mr. Wildonger reviewed the document with me.

FAP Meeting – August 21, 2013 – I met with Mr. Wildonger and was given a copy of a second version (revised) of my 2013-2014 FAP. Mr. Wildonger reviewed the document with me.

FAP Meeting – August 23, 2013 – I met with Mr. Wildonger again to discuss the 2013-2014 FAP and the due dates for specific performance competencies.

FAP Meeting – September 11, 2013 – I met with Mr. Wildonger to review my plans/documents for the six FAP performance competencies that were due and I had submitted to Mr. Wildonger via email.

The FAP performance competencies – plans and documents – and the discussion pertaining to each were as follows:

- FAP competency 2 (2), submitted – 8/23/13. NO DISCUSSION (Copy of email attached – Appendix A)

- FAP competency 1 (3), submitted – 9/6/13. NO DISCUSSION (Copy of email attached – Appendix A)

- FAP competency 1 (3), submitted – 9/6/13. NO DISCUSSION (Copy of email attached – Appendix A)

- FAP competency 2 (1), submitted – 9/6/13. NO DISCUSSION (Copy of email attached – Appendix A)

- FAP competency 3 (3), submitted – 9/6/13. NO DISCUSSION (Copy of email attached – Appendix A)

- FAP competency 5 (1), submitted – 9/4/13. Mr. Wildonger noted that the plan was submitted late. Due 8/30/13. (Copy of email attached – Appendix A)

During the September 11, 2013 FAP Meeting, Mr. Wildonger acknowledged receiving the FAP plans/documents I had submitted to him. Mr. Wildonger did not ask any questions or offer any feedback. No discussion regarding my plans/documents. No suggestions for consideration.

FAP competency 3 (1), was due on 9/30/13. Complying with the due date was not possible Re: Human Resources Office did not provide NHQT (PA Form #425). Please see my email to Mr. Wildonger 9/27/13, with email from Christina Mazzella (9/16/13) attached. (Copy of emails attached – Appendix A)

No other FAP Meetings were scheduled by Mr. Wildonger between September 12, 2013 and February 18, 2014.

Please note: During the supervision of my 2012-2013 FAP, my supervisor Susan Lozada met with me for 21 FAP Meetings during the same time period (Susan Lozada/Jose Rosado FAP Meetings 2012-2013 attached – Appendix B)

On the following dates: November 21, 2013, December 6, 2013 and December 13, 2013, I email Mr. Wildonger (as my direct supervisor) regarding specific concerns and requested to meet with him regarding my concerns. The Subject of my emails and request for meetings is as follows:

- November 21, 2013 – Subject: FAP Competency 1 (2). I requested a meeting with Mr. Wildonger – Mr. Wildonger DID NOT RESPOND TO MY EMAIL. (Copy of email attached – Appendix C)

- December 6, 2013 – Subject: Restructuring of Alternative Education (IBEAM) – Need for Additional Resources/Support. I requested a meeting with Mr. Wildonger – Mr. Wildonger DID NOT RESPOND TO MY EMAIL. (Copy of email attached – Appendix C)

- December 13, 2013 – Subject: District Non-Compliance (NHQT – Staffing & Special Education Students Assigned to Alternative Education) Unfair Evaluation/FAP. I requested a meeting with Mr. Wildonger – Mr. Wildonger DID NOT RESPOND TO MY EMAIL. (Copy of email attached – Appendix C).

On November 27, 2013, I emailed Mr. Wildonger (Subject: AEDY/Special Education – Compliance Concerns) regarding a directive he issued to me during a meeting on November 26, 2013. In the email I informed Mr. Wildonger that "I cannot comply with your directive to move the special education students into the AEDY program." "I believe that this action would be illegal and unethical." "Please consider one of the other options I proposed during our meeting yesterday…." Mr. Wildonger did not respond to my email with a response email. Instead, during a meeting later that day, which I was called into, I was asked to review the options I had proposed and an appropriate option was agreed upon. (Copy of email attached – Appendix D).

On May 6, 2014, I met with Mr. Wildonger to review my Mid-Year FAP Evaluation. The meeting was also attended by Christina Mazzella and Robert Wheeler. I acknowledged receiving a copy via email prior to the meeting. Mr. Wildonger asked if I needed for him to read the 18 page document to me, I said that would not be necessary.

Mr. Wildonger then proceeded to give me a document (memorandum) regarding a list of documents I was to provide to him in 10 days (May 16, 2014). (Copy of memorandum attached – Appendix E).

Immediately after receiving the memorandum (noting the list of documents Mr. Wildonger required me to provide), Christina Mazzella gave me a letter placing me on Administrative Suspension with pay.

Although I was placed on Administrative Suspension with pay, I was required to complete the task assigned by Mr. Wildonger.

Please see the attached emails – (Appendix F) - regarding my efforts to gain access to the files and documents required to complete the assigned task.

On Thursday, May 15, 2014, I reported to the Administration Center at 12:00 noon – as directed – to review the files and documents I had requested and to complete the assigned task.

Upon reviewing the files and documents which were retrieved and brought to Christina Mazzella's office, I found that several of the files and documents I requested were not included with the files and documents that had been retrieved and provided to me. I also found an email addressed to Jacqulyn Alotta (not from me) and a file belonging to Jacqulyn Alotta along with my files and documents. I also found an email addressed to Candice Avrich (not from me) included in my files and documents. I gave these files and documents to Christina Mazzella and asked that she note that those documents were included with my files and documents.

List of Documentation to be provided by Mr. Rosado within 10 days (May 16, 2014).
Documents were provided to Mr. Wildonger on May 16, 2014 as directed.

1. Competency 2, No. 2: The required file/documentation was not retrieved and provided for me at the Administration Center as stated by Mr. Wildonger. Specifically a file on Sarah Lucci – a teacher at the 4th and Allen Building.

2. Competency 2, No. 3: On Wednesday, January 29, 2014, I received an email from Susan Elliott, Raub Middle School principal. The subject of the email was: video (Copy of email attached – Appendix G). In the email Mrs. Elliott states "the video is sexual in nature." She also indicated that student #103276 was in possession of the video. This student is a PM VISTA student. On Thursday, January 30, 2014, I confirmed that the student was in attendance at 4th and Allen. I was also made aware that the video in question could be on her cell phone. Beginning at 12:00 noon – 4:30 PM, I was actively involved in a potential Sexual Harassment Investigation. I do not recall whether I saw or spoke with John Monahan while he waited in the office. During the course of the investigation I consulted with Mr. Wildonger and Mr. Makhoul. Mr. Makhoul visited the building and was present when the student and parent met with an officer from the Allentown Police Department.

3. Competency 2, No. 3: During the Alternative Education Opening of School – Faculty Meeting (Monday, August 26, 2013) I specifically spoke about Purchase Requisitions (Books and Resources). I asked teachers to complete an inventory and forward purchase orders to me for any requests regarding books and instructional resources. Mr. Troxell was in attendance during the faculty meeting (Agenda and Acknowledgement Form attached – Appendix H). On September 10, 2013, during the Lehigh Street Campus Faculty Meeting, I again spoke about Purchase Requisitions and gave teachers copies of the purchase requisition form. I asked if teachers had completed their inventories (books/Instructional resources) and if they needed books and/or instructional resources they should see me regarding purchase requisitions. Mr. Troxell was in attendance during the faculty meeting (Agenda and Sign-In Sheet attached – Appendix H).

4. Competency 2, No.3: Consistent walkthroughs with the SOI's was not possible due to the constant turnover (resignations/reassignments) of the SOI'S. Multiple Supervisor of Instruction Rotation Schedules were put out by Dr. Murray (Copies of the multiple schedules are attached – Appendix I). Dr. Murray and I worked closely to provide as much support as possible for the

alternative education teachers. Scheduling conflicts – on the part of the SOI's - often caused the SOI's to miss a scheduled visit. Conflicts on my part due to attending to other administrative duties (code of conduct, parent conference, incident investigations and other duties) also presented a challenge. Completed walkthroughs /communications between Dr. Murray, the SOI's and myself / revised SOI Rotation Schedules and other documents pertaining to walkthroughs are attached in Appendix I).

5.   Competency 2, No. 4: I recognized staff success during "morning circle" (IBEAM), In-Service Announcements, Faculty Meeting Announcements, individual contacts with staff and the creation of a staff appreciation bulletin board located in the main office at IBEAM (I contributed staff appreciation notes on the bulletin board).

6.   Competency 2, No. 5a: Strategies/training on how to reduce incidents of student discipline and reduce errors in Sapphire reporting was provided on the following dates: 8/26/13 (all staff), 9/9/13 (IBEAM staff), 9/10/13 (Lehigh Street Campus staff), 9/25/13 (Lehigh Street Campus – ALC staff). (Copies of Agendas, notes and Sign-In Sheets are attached – Appendix J).

7.   Competency 2, No. 5a: The issue regarding Sapphire errors was compounded by the fact that all of the alternative education programs located at the Lehigh Street Campus were moved to the 4th and Allen Building one month after the school year. On 9/23/13 course Maintenance was completed for all alternative education program located at the Lehigh Street Campus. On 10/21/13, new homerooms were added (Upon move to the 4th and Allen Building). The counselors (Jen Carter and Damaris Soto) communicated with Robin Powlus and Nancy Conway regarding adding homerooms, classrooms and student schedules. Most of the errors were corrected in a timely manner. The counselors experienced some problems with the system (could not delete courses and save changes). I worked with the counselors and Robin Powlus to address the concerns. (Copies of relevant documents are attached – Appendix K).

8.   Competency 2, No. 6: Staff recognition regarding successes in improving accuracy of entries made in Sapphire over the first two quarters was accomplished by making announcements and having discussions during "Morning Circle" (IBEAM), individual contacts with staff, team meetings, role-call meetings and faculty meetings.

9.   Competency 3, No. 7: Please see response to Competency 2, No.3 and Appendix I

10. Competency 4, No. 1: Files and documents (Rosters) pertaining to this Competency were not retrieved from my office and made available to me for the purpose of this report as requested.

11. Competency 4, No.3: Records pertaining to my contacts with parents regarding concerns they have reported (Copies of my communications with parents are attached – Appendix L).

12. Competency 4, No. 4: Please refer to Appendix J for Professional Development/Training (Agenda, Dates, Sign-In Sheets) where directions were provided regarding completing a Sapphire Discipline referral (Documentation of Interventions, Behavior Specialist Intervention, Refocus Room, Classroom Management Plan, Describe Behaviors – do not define)

13. Competency 4, No. 5: The roles of CIS staff (at IBEAM and The Lehigh Street Campus) were discussed and reviewed during the Opening of school Faculty Meeting (8/26/13). Agenda and Sign-In Sheets can be found in Appendix J). Specifically we discussed CIS staff interventions in support of the Behavior Specialists and in the Refocus/ATS Room. Also Ms. Grim, LSW completing Threat Assessments at IBEAM. A CIS SITE PLAN was also created. This SITE PLAN clearly identifies CIS staff and roles at IBEAM (Copy of CIS SITE PLAN is attached – Appendix M). The two CIS staff at the Lehigh Street Campus/4th and Allen, facilitate student groups.

14. Competency 5, No. 1: This information was included in the FAP Competency 5, #1, submitted on September 4, 2013 (Copy attached – Appendix N).

15. Competency 5, No. 4: Please see my emails of 1/9/14, (1/2 day vacation, Rescinding ½ day vacation Request). I acknowledged that I did not make a proper request to you as my supervisor. However, I still remain very troubled by your reaction towards me in Mr. Perez's office later that morning. (Copies of emails and Harassment Complaint Narrative are attached – Appendix O).

Response to evaluations provided regarding other Competencies:

Competency 1 (1b): Mr. Wildonger noted that a meeting took place on February 10, 2014 with two Middle School Principals regarding – Procedures and protocols set forth in the Student Case Management Binder are not being followed (Please note - The Student Case Management Binder was Introduced and Implemented for the first time at the beginning of the 2013-2014 school year). During this meeting the following acknowledgements/ statements were made:

- Mr. Wildonger – "We all have to own it......we are here to understand what is going on"
- Mr. Price – "The process is flawed"
- Mr. Wildonger – "Communication between the counselors and administrators at both ends (home school and alternative education) not happening"
- Daria Custer – "All forms should be revised"
- Mr. Wildonger – "Pieces of the book that need to be corrected"
- Ms. Mazzella – "Needs fine tuning....first year...realization that we have to fine tune and change things...we are making progress"

Competency 1 (2a): Mr. Wildonger noted "You also stated that a complete schedule of formative and summative evaluations was not possible because of three instructional vacancies on your staff, but that you would complete a tentative schedule of formative and summative evaluations beginning on Monday, September 16, 2013. I have no record of receiving this document from you, on September 16, or later"

- On September 12, 2013, I sent an email to Mr. Wildonger (Re: Observation Schedule). The email noted that the observations were scheduled and "observations are noted in my daily calendar which you have access to"

Competency 2 (2): Mr. Wildonger noted "before the first teacher work day of 2013-2014 school year, your objective was to develop a plan of professional development ("PD") for yourself that specifically included PD in Teachscape and differentiated Supervision.

- On August 22, 2013, I attended a Teachscape traing session provided by Ms. Kruger. During the training session Ms. Kruger made the following assessment regarding the implementation of Teachscape by the Allentown School District – "misunderstanding between Teachscape and the state.....Confused....at a loss....Honest to God we are not real comfortable with this'
- On November 21, 2013 I emailed Mr. Wildonger regarding the implementation of Teachscape. I requested a meeting with him to discuss my concerns – Mr. Wildonger DID NOT RESPOND TO MY EMAIL AND REQUEST FOR A MEETING (Copy of the email is attached - APPENDIX C)

Competency 2 (4): Mr. Wildonger noted concerns regarding "response time to Sapphire referrals."

- On December 6, 2013, I emailed Mr. Wildonger (Re: Restructuring of Alternative Education (IBEAM) – Need for Additional Resources/Support). Student Discipline (Sapphire Referrals) was one of the concerns noted in my email to Mr. Wildonger. I requested a meeting with Mr. Wildomger to discuss my concerns – Mr. Wildonger DID NOT RESPOND TO MY EMAIL AND A REQUEST FOR A MEETING.

Competency 2 (8): Please see response to Competency 1 (1b)

REC'D JUN 1 6 2014

KINGSPRY

June 12, 2014

JEROME B. FRANK
DONALD F. SPRY II
DOMENIC P. SBROCCHI
KIRBY G. UPRIGHT, LLM, CPA
KENT H. HERMAN
TERENCE L. FAUL
JOHN E. FREUND, III
JEFFREY T. TUCKER
GLENNA M. HAZELTINE
JAMES F. SWARTZ, III*
KEVIN C. REID
PAUL S. FRANK
BRIAN J. TAYLOR
MICHAEL A. GAUL
ELIZABETH M. KELLY
ELLEN C. SCHURDAK
KRISTINE RODDICK
REBECCA A. YOUNG
DOROTA GASIENICA-KOZAK
JESSICA F. MOYER
LUCAS J. REPKA
ERIN D. GILSBACH
CATHERINE L. STEHLIN
AVERY E. SMITH
KEELY J. COLLINS
KARLEY BIGGS SEBIA
JONATHAN M. HUERTA

Thomas L. Kelly
36 East Second Street
P.O. Box 1048
Media, PA 19063-0848

Re: Allentown School District/Jose Rosado, Sr.

Dear Mr. Kelly:

By this letter I am acknowledging receipt of your voice message left on today's date, in which you confirmed your availability for a *Loudermill* hearing on **July 15, 2014, at 10:00 A.M.** at the Allentown School District Administration Center, 31 S. Penn Street, Allentown PA 18101. Please report to the second floor reception desk and you will be directed to the room of the hearing from there. No separate letter of notice will be sent to Mr. Rosado by the District; it is anticipated that you will communicate to him with this information. It is also understood that you will contact me in the event that Mr. Rosado is not cleared to attend the hearing by his doctor.

This hearing will be in the nature of a meeting, not a formal hearing. In the near future, I will send a letter to inform you of issues are of concern to the District and what actions or inactions are believed to be attributable to Mr. Rosado, as per your prior request for same.

OF COUNSEL:
E. DRUMMOND KING
JAMES J. RAVELLE, Ph.D., JD.
PAUL K. BLUNT
KATHLEEN CONN, Ph.D., JD., LLM

AFFILIATED WITH:
WEISS BURKARDT KRAMER, LLC
PITTSBURGH, PA 15219

*Certified Civil Trial
Advocate by National
Board of Trial Advocacy
("A PA Supreme Court
Approved Agency")

Very truly yours,

John E. Freund, III, Esquire

C: David M. Wildonger
Christina Mazzella
Elizabeth Kelly, Esquire

KING, SPRY, HERMAN, FREUND & FAUL, LLC • ATTORNEYS & COUNSELORS AT LAW
ONE WEST BROAD STREET • SUITE 700 • BETHLEHEM, PA 18018 • TEL: 610-332-0390 • FAX: 610-332-0314

ALLENTOWN ❖ BETHLEHEM ❖ STROUDSBURG

www.kingspry.com

CHRISTINA MAZZELLA

Executive Director of Human Resources
mazzellac@allentownsd.org

31 South Penn Street ■ P.O. Box 328 ■ Allentown, PA 18105
Administration Center ■ 484-765-4231 ■ Fax: 484-765-4140

July 25, 2014

Certified Mail

José Rosado, Sr.
918 N. Bergen Street
Fountain Hill, PA 18015

Dear Mr. Rosado:

By this letter, you are hereby notified that effective Monday, July 21, 2014, you shall be suspended without pay. The suspension shall continue while the recommendation to terminate your employment as Director of Alternative Education is pending, until such time as the District's Board of School Directors acts on the recommendation.

During this period of unpaid suspension, you are neither required nor permitted to report to work. You are directed to remain away from all District buildings and property, and all of your contact with the District should be made through your legal counsel.

Sincerely,

Christina Mazzella
Executive Director of Human Resources

C: Dr. C. Russell Mayo
        David M. Wildonger
        Thomas L. Kelly, Esquire
        John E. Freund, III, Esquire
        Kristine M. Roddick, Esquire

SCHOOL DISTRICT

31 South Penn Street • P.O. Box 328 • Allentown, PA 18105
Administration Center • 484-765-4000 • Fax: 484-765-4085

**VIA FIRST CLASS MAIL
AND CERTIFIED MAIL, RETURN RECEIPT REQUESTED**

July 28, 2014

José Rosado, Sr.
918 N Bergen Street
Fountain Hill, PA 18015

Via Email & United States Mail, First Class

Re: Notice of Charges and Hearing

Dear Mr. Rosado:

You are hereby notified pursuant to Article XI of the Public School Code of 1949, *as amended,* and the Local Agency Law, the Allentown School District Board of Directors ("Board") will conduct a hearing for the purpose of determining whether Mr. Rosado should be dismissed from his employment with the School District as a professional Employee, which is tentatively scheduled for **Tuesday, August 12, 2014**, at 10:00 a.m. in the public hearing room of the Allentown School District Administration Center, 31 S. Penn Street, Allentown, PA 18105.

You are charged by the Allentown School District Administration ("Administration") with (1) Persistent Negligence in the Performance of Duties, (2) Willful Neglect of Duties, and (3) Intemperance, as contemplated by the School Code of 1949, *as amended*, arising out of the following:

A. In 2013-14, you failed or refused to address student discipline referrals in a timely manner, and did so after he was informed that his response to student discipline matters was not timely in the 2012-13 school year and that this failure caused a perception among teaching staff that he did not care about staff safety or student violations of the District's Code of Conduct and was directed to improve his response to student discipline referrals.

{00157609}

SCHOOL DISTRICT

31 South Penn Street ▪ P.O. Box 328 ▪ Allentown, PA 18105
Administration Center ▪ 484-765-4000 ▪ Fax: 484-765-4085

DIRECTORS
ROBERT E. SMITH, JR.
President

DEBRA H. LAMB
Vice President

SCOTT ARMSTRONG
ELLEN B. BISHOP, M.D.
CE-CE GERLACH
ELIZABETH MARTINEZ
CHARLES F. THIEL
MICHAEL E. WELSH
DAVID F. ZIMMERMAN

OFFICERS
C. RUSSELL MAYO, Ed. D.
Superintendent of Schools

JANET MORILLO
School Board Secretary

John R. Clark, Ed. D.
Treasurer

John E. Freund, III
Solicitor

B. In 2013-14, you failed or refused to ensure that students' home schools received timely and informative information about students and their progress in the alternative education programs when the students were transitioning back to the home schools after he was directed to improve his communication and rapport with principals, particularly in the student transition process.

C. In 2013-14, you failed or refused to take steps to ensure that his staff followed the procedures outlined in the Student Case Management Binder for tracking and documenting the progress of students, including completing the Student Success Plans and providing them to the home schools, and your failure or refusal occurred after you were specifically directed in writing to be thoroughly familiar with the Student Case Management Binder and that as Director of Alternative Education, you were responsible for keeping others informed about the alternative education procedures and protocols contained in it.

D. In 2012-13 and in 2013-14, you failed or refused to complete a schedule for the observation and evaluation of all teaching and other professional employees under your supervision, and this failure or refusal occurred after you were directed in writing to complete such a schedule at or before the commencement of both school years.

E. In 2013-14, you failed or refused to complete training in professional development in Teachscape, a program that was purchased by the District to assist administrators in using the mandatory evaluation procedure for the District's professional employees. You failed to take the initial Teachscape tests in Focus 1 and 2 on or before February 18, 2014. This failure or refusal occurred after he was specifically directed, in writing, to complete professional development in Teachscape and in observation and evaluation of professionals.

F. As of February 18, 2014, you failed or refused to take steps necessary to ensure that teachers under your supervision had activated their Teachscape accounts, so they could be evaluated using the new evaluation method mandated under the School Code.

G. You failed or refused to give a presentation on Teachscape to your teaching staff, but directed a Supervisor of Instruction to do so. You also failed to be present for one of the

{00157609}

249

31 South Penn Street ▪ P.O. Box 328 ▪ Allentown, PA 18105
Administration Center ▪ 484-765-4000 ▪ Fax: 484-765-4085

Teachscape presentations and one of the question and answer sessions, and thereby failed to show support for the Teachscape tool.

H. In 2013-14, you failed or refused to develop a written schedule of walkthroughs to be conducted by you and the supervisors of instruction to provide feedback to the teaching professionals under your supervision, thereby failing to maximize your opportunities to provide useful feedback to teachers under your supervision. Your failure or refusal in this regard occurred after you were specifically directed, in writing, to develop such a schedule.

I. You failed to take necessary steps to ensure that teachers under your supervision had the necessary books and other materials needed to teach the state approved curriculum. In fact, books and materials were available elsewhere in the District, and were obtained by others for the teachers under your supervision.

J. You demonstrated on numerous occasions in 2012, 2013, and 2014, and you displayed a poor temperament and did not conduct yourself in accordance with a demeanor that is appropriate for an instructional leader. You used body language that was disrespectful of others in the workplace, including but not limited to your supervisor, and persisted in the use and display of such body language after being specifically directed in writing to stop.

You have the right to a hearing pursuant to Section 1121 through 1132 of the School Code, as set forth herein and as tentatively scheduled as discussed in the first paragraph of this notice.

At the School Code hearing, you shall have the following rights:

(1) The right to be represented by counsel;
(2) The right to hear the witnesses and evidence against you and to cross examine said witnesses;
(3) The right to present witnesses and evidence on your own behalf and to testify on your own behalf;

{00157609}

250

SCHOOL DISTRICT

31 South Penn Street ▪ P.O. Box 328 ▪ Allentown, PA 18105
Administration Center ▪ 484-765-4000 ▪ Fax: 484-765-4085

DIRECTORS
ROBERT E. SMITH, JR.
President

DEBRA H. LAMB
Vice President

SCOTT ARMSTRONG
ELLEN B. BISHOP, M.D.
CE-CE GERLACH
ELIZABETH MARTINEZ
CHARLES F. THIEL
MICHAEL E. WELSH
DAVID F. ZIMMERMAN

OFFICERS
C. RUSSELL MAYO, Ed. D.
Superintendent of Schools

JANET MORILLO
School Board Secretary

John R. Clark, Ed. D.
Treasurer

John E. Freund, III
Solicitor

(4) The right to present evidence as to whether discharge or some lesser personnel action is appropriate under the circumstances;

(5) The right to have your choice of either a public or private hearing; and

(6) All other rights guaranteed by the Constitution and applicable law.

The hearing will be stenographically recorded before a hearing officer, and a transcript of the hearing shall be provided to you upon your request and willingness to pay the cost of the transcription to the court stenographer. The Board's decision shall be prepared in writing as an adjudication that specifies the action taken by the Board and the reasons therefor.

If you intend to be represented by legal counsel at the hearing, please contact or have your legal counsel contact the School District Solicitor who will be representing the administration in the prosecution of this case, **to confirm your attendance at the hearing no later than Monday, August 4, 2014.** His name, phone number, and address are as follows:

John E. Freund, III, Esquire
King, Spry, Herman, Freund & Faul, LLC
One West Broad Street, Suite 700
Bethlehem, PA 18018
(610) 332-0390

If you have not already done so, you are hereby directed immediately contact Christina Mazzella, the Executive Director of Human Resources, to surrender and deliver any and all papers, property and effects of the Allentown School District in your possession including any keys to District property.

ATTEST:

THE BOARD OF DIRECTORS OF THE
ALLENTOWN SCHOOL DISTRICT

By:

By:

{00157609}

251

SCHOOL DISTRICT

31 South Penn Street ▪ P.O. Box 328 ▪ Allentown, PA 18105
Administration Center ▪ 484-765-4000 ▪ Fax: 484-765-4085

DIRECTORS

ROBERT E. SMITH, JR.
President

DEBRA H. LAMB
Vice President

SCOTT ARMSTRONG
ELLEN B. BISHOP, M.D.
CE-CE GERLACH
ELIZABETH MARTINEZ
CHARLES F. THIEL
MICHAEL E. WELSH
DAVID F. ZIMMERMAN

OFFICERS

C. RUSSELL MAYO, Ed. D.
Superintendent of Schools

JANET MORILLO
School Board Secretary

John R. Clark, Ed. D.
Treasurer

John E. Freund, III
Solicitor

Janet Morillo, Secretary   Robert E. Smith, Jr., President

C: Dr. C. Russell Mayo
      David M. Wildonger
      Christina R. Mazzella
      John E. Freund, III, Esquire
      Kristine M. Roddick, Esquire

{00157609}

THE DEPOSITIONS

As part of the proceedings moving toward a trial for a federal law suite, each of the parties, including C. Russell Mayo, David M. Wildonger and myself, were deposed. In addition to the interested parties, Susan Lozada was also deposed as a witness. In this chapter I provide excerpt from each of the sworn depositions.

I encourage the reader to compare the testimony given during the sworn depositions with the documentation and other evidence provided in the prior chapters in an effort to identify any discrepancies between the documentation and the sworn statements provided.

Are the discrepancies, if any, the result of indifference, incompetence or just false and untrue statements?

IN THE UNITED STATES DISTRICT COURT

FOR THE EASTERN DISTRICT

OF PENNSYLVANIA

* * * * * * * *

JOSE ROSADO,   *

    Plaintiff   *   Case No.

    vs.   *   15-0252

C. RUSSELL MAYO, Ed.D., *

DAVID WILDONGER and   *

ALLENTOWN SCHOOL   *

DISTRICT   *

    Defendant   *

* * * * * * * *

DEPOSITION OF

JOSE ROSADO

November 19, 2015

SARGENT'S COURT REPORTING SERVICE, INC.
(814) 536-8908

PROCEEDINGS

JOSE ROSADO, HAVING BEEN DULY SWORN, TESTIFIED AS FOLLOWS:

EXAMINIATION
BY ATTORNEY FREUND:

Q. I suspect we'll be a few hours today, so that if you need a break for any reason whatsoever, just ask and we'll take a break.

 You can confer with Mr. Orloski at any time you want. However, if there is a question on the table, you have to answer that question before you can confer with counsel. Do you understand that?

A. Yes, I do …

Q. All right. Let's start now with some background on you. Give me your full name?

A. Jose Rosado…

Q. What is your work professionally before Allentown?

A. Prior to Allentown I worked with the Bethlehem Area School District. I was hired by the Bethlehem Area School District, I believe it was March of 1987. And I worked with the Bethlehem School District for 22, plus years until I left in November of 2009.

Q. Okay. What was your position or positions in Bethlehem?

A. Started as a guidance counselor at Liberty High School. Director of Peer Counseling Program, Liberty High School; worked in that position for eight years.

 After leaving that position I transitioned over to East Hills Middle School for one year.

 Then I took an administrative position at Broughal Middle School as an assistant principal. I want to say that was another eight years. I may be off a little bit on the math.

 And then East Hills Middle School as an assistant principal for approximately five years.

 I eventually left the Bethlehem Area School District in November of 2009 and took the position with the Allentown School District.

Q. Why did you leave the Bethlehem School District?

A. I saw the posting for the position in the Allentown School District, Director of Alternative Education, and I thought it was a good opportunity, given my background with Bethlehem, having worked with at risk or challenged student population, and urban education was an interest. I thought the position would be a good fit for me.

 I left the Bethlehem Area School District on very good terms, was never rated anything other than satisfactory, never had any issues with my performance.

 And I just thought that it was a good opportunity. I was attracted by the position and the professional opportunities to serve in that capacity in Allentown…

Q. All right. So when you started the job in Allentown, tell me what were your responsibilities as director of community and student services?

A. Primarily was to oversee the alternative education programs. When I started in Allentown, we had multiple programs at multiple sites. I believe there were probably four different sites within the city where the programs were being housed or offered. So I had to travel between the sites to oversee staff and oversee the program in general.

Q. Can you tell me what those sites were?

A. There was one site, which was the Vista II site. And that was at the Boys and Girls Club on Seventh Street, I believe it was, in Allentown.

Q. Okay.

A. There was a second site at I believe it was Sixth and Green, which was also a Boys and Girls Club facility. And that's where we housed the Vista I program.

We had two other programs. One was housed at the Fairgrounds facility, the Fairgrounds building. I don't recall the address. There we had the CIS program, which was an AEDY program, and we also had our what was called at that time Advanced program and Second Chance program. They were two different locations within the Fairground building.

I'm trying to think. Boys Club, Boys Club, Fairgrounds. I believe those were — I believe that was where we were at.

Q. Okay. And what was it your responsibility then for all those four sites?

A. yes.

Q. Were you the principal for all those four sites?

A. Yes, I was.

Q. And were you the administrator who had overall responsibility for the Vista program?

A. Yes.

Q. And the IBEAM program?

A. Let me just go back. I did not include the IBEAM program. When I was first hired by the Allentown School District, the IBEAM program didn't exist.

So it was the following school year. That would have been — I think it would have been 2010-2011 school year that we implemented the IBEAM program. So that would have been an additional site to the ones that I've already mentioned.

Q. Was that your responsibility?

A. Yes, it was my responsibility as well. So I had Vista I, Vista II, Advanced, Second Chance, and the IBEAM program. Those five programs at those multiple sites.

Q. Mr. Rosado, please be patient with us here a little bit, because there may be people that read this transcript that are not familiar with some of these acronyms as some of us.

A. Yes.

Attorney Orloski: Particularly me.

Attorney Freund: Well I wasn't thinking of you Richard. But I was actually thinking of any court official who might have an opportunity to look at this.

BY ATTORNEY FREUND:

Q. First of all, AEDY, what is that acronym?

A. That's Pennsylvania Department of Education, Alternative Education for Disruptive Youth.

Q. Okay. And let's get really simple. Give us your definition of alternative education?

A. Well, the state program for Alternative Education for Disruptive Youth is specifically a program designed to work with students that have had issues of behavior misconduct in the schools. It is a temporary exclusionary program designed to provide interventions for students to help them be successful in their regular home school environment.

Q. Would you say it's a punishment to be placed in that program?

A. It should not be a punishment. However, some students have viewed it as such.

Q. Okay.

A. And unfortunately educators sometimes view it as such. But it's not designed at the state level PDE to be punitive.

Q. It's to be what, corrective?

A. Yes. Again, it's a corrective program designed to provide interventions...

Q. all right. Now, tell us, what is the Vista program? And, if it's an acronym, tell us what that it is?

A. I don't know where Vista came from. The Vista program was in place before I got there. Vista is an expulsion program. It is not an AEDY program.

Q. Not AEDY?

A. No, Vista I and Vista II are not AEDY.

Q. But, nevertheless, you had responsibility for those programs?

A. Yes.

Q. Vista I and Vista II?

A. Vista I and Vista II.

Q. Okay. What is it?

Attorney Orloski: Let's do this one at a time, Vista I and then —.

Attorney Freund: Well, we're going to break those down.

A. Vista I is a middle school expulsion program serving students in grades six, seven, and eight. Vista II is a high school program, again, an expulsion program, serving students nine through twelve. And students are placed there when they are expelled from the School District, so that is a disciplinary program. Vista programs are —.

BY ATTORNEY FREUND:

Q. And tell who's eligible for it, what grades and —.

A. May I go back again? In addition to IBEAM, which is the secondary program, we also had ALC, which is the middle school AEDY program...

Q. Okay. Were there any other programs that you oversaw that were in Boys and Girls Clubs buildings on Sixth and green or Seventh Street?

A. Sixth and Green, when I started with the Allentown School District, the ALC programs were being offered in each one — one classroom in each of the four middle schools.

Q. All right. Slow down.

Attorney Orloski: When you say ALC —?

A. The AEDY programs.

Attorney Orloski: And that's —?

A. Alternative Education for Disruptive Youth. So when I started in the district, each of the middle schools had one classroom where they were providing the AEDY alternative programs to students within each of those schools.

Attorney Orloski: Which schools?

A. South Mountain, Trexler, Raub, Harrison-Morton.

By Attorney Freund:

Q. So, there's one class of —

A. AEDY.

Q. — AEDY in each.

A. In each.

Attorney Orloski: Those are non-high school classes?

A. Middle school.

By Attorney Freund:

Q. That would have been the ALC program, right?

A. Yes.

Q. Okay. Now, did that change then?

A. yes. As part of my responsibilities as the director of community and students services, obviously the AEDY programs fell under my supervision.

When I visited those schools to visit those programs, what I found was that the District was operating out of compliance with AEDY in many, many ways.

Q. Okay. We'll get to that, but that's not what I'm interested in right now. What I'm interested to know is what programs were in what facilities?

A. Those — the AEDY — middle school's AEDY's operated one classroom for students six through eight in each of those buildings with one teacher.

Q. All right. Did that change during your tenure there?

A. Yes. Because, again, I —.

Q. I don't care why. Just tell me whether it changed or not.

A. I reconstructed the ALC programs and took those classrooms, and the staff that was assigned to each of those classrooms, and moved them out of those buildings.

And principals certainly were not pleased with that, but because I thought that we showed that they were operating out of compliance, we moved them out and moved the ALC into the Sixth and green building ...

By Attorney Freund:

Q. When you first went to work for Allentown as director of community and students services —

A. yes.

Q. To whom did you report?

A. Susan Lozada, L O Z A D A. Susan Lozada.

Q. All right. And do you know what her title was?

A. Executive director of community and student services.

Q. Now, at some point Ms. Lozada left the employ of the District. Do you remember when that was?

A. She left the District I believe it was in June. And at the end of the — June of 2013, the end of the school year.

Q. Okay. After she left the District who was your direct report?

A. When she left the District, David Wildonger took over the responsibility of supervising me. Susan Lozada was my supervisor up until the end of the 2012-2013 school year.

Attorney Orloski: But he didn't get her job?

A. No. And Susan Lozada did not complete my evaluation for the 2012-2013 school year, although she was my direct supervisor and supervised my FAP during that school year. David Wildonger assumed that responsibility, even though he did not supervise me during 2012-2013. And Susan Lozada, document number 21, clearly stated that she intended to complete my FAP and my evaluation for that school year.

BY ATTORNEY FREUND:

Q. Okay. Now, was Susan Lozada your direct report from the time that you first — I'm sorry, from the time you first began with Allentown up until she left?

A. Yes, she was.

Q. Okay. And during that time she had placed you on this FAP, correct?

A. There were —

Q. Try to focus on my question. Did she place you on an FAP?

A. There were multiple FAPs. And she did place me on a FAP, yes.

Q. How many FAPs did she put you on?

A. There was an FAP that was a result of a suspension for a harassment complaint filed by Ryan Miller. That first FAP is dated — and it's document number 13 dated May 4th of 2012.

Q. Okay. That's FAP number one?

A. Yes.

Q. Okay.

A. Now —

Q. What's FAP number two?

A. FAP number two is number 14.

Attorney Orloski: You're talking about our numbering?

A. The document numbers, I guess, the discovery documents.

ATTORNEY FREUND: Okay. We'll figure that out.

A. I was called into a meeting by Susan and David Wildonger, also attended by Mr. Wheeler and Mr. Cote, on June 12th, 2012, for the purpose of placing me on an FAP.

BY ATTORNEY FREUND:

Q. At the start of the meeting, as we were all in the meeting, Susan and Dave looked at one another, I guess trying to determine whose meeting it was, and who was going to run the meeting. Dave motioned to Susan to start the meeting.

ATTORNEY ORLOKI: David meaning?

A. David Wildonger. Susan said to Dave, or suggested to Dave, it's not my meeting. And at that point David asked Susan to meet with him outside of the office. They were outside of the office for a few minutes. My recollection. And then they both came in, and Susan started to run the meeting regarding the Focused Assistance Plan of June of 2012.

BY ATTORNEY FREUND:

Q.   **That's the second FAP you're on, right?**

A.   Yes. But there's multiple documents for this, so I need to show what — the FAP. The first document states, "This plan is based on the outcome of an investigation into a complaint against you by a staff member."

Q.   **That was a Mr. Miller, correct?**

A.   Yes. That was my understanding. And that's what I was told at the time.

Q.   **All right.**

A.   So during that meeting I asked or I stated I'm appealing that suspension. So —

ATTORNEY ORLOSKI: First FAP?

A.   Yes, the first FAP. So I questioned Mr. Wildonger and those that were in the room. I said to them, if the suspension is overturned on appeal, does the FAP, is it voided? Does it go away? Because, based on what I'm reading there, the FAP was based on the investigation. Mr. Wildonger then said, no, the FAP is not based on the investigation, rather it's based on the next document. And he said that it was based on my performance and evaluation.

I then said to Mr. Wildonger, the FAP does not state that. The FAP clearly states that the FAP is the outcome of an investigation of a complaint against me. Mr. Wildonger then said, the FAP will be changed to show that it is not based on the investigation, rather it's based on my performance expectations.

I then said to Mr. Wildonger, I was rated overall satisfactory for that school year, which would have been the '11-'12 school year. I was rated satisfactory. And I asked him, is it standard to place an administrator on an FAP if they have a progressing in certain area of their evaluation but overall satisfactory?

And Mr. Wildonger said, yes, that is standard. I have since found out that that is not true. Attorney Freund: Okay.

A.   So there were two FAP's. And my recollection is that I didn't sign either one, because again, I didn't understand clearly why I was being placed on the FAP.

First they say it's a complaint of an investigation. And when I asked about the complaint into an investigation, I asked was that the Miller complaint. And they acknowledged that. Yes, it was in fact the Miller complaint. That's why I asked about the appeal…

Q.   **So you now have — while you were in the employ of Allentown School District you had a total of two FAPs or more?**

A.   I believe there was a third. Yes, a third FAP.

Q.   **Okay. What was the third — when was that issued?**

A.   At the end of the '11-'12 school year, the FAP for '11-'12 — I'm sorry, let me go back. This was '12. This here was '12-'13. So I was placed on the second one for the '12-'13 school year.

I was supervised throughout that school year by Susan Lozada. And we did submit the FAP binder, including all of my meetings with Susan Lozada, the FAP meetings and what have you, which showed satisfactory progress.

Susan then stated to me in an email that she intended on completing my FAP and evaluation for that year, however, she had also indicated that she was going to be resigning.

So at that point Dave then took over the responsibility of completing my FAP and my evaluation for the 2012-2013 school year. And Dave then placed me on an FAP for unsatisfactory progress.

Q. So that was a performance-based FAP as well, correct?

A. That was a performance-based FAP issued by David Wildonger, who did not supervise me during the — that particular school year...

SHORT BREAK TAKEN BY ATTORNEY FREUND:

Q. I think when we broke —.

Attorney Orloski: He wants to correct something on the record.

Attorney Freund: Go ahead.

A. I just wanted to amend or clarify my response to the first Focused Assistance Plan that I was placed on due to an investigation of a complaint against me by a staff member.

I just want to state that the Focused Assistance Plan was the result of a suspension based on a harassment complaint made by Ryan Miller against me. I was found to have harassed Ryan Miller. Subsequent to that Ryan Miller filed a second harassment complaint against me. And after that harassment complaint was investigated the District determined that Ryan Miller made false accusations, allegations against me, and that I did not in fact harass him, and that his claim of harassment was false.

And the District found that he falsified and made improper harassment allegations against me. Based on that second investigation or that second charge of harassment made by Ryan Miller, I then asked that the first FAP and three-day suspension that resulted from that, I asked that it be voided as a result of the fact that the District had now found that Ryan Miller was not credible, and had in fact lied during an investigation, and made false allegations and false charges of harassment against me.

And the District refused to rescind that first Focused Assistance Plan, even though they were the ones that investigated and determined that Ryan Miller did in fact make a false claim and lied during the investigation of such harassment charge against me.

Attorney Orloski: He was disciplined too, wasn't he?

A. He was also disciplined as a result of making false allegations against me, and also for lying during the course of that investigation. So, again, therefore, given those facts, that the District had determined or had discredited Ryan Miller, I thought that it would be reasonable that they would void the three-day suspension and also void the Focused Assistance Plan, the first Focused Assistance Plan against me dated May 4. 2012.

And the District refused to void the suspension, and also refused to void the Focused Assistance Plan which was based on the first harassment charge or charge that Ryan Miller made against me...

Q. Okay. Bottom line is you had some performance issues, at least as far as your supervisors were concerned, right?

A. As far as David Wildonger was concerned, yes...

Q. Okay. So there had been and there were during your administration of the AEDY, special education students in AEDY programs?

A. We would literally have special education students show up at our doorstep the day they were instructed by either administrator at the home school, or a representative of special education without my knowledge of what you just went through there...

Q. **Okay. Tell me the authority, if you know it, why an IEP team has decided that the AEDY program is an LRE, why there needs to be any additional due process for that placement of that student?**

A. It would have to comply with the application that the District put into place. So if it's included in the application then it would be acceptable.

Q. **Why do you think that that's true?**

A. Because the application that we submit is our application. That's what we are held to by the state.

Q. **Okay. Now, you also during the time that you were administrator you had — within the same facilities in which you operated your alternative education program you also had ES or emotional support students, correct?**

A. ES students —

Q. **Emotional support programs, ES?**

A. Could you restate that?

Q. **There were ES kids in the same facilities as you ran your programs. Would you agree with that?**

A. Students that were placed in the alternative program through the special ed. department, yes.

Q. **Okay.**

A. May I clarify one thing please?

Q. **Go ahead.**

A. When I reported the district, back in November of 2011, as operating out of compliance, the Office of Alternative Education for Disruptive Youth did a compliance-monitoring visit at the IBEAM site.

I was directed by the superintendent of schools to move students into alternative education, regular ed. and special ed. in violation of AEDY and due process.

Q. **Well —.**

A. The state came in and did a compliance-monitoring visit. At that time we had regular education and special education students at IBEAM. The state determined that the students were being moved into AEDY out of compliance and the District was cited.

We then had to move into a corrective action plan, and we had to then at that point communicate back to home schools that students would not be allowed to be moved into the AEDY unless they were in compliance.

The special education students that were in IBEAM at that point had to be removed, because they were being moved into alternative education by the executive director of special education without following the compliance of AEDY.

So at that point the state, you know, said that in your AEDY program you can only have regular education students, only regular education students in AEDY.

The way that the District got around that was saying they were going to put these special education students into my building, but at that point after the compliance visit they were not supposed to be AEDY…

Q. **All right. Now, in 31 you say that 98 percent of the students are African-American, Hispanic, or other students of color. Do you mean the students in programs under your control or do you mean in the School District?**

A. I mean specifically to alternative education. Approximately 98 percent, yes, in alternative education.

Q. **Okay. Are you making any allegations of racial bias?**

A. On the part of the District against the students or myself?

Q. **On the part of the District against the students?**

A. I think that the non-compliance visit that was conducted by the state clearly shows that the District violated students' civil rights and due process rights, and that the majority of the students were African-American and Latino, and the District knew that and willingly violated their rights and discriminated against the students.

Q. **Okay. Let me ask you this. If the students were placed in your program by virtue of an IEP and a NOREP, what rights of theirs were violated in your opinion?**

A. If the students was place in the program because of an IEP or a NOREP.

Q. **Yes.**

A. Well, according to the compliance visit by the state, there were special education students that were not properly placed there. And that would be in the documentation provided by the state. I believe one student that was a special education student that was placed there, the behavior was in fact a manifestation of his disability. And the District still, knowing that the behavior was a manifestation of his disability, placed that student there. So that's one example…

Q. **Let's look at Paragraph 33 in your complaint. You say there, once defendants, C. Russell Mayo, Ed. D., and David Wildonger, assumed chief administrative positions as superintendent and chief of operations, the attitude changed and quality educations for students was secondary to reducing costs and re-assigning students to programs that were cheaper but inadequate for the needs of special education students.**

A. Yes.

Q. **What costs would be reduced in assigning special education students to your programming, if in fact that's what their IEP called for?**

A. When we first started the IBEAM program, as I had stated earlier, we offered the site services. That was the therapeutic support, the school psychologist, the psychiatrics, and all of those services. That was the first year.

At the end of that first year those services were discontinued. So those students were placed at IBEAM because they were specifically going to receive those site services, when they were initially placed there, they were receiving those services.

When the District then discontinued those site services, those students then should have been placed in an IU program or another program that could meet their specific needs. But when the services were discontinued, they kept the students at the IBEAM program without providing them the appropriate services that got them placed there. So the services were in place when they were referred. The District took the services out but left the kids there...

Q. Okay. Now, let's go back and look at number 34 here. You say that when the Defendant Mayo became superintendent, and while you were principal at William Penn Building, you determined — let's see — that principals from other regular education schools were referring minority students to alternative education who did not otherwise meet the standards of disruptive students.

A. Yes.

Q. Okay. Now, just, again, so we have some basic agreement a disruptive student, that's not a special ed. term, right?

A. No.

Q. That's an alternative education term —

A. Yes.

Q. — right? Now, you agree with me that more than 50 percent of the student population in Allentown is minority?

A. Yes.

Q. Okay. So what is the basis of your statement that they were referring minority kids who didn't receive — who didn't meet the standards as disruptive students?

A. The standards established by AEDY.

Q. Well, what didn't they meet?

A. For the regular education students the Office of AEDY requires that the School Districts not only document student infractions, but also document interventions that were implemented and completed by the school, behavioral interventions, SAP interventions, and that they document that the school made attempts to correct the disruptive behaviors before referring them to the AEDY program.

Q. Okay.

A. Part of that also includes the due process to inform the family and obtain the signature, or at least inform the family that the students are being moved in. The District was submitting referrals that did not meet the standard established by AEDY...

Q. Okay. In Paragraph 37 you say, At some point in November 2011 plaintiff — that's you — was called to a meeting with the Defendant Mayo, who accused you of interfering with, quote, automatic placements from other principals who wanted the students out of their schools and into alternative education programs. Is that a true statement?

A. Yes, it is.

Q. All right. Did you hear Dr. Mayo use a term "automatic placement"?

A. I have my notes from that meeting, and they were provided as documentation for discovery. The meeting actually took place on November 2nd of 2011. In attendance were Dr. Mayo, Susan Lozada, and myself.

Dr. Mayo said that he had heard from principals that I was blocking students from moving into alternative education. I said that I was doing no such thing, that there was a standard to move students into AEDY, and that the principals were submitting incomplete referrals for students into AEDY.

I had communicated with the principals what was needed to comply with AEDY to move students into alternative ed. Dr. Mayo said, quote, We need to fast track students into alternative education, end quote. I informed Dr. Mayo of an AEDY regional meeting with Drew Schuckman that I had attended just a week or so prior to that.

Dr. Mayo replied, quote, We are operating under a state of emergency, end quote, and directed me to, quote, Expedite all alternative education placements, expedite the process, and directed me to move those referrals that I currently was — that I currently had received, to move all of those students into AEDY…

Q. All right. Well, you say that you were accused of blocking these kids. What did you do that constituted blocking their transfer?

A. That was the superintendent's term. He said that the principals have accused me of blocking students from moving into alternative education.

Q. But were you blocking them?

A. No. The expectation was that it was an automatic, status quo, past practice. I'm the principal at School A, I send you the referral, you rubber-stamp it, move the kid in. That was past practice. That was the status quo.

Since I didn't do that, because I was reviewing the referrals and holding them to the standards set by the sate, the principals at the home school were accusing me of blocking that. And that's what the superintendent communicated to me, that he was told by principals at the home school that I was in fact, quote, blocking kids from moving into alternative education.

Q. When a kid is transferred into one of your AEDY programs, they're accompanied with certain documentation, correct?

A. Regular education?

Q. Yeah, regular education.

A. That is the AEDY referral, yes.

Q. Right. And so are you saying that some of these forms were deficient, they weren't filled out right?

A. They were incomplete, yes.

Q. Okay. Well, wasn't it your job to call principals and say fill them out?

A. That's what I did, yes. I would call the principals and explain to them that this referral is incomplete and it requires them to include the interventions, to hold that due process meeting.

The principals, instead of — and I'm not generalizing, but in many cases the principals, instead of doing what they were expected to do to comply with AEDY, they went over my head and complained to the superintendent and accused me of blocking them…

Q. So were they just ignoring you or what?

A. I don't — I can't say what their reasoning for their intentions were other than it had been done that way and they wanted to continue to do it that way.

I know that many of them, to me, and it was common knowledge, would complain that it was too much work. I did hear that from some — and even during that meeting that took place at the elementary school after the compliance visit, there were comments about how intensive it is to do this.

Q. **Let me ask you this. When you had a principal say that it's too much work, did you report that to your superior, that this principal was saying, gee, this is too much work to fill out the form?**

A. They were saying it directly to — in those meetings. Susan Lozada was aware of the pushback, for lack of a better word, from the administrators. Susan Lozada was aware, Dave Wildonger was aware, and Russell Mayo was aware that the home schools were — I don't know what the right word is — concerned or objecting to the completing of these referrals.

Q. **All right. What your testimony is, is that once the compliance report came down the superintendent made everybody aware of the non-compliance and said they had to comply, right?**

A. After the complaint he did say that they had to comply, yes.

Q. **All right.**

A. And then after that, principals continued to send referrals in that were incomplete and I would send them back. And I certainly wasn't making any friends in the District.

And then after the compliance visit special ed was removed from alternative education, so the District was able to continue to backdoor special education students into alternative education and not be held accountable to the compliance report...

Q. **All right. Let's go back to your notes here. From what I can understand it says informed of AEDY, then it says regional meeting, re: Drew Schuckman.**

A. Yes.

Q. **Was he from the Department of Education?**

A. Drew Schuckman was the one that eventually did the compliance-monitoring visit. He was the state coordinator for AEDY.

Q. **Okay. Now, who was informed of the AEDY regional meeting?**

A. When Dr. Mayo said to me fast track these students into alternative ed., I told him, look, I just attended a meeting a week or two prior to this. It was an AEDY regional meeting with Drew Schuckman. And Drew Schuckman talked about proper procedures for moving students into AEDY. And I said the interventions must be completed. That's one of the things — Mayo replied to that by saying we are operating under a state of emergency.

Q. **What was the emergency?**

A. I don't know. That's Mayo's term.

Q. **Did you ask him?**

A. Well, I remember him saying that the teachers were complaining that the schools were unsafe. I think there was some media attention going on at that time at Allen High School. But I do recall him saying something about the teachers' union and the teachers feeling unsafe.

He also sent out a newsletter, which I think I also included as a document in — for discovery, where he did say something about —- used that same language, fast tracking students into alternative education. But that is a document that I submitted as part of discovery.

But I believe he was — I don't know if I want to say I believe, but the impression that Susan and I both got, because Susan and I talked about it afterwards, that he was getting pressure from the teachers' union and the administrators to move disruptive students out of the home schools and into alternative education. That's the impression that I got. But he did mention the teachers' union, did in fact say — those are his words, we are operating under a state of emergency.

And I told him that, you know, we still cannot violate students' rights. We can't move students into alternative education and violate their rights because the teacher's union is upset, or the principal's want these students moved out. We still have to protect the due process and civil rights of the students…

Q. **Now, you said that you contacted the state. How did you contact them?**

A. By phone.

Q. **Who did you speak with?**

A. The first call I made was to Alfredo Gonzalez. And those are in my discovery notes as well. I contacted Alfredo Gonzalez, and I explained to him the fact that I was directed to move these students into alternative education. I believe I made that call on December seventh. Spoke with Alfredo Gonzalez.

Alfredo Gonzalez then said, you know, this is a serious accusation; you're reporting your own program. I said yes, I'm reporting my own program, my superintendent directed me to do this. I believe it's unethical; it's illegal, so I'm reporting it.

And at that point he said, well, you now, I'm going to report this to Drew Schuckman, and I'll have Drew Schuckman call you. Shortly after that Drew Schuckman called me. And, as I testified earlier, I was in a meeting with Drew Schuckman probably a week or two prior to that. I explained to Drew Schuckman what I was directed to do.

And then Drew Schuckman said to me, we are going to schedule a compliance visit. And that's when he sent the email dated December 8th. He sent that to me, cc'd Mr. Gonzalez on that…

Q. **All right. On number 43, Paragraph 43, in your complaint, you say there that you filed a charge of discrimination and race retaliation because of false charges directed at you because you're Hispanic, and it said you were attempting to protect Latino and African-American students from abuse. That charge, if I recall, was ultimately dismissed, was it not?**

A. I believe so.

Q. **Well, let me ask you this. Why do you feel that you were being discriminated against because you were trying to protect Latino and African-American students?**

A. Well, there are several factors here. Number one, the fact that I reported — the superintendent reported the District for violations of AEDY. I believe that the superintendent at some point became aware that I had filed that complaint.

Then also looking at the harassment complaint that was filed against me by Ryan Miller, filed a harassment complaint against me alleging that I harassed him —

Q. **Now, Ryan Miller was your subordinate, correct?**

A. He was a teacher under me, yes.

Q. **Okay, Was he white? Black —**

A. White.

Q. White?

A. He was actually —- what had happen was — and these are documents that you have — he was engaging in inappropriate behaviors with students, instigating, provoking, demeaning kids, and also sending students out of class to the re-focus room for all sorts of issues.

When I would attempt to speak with Mr. Miller about his interactions with students, he would refuse to meet with me without the specific presence of the union president. Not the building rep., but the union president. So he was refusing to meet with me.

He would write discipline referrals. And if I had questions regarding the discipline referrals that he was writing on students, if I had questions for him, again, he would refuse to meet with me. He was confrontational with students. He was confrontational with me...

A. So Ryan Miller was being confrontational with me. I then sent several emails to my supervisor, and to Rita Perez, indicating some concerns that I had with Ryan Miller. The emails are here. It's number five in our documents. Concerns regarding Ryan Miller, student interactions. It's dated February 15th or 2012.

Proceeding with meeting with Ryan Miller concerns at IBEAM Academy, dated February 15th. Ryan Miller, confrontational behavior directed at principal, dated February 16th. In those emails to my supervisor, Susan Lozada, and copied to Dr. Regina Cesario and Rita Perez, I outline concerns and the fact that this teacher refused to meet with me. And in those emails I expressed concerns that the teacher was creating an unsafe work environment and an unhealthy learning environment for students.

And I asked that since he refused to meet with me that the administration look into — Rita Perez look into investigating the concerns that I was bringing forth to them. I was then told by my supervisor, Susan Lozada, and also Robert Wheeler, that since I had put this into writing that the District now would have to investigate the concerns that I was bringing to their attention.

So the last email was dated February 16th. As of March 8th of 2012 there was still no response from downtown, from the administration center. There was no response. And the teacher continued to create an unsafe work environment and unhealthy learning environment for students.

By Attorney Freund:

Q. Well, how does your difficulty with your subordinate, how is that discrimination, retaliation against you for protecting Hispanic and African-American students?

A. When I re-assigned === on March 8th I re-assigned Ryan Miller. And I made it very clear in my opinion Ryan Miller's conduct has created a hostile work environment for staff and unhealthy work environment for students. As such, I have made the administrative decision to change Ryan Miller's schedule in effort to minimize his interactions with students and staff until such time that an appropriate investigation is conducted to address the nature of my concerns.

So when I did that, then at that point Rita Perez and the administration had no choice. They disregarded me for a month. At that point they came in, Ryan Miller then countered and said that I was harassing him.

So at that point Rita indicated that she was going to conduct an investigation. I said, Rita, my concerns are very clear. I'm not suggesting or alleging that Ryan Miller is harassing me, I'm alleging that Ryan Miller is creating an unhealthy — exactly what I wrote there, hostile work environment, unhealthy learning environment. He countered that I was harassing him. Rita then conducts this investigation. At the end of the investigation it's found that Ryan Miller did not harass me.

And I said, Rita, I never alleged that he harassed me. Very clearly right here is what my concerns were. So they said that the investigation concluded, that he never harassed me.

I said how about my concerns here? They never investigated my concerns. They never interviewed students or staff regarding my concerns of work environment and students.

So what happened was I was then suspended for three days for harassment. Subsequently — oh, and Ryan Miller was found not to have harassed me, which I never alleged.

Subsequently, as I've stated before, Ryan Miller files a second harassment charge against me. And now the District determines that he lied. He made a false report, provided false statements, and lied during the investigation.

I then asked the District to void my suspension, void the FAP, because it's obvious now that that is all based on somebody that provided false information.

The District refused to do that. I believe that that was retaliation and discrimination against me, because they refused to void my suspension and the first FAP that were based on fraudulent information or false accusations made by —

Q. **I thought you said before that you corrected our testimony and said the first FAP was not based on your situation with Mr. Miller?**

A. The May 4th FAP, which was in effect for maybe a month, that was based on that. Then in June they wanted to put me on the second FAP, and they said it's based on the investigation of Ryan Miller.

Q. **Okay. Now —.**

A. Then they said, no when I challenged that, they said, we, no, it's based on your performance evaluation.

Q. **Your supervisor during all of this was Susan Lozada, correct?**

A. Susan Lozada was my supervisor, but she was directed, directed to implement the May 4th FAP and the June12th FAP.

Q. **Who told you she was directed?**

A. She told me that.

Q. **All right. And she was a Hispanic woman too, right?**

A. Yes. Now, based on what took place on June 12th, and I testified to this earlier, at the very start of the meeting Susan Lozada and Dave Wildonger looked at each other like, okay, who's in charge here?

And Susan says, Dave, this is your meeting. Dave says, No, it's your meeting. And that's when Dave took her out of the office and had that conversation with her. My understanding that Susan shared with me was Dave directed her to move forwards with that FAP.

When I said to Dave, Hey, look-it, you're placing me on this FAP because of an investigation with Ryan Miller, at that point I said, Well, I'm appealing that. So I said if the suspension and FAP get turned over as a result of that appeal, does this go away.

Dave is the one that said no, not Susan. Dave is the one that said, no, you're being placed on a FAP because of your performance evaluation. Susan did my evaluation and rated me satisfactory. So if you look at that evaluation, I'm rated satisfactory by Susan but I'm placed on a FAP.

Susan did not have any — she was not in agreement. She was directed to do that. Because there's a clear contradiction between being rated satisfactory and being placed on a FAP.

When I asked Dave Wildonger is it standard to place an administrator on a FAP when they have a couple areas of progressing but overall satisfactory, Dave Wildonger said yes, this is standard. Again, since then I have found that's not true.

In my mind he discriminated against me and retaliated against me and put me unjustifiably on a FAP. And Liz was in on a meeting also —.

Attorney Orloski? Liz who?

A: Liz Kelly. I'm sorry Liz Kelly was in on a meeting when we were doing a progress report of the FAP. And during that — prior to moving into that — let me find it here. I read for the record my recollection of where we were. On April 5th of 2013 we had a Focused Assistance Plan ongoing status. And this Focused Assistance Plan again is based on your '11-'12 evaluation, which was satisfactory, and specific performance expectations listed below. Prior to the meeting — and the meeting was 4/5/13 FAP meeting. In attendance were Susan Lozada, David Wildonger, Liz Kelly, and Bob Wheeler.

And these are my — you have this documentation as well. Prior to going into the FAP review I stated for the record, talked about correspondence that are from Attorney Kenupis, who was representing me at the time, to John Freund regarding EECO charges, specific language regarding FAP. And then — and I read exactly from these. I said I want to put this on record. FAP could lead to termination, per the EECO. I was on a FAP, May 4, 2012, the first one.

Outcome of investigation into complaint by staff, Ryan Miller, three-day suspension without pay. I signed that FAP, complied and completed performance expectations, activities, and objectives related to that FAP. June 12, 2012, outcome of investigation into a complaint against you by a staff member, Miller. Three-day suspension without pay. And that was the May 4th FAP.

By Attorney Freund:

Q. Okay. And you've been reading from the notes of — what is that?

A. These are — this is exactly what I said during that meeting that Liz was at.

Q. And those are notes you took during the meeting?

A. Yes. And I stated to Mr. Wildonger that I had appealed the suspension. Since the FAP was based on the investigation of suspension, if the suspension is withdrawn on appeal, would the FAP also be withdrawn?

Mr. Wildonger told me no. He said the FAP was based on my '11-'12 evaluation progressing and performance areas. I told Mr. Wildonger that my overall evaluation was satisfactory.

I asked Mr. Wildonger if it was standard for administrators to be placed on an FAP for being evaluated progressive in specific performance areas but overall satisfactory. He said yes. And, again, Liz was present when — as I read this.

270

I pointed out to Mr. Wildonger that the FAP did not note or make mention of my evaluation. The FAP was specific to the outcome of the investigation into a complaint by Ryan Miller. Mr. Wildonger told me the FAP would be changed to reflect that the FAP was based on my overall evaluation — my overall 2011 evaluation, which was satisfactory.

So, again, the allegations of discrimination and retaliation are tied to that, that it was a false FAP, and that Mr. Wildonger knows that the initial FAP was based on false information provided by a teacher that the District has determined — .

Q. All right. So Mr. Wildonger did not feel that the second FAP should be withdrawn and you did. You wanted it withdrawn, right?

A. I wanted the first and second FAPs withdrawn.

Q. Okay. And he disagreed, and you feel that that constitutes discrimination?

A. Discrimination and retaliation…

Q. Okay. I don't have a question for you. Let's talk about Ms. Kelly here for a second.

A. Excuse me?

Q. Let's talk about Attorney Kelly here for a second. You have on Paragraph 44D, it says that you reported misconduct of the interim director to her. What misconduct did you report?…

A. There were several situations that Ms. Kelly was made aware of from me. One in specific was I filed a harassment complaint on behalf of my staff, students, and parents, regarding inappropriate behavior for Ryan Miller. I submitted that complaint to Ms. Kelly. And, again, I was not alleging that Ryan Miller was harassing me, rather that he was harassing students, staff, and parents.

I followed the District procedure in submitting that referral to Liz Kelly for investigation, and the complaint was never acted upon or closed out, or to my understanding, the best of my recollection, there was never an investigation that took place.

Q. Okay. So that's about Ryan Miller in 44D?

A. Yes. Let me read the question again, if I may, please? There were other situations; again, referring to Ryan Miller, and golly, I've got to get this name. Mr. Cunningham. I forget the first name. Improper conduct and matters that I was investigating where I wanted to issue some type of either verbal or written reprimand or other. Where I would investigate those cases, make recommendations to Ms. Kelly, and I wouldn't receive a response on how to proceed, or whether or not I could issue the discipline that I was recommending, because Ms. Kelly would not respond to me in a timely manner to address those concerns.

Most, if not all, of those documents were introduced or provided in our discovery documents. Most refer to alleged inappropriate conduct on the part of Ryan Miller and I forget Mr. Cunningham's first name.

Q. All right. Let's go back to Exhibit 5 for a minute. After the corrective action plan was submitted — I take it this was submitted to PDE, correct?

A. Yes.

Q. All right. After that the findings that were contained in the PDE report were withdrawn, were they not?

A. They weren't withdrawn. What happened was that the District, after we submitted our corrective action plan, after we submitted our corrective action plan, they did a follow-up visit. And all of that specifically would be in the documents. And when they did the follow-up visit, they said that we were at that point operating under compliance. Not the initial non-compliance, that was never withdrawn, it was just that we corrected what we were doing wrong.

Q. **All right.**

A. And at that point the state said that we were no longer under corrective action and that we were operating within AEDY guidelines.

Q. **Okay. Now I'm going to suggest to you that I believe we have a document that uses the term — let me see if we can find that. Now, if I'm correct, wasn't there another audit in a regular cycle of audits for the '13-'14 school year?**

A. There were other audits, yes. I mean I don't know what specifically you're talking about.

Q. **What I'm getting to is there was a '13-'14 audit in which there were no negative findings. Do you remember that?**

A. I was still — yeah, there were no — I was still there '13-'14? Was I? I was there –

Q. **You didn't leave until '15.**

A. Yeah. So any follow-up visit, I was never told that we were out of compliance during any subsequent visit while I was an administrator there.

Q. **Okay. So basically it's your understanding that the corrective action plan and whatever action was taken there satisfied whatever the department's concerns were in its original plan?**

A. And, as you noted, I was the primary person responsible for implementing the corrective action plan, as you had mentioned before.

Q. **With the same obligations that you had before the non-compliance report was submitted.**

A. That I knew that we were out of compliance and reported that myself.

Attorney Freund: Let's take five minutes for a break.

Short break taken.

Deposition concluded at 3:51 P.M.

IN THE UNITED STATES DISTRICT COURT
FOR THE EASTERN DISTRICT OF PENNSYLVANIA

JOSE ROSADO,   :   CIVIL ACTION
   Plaintiff   :
            :   No. 15-CV-2390
  vs.   :
            :
C. RUSSELL MAYO, Ed.D., :
DAVID WILDONGER, and   :
ALLENTOWN SCHOOL   :
DISTRICT,   :
   Defendants   :

ORIGINAL

DEPOSITION OF C. RUSSELL MAYO - VOLUME I

Taken in the law offices of King, Spry, Herman, Freund and Faul, One West Broad Street, Bethlehem, Pennsylvania, on Wednesday, December 2, 2015, commencing at 10:29 a.m., before James P. Gallagher III, Registered Diplomate Reporter.

* * *

GALLAGHER REPORTING & VIDEO, LLC
Mill Run Office Center
1275 Glenlivet Drive, Suite 100
Allentown, PA 18106
(800) 366-2980 / (610) 439-0504
Gallagherreporting@verizon.net

PROCEEDINGS

C. RUSSELL MAYO, HAVING BEEN DULY SWORN, WAS EXAMINED AND TESTIFIED AS FOLLOWS:

EXAMINATION
BY: MR. ORLOSKI:

Q. Doctor, my name is Rick Orloski. I represent Jose Rosado concerning a lawsuit he has filed against you and others at the Allentown School District. We're here today to get your version of events. The way the system is supposed to work I'm supposed to ask easily understood questions and get honest answers. I don't always succeed. Sometimes my questions confuse people. If the question is confusing don't answer it. You're here with very distinguished counsel—two distinguished counsel. Tell them the question is confusing and on the record we'll clarify it for you so the question will not be confusing.
   Are you with me so far? Say yes or no. Are you with me so far?
A. I am with you, yes...
Q. Please state you full name for the record.
A. C, I use my first initial C, Russell with two Ss and two Ls, Mayo, M A Y O.
Q. And where are you employed today?
A. Allentown School District
Q. In what capacity?
A. Superintendent of schools.
Q. And who do you report to as a superintendent of schools?
A. Well, I report to a nine-member board, governing board.
Q. When were you hired?
A. I was hired as superintendent August 18, 2011...
Q. Now, for deputy superintendent, is there a special certificate for that?
A. Superintendent. It's – to my knowledge, it's you have to qualify to be a superintendent. There may be a separate one for that, but as I recall, I had – I did have a commission as deputy superintendent. So I'm not sure if a commission in Pennsylvania is equivalent to a certification in Virginia, but basically they all have their expectations and standards...
Q. Is there a deputy superintendent in the Allentown School District today?
A. No.
Q. Why not?
A. I reorganized the first year I was selected as superintendent, which was the second year after acting. And in my judgment I thought it was more effective to have a chief academic officer, also known as CAO, a chief operating officer, and a chief financial officer. Three of those positions had existed in the past. One of them was considered a deputy position that I held.
Q. When you came to Allentown you were a deputy superintendent, correct?
A. I came as deputy superintendent in July 1, 2004.
Q. And you had that job until when?

A. Until August the 18th, 2011.

Q. **And August 18th, 2011 you were acting superintendent?**

A. I became acting superintendent August 18th, 2011…

Q. **During your tenure you were a deputy superintendent or a superintendent; you never had a chief operations officer?**

A. The deputy position that I occupied turned into the chief operations officer position basically, but seriously modified and reworked.

Q. **I thought I heard you just say when you came you reorganized and created those three positions? Did I hear you –**

A. I said I reorganized. I don't know – I didn't mean to imply I created the. I did create COO, chief operations officer, because that would have been the slot, although not all the responsibilities, of the deputy. And what I may have forgotten is that we had a superintendent for one year prior to my acting year who changed the names of those positions – not mine, but the other two, to chief academic officer and chief financial officer, I believe. He was the one who changed them.

Q. **But you don't have a deputy superintendent?**

A. I do not have a deputy superintendent.

Q. **And you never had a deputy superintendent?**

A. That is correct.

Q. **Do you know David Wildonger?**

A. Do I know David Wildonger?

Q. **Yes.**

A. Yes.

Q. **And how do you know him?**

A. Well, I've known him since 2004 when I came to the district, and he is currently serving as chief operations officer since July 1, 2012.

Q. **I thought I asked you who the chief operations officer was and you said there was none?**

A. There is a current chief operations officer that I reorganized when I reorganized.

Q. **And who's that?**

A. David Wildonger. Prior to his taking the position in 2012 there was no chief operations officer. It was a deputy, which I served as.

Q. **Did David Wildonger have the necessary certificated to become a deputy superintendent?**

A. He did not.

Q. **Does he have them today?**

A. No, I don't think so…

Q. **Do you know a Susan Lozada?**

A. Yes.

Q. **How do you know her?**

A. I've known Susan since about 1999 when I first came to the valley. She was a student in my classes at Lehigh.

Q. **That was – so you were the professor and she was a student?**

A. Correct.

Q. **Was she working at that time?**

A. She worked in the Parkland School District at the time teaching Spanish. I believe she was a Spanish teacher for the Parkland School District.

Q. **At some point did she join the Allentown School District?**

A. She did. And I'm not sure when, but I believe it may have been a year before I came to Allentown, because I did not know right away when she joined, but discovered she was working for the Allentown School District when I became deputy superintendent.

Q. **Did you interact with her in the course of her employment with Allentown School District?**

A. As time went on more and more, because she was eventually promoted to the position of, I believe, executive director of community and student services. She replaced Ralph Daubert, who retired.

Q. **Is she still there today?**

A. No...

Q. **What were the circumstances surrounding her leaving Allentown School District?**

A. She resigned.

Q. **Voluntarily or involuntarily?**

A. To my knowledge voluntarily, because I was fine with her work. She never received any kind of dissatisfying comments from me, verbal or otherwise.

Q. **Would you have been her immediate supervisor?**

A. Let me think. No.

Q. **Who would have been her supervisor?**

A. David Wildonger, chief operations officer.

Q. **Did he ever complain about her to you?**

A. I don't recall complaints from him about her.

Q. **What's her background?**

A. I believe Hispanic.

Q. **And did she in fact supervise Jose Rosado while she was there?**

A. Yes.

Q. **So she departed, and you think voluntarily, correct?**

A. I don't recall any indication from her otherwise. I know there was publicity surrounding it. I'm not naïve to what was in the media, but that was not consistent with our conversations and my relationship with her, which went back to 1999.

Q. **What was the publicity in the media?**

A. Well, she was tied with Jose Rosado and this theme of racism, and termination of minorities. When Jose began to feel pressure from his job and the dissatisfaction we had for his performance her name was looped into it. I never saw, heard or otherwise believe she was directly involved in it. Her name just kept being brought into it as an example, as I recall, of one of more minority administrator who's been pushed out of the district, or leaving the district, or whatever...

Q. **When you heard – read the publicity that she was forced out did you check with anybody to see if that was accurate?**

A. I didn't have to. You know, I knew her work and I knew the position of her supervisor, which was not dissatisfaction with her work.

Q. **Well could it – her supervisor was Wildonger, right?**

A. Correct.

Q. **Could she have been forced out even though she was a good employee by Wildonger just because she's Hispanic?**

A. No, I don't believe that. I have no indications, one, that she was forced, or two, that it was because she was Hispanic...

Q. **Did you ever interact with her while she was Jose Rosado's supervisor?**

A. Occasionally.

Q. **Did she ever complain to you about his – about the performance of Jose Rosado?**

A. I don't recall direct complaints from her to me. I do recall that there was an evaluation, at least one she did on Jose, in which there were some unsatisfactories. But as far as verbally sitting down with me and complaining to me about Jose, I don't recall any session or meeting.

Q. **Do you know Elizabeth Kelly?**

A. I do.

Q. **How do you know her?**

A. She is one of our attorneys in the solicitor's office.

Q. **Do you have a solicitor's office?**

A. We are sitting in it now.

Q. **We're at a private law firm, correct?**

A. Correct. We haven't hired a solicitor. We retain a law firm on the side.

Q. **Okay. So to the extent you've identified her as a solicitor –**

A. I said she was in the solicitor's office. To me this is the solicitor's office.

Q. **Now, in addition to functioning as an attorney did she ever work directly at the Allentown School District?**

A. She helped us for a number of months, might have been as much as a year in our HR department.

Q. **What was her position in the HR department?**

A. She was basically head of the HR department.

Q. **And –**

A. Human Resources is, of course, what I mean by HR.

Q. **Approximately when was she the head of the HR department?**

A. I'm sorry?

Q. **Approximately when was she the head of the HR department?**

A. I'll have to try to figure it out by my tenure as superintendent. I'm going to say it was probably 2012 to '13.

Q. **Did she have an office at the – at the administrative office or a school?**

A. She used the office of the current executive director of HR.

Q. **Where was that?**

A. In the central office of the school district.

Q. **Was she in fact an employee of the school district?**

A. I don't think so. The reason I say I don't think so, I believe she was basically on loan at a fee from the solicitor's office.

Q. **But she functioned as the head of the HR department, correct?**

A. Together with Wildonger and myself, and she did lead the HR department and give us legal advice on it, as well as guide those who were employed there.

Q. **Was she there as a lawyer or as the head of the HR department?**

A. I'd have to say yes.

Q. **Well, I think the question was, was she there as a lawyer or head?**

A. Yes, she was both.

Q. **She was both. Did she bill for the role as a lawyer?**

A. We were billed for both at the time she was serving…

Q. **So she was on loan, but you were paying for the loan?**

A. We were paying fees to the law firm for her time…

Q. **So while she was head of the HR department, who was Elizabeth Kelly's supervisor?**

A. David Wildonger, if you can consider her to have a supervisor. We pretty well depended on Liz from a legal point of view and an HR point of view to take us where we needed to go for a temporary period of time. It was not intended to be long term, meaning more than a year probably. And David Wildonger would have still had responsibility for HR, but we had a healthy respect for Elizabeth Kelly's credentials as well as her experience, and we had worked with her previously, so –…

Q. **You know Jose Rosado, correct?**

A. I do.

Q. **What's his ethnicity?**

A. I believe he's Hispanic…

Q. **Do you know what certifications he had?**

A. No, I don't know. I know he was endorsed as a principal – I mean as an administrator, or he wouldn't have been able to have the job…

Q. **When was he hired?**

A. I'm not sure. It was before I was superintendent. He was hired by Karen Angelo who was prior to Jerry Zahorchak who was superintendent for a year. So he had to be hired somewhere around – gosh, probably somewhere around 2008…

Q. **What was he hired – what was the position he was hired for?**

A. Director of – I don't remember the rest of the title, whether it was community and student services, because we had an executive director, or if we called him director of alternative education. I believe the latter, but can't be sure.

Q. **Okay. Director of alternative education, what is alternative education in the School District of Allentown at the time he was hired to be the director?**

A. It was separately housed programs. I don't remember the names of all of them, but they were, as I recall, located in partial buildings, leased, so we could have programs for our kids who needed restoring to the regular educational program, as well as expulsions, who could not be restored immediately, had to be out for a period of time, which is the – alternative jargon in education for programs for disruptive youth…

Q. **So basically it's the kids with problems?**

A.   Yes…

Q.   **Now, the alternative ed is not for students with disabilities, learning disabilities, correct?**

A.   That depends on the IEP committee and decisions made under the IDEA.

Q.   **So are you saying that students with academic – learning disabilities could be placed in the alternative education program even thought they weren't disruptive?**

MR. FREUND: Objection. You can answer.

A   I don't think we would even try to place students in alternative education unless they were disruptive in some way, and in the case of special needs students, unless it had gone to their committee, the IEP committee.

Q.   **So a special needs student first had to be disruptive before they would be placed in the alternative education program?**

A.   The alternative education program is for disruptive students. It's not for special needs students unless they have been disruptive, and their IEP committee placement is determined to be best done there…

Q.   **Do principals have the right to or the option of referring students to the alternative education program?**

A.   They can refer them to the alternative education program. And then there's due process procedure to follow, which is what the person in charge of alternative ed oversees.

Q.   **So who gets – are there any type of regulations, administrative regulations from the Department of Education about transferring students into the alternative education program?**

A.   There is due process, standard due process, which is a part of the regulations. There is – you're talking about from the time of the disruption to the recommendation to the placement?

Q.   **I'm trying to – can a teacher or principal just say, I want this student placed in the alternative education program, and then it happens automatically?**

A.   No.

Q.   **It can't happen that way, right?**

A.   No.

Q.   **Why not?**

A.   Well, there has to be documentation, there has to be evidence. A principal alone does not have the authority to make that happen without consideration from the alternative ed administrator, other staff that advises on that. They have to make a case for it basically.

Q.   **And the case involving – involves documentation, correct?**

A.   It involves documentation of the disruptive behavior, yes.

Q.   **So, and that's done by the principal that's making the referral, correct?**

A.   Or the staff, or designee, yes.

Q.   **So if a referral is made by a principal who doesn't include evidence of the disruptive behavior, or evidence of any documentation, the director of alternative education program should not accept that student into the program correct?**

MR. FREUND: Objection. You can answer.

A.   I think the director – the person responsible for alternative ed needs to open lines of communication pretty quickly and say, what is supposed to happen here, why are you recommending this person, can you show me the documentation, et cetera. Communication is very important in that case. I don't believe you'll find any principal just recommending arbitrarily a student to alternative ed without showing some kind of episode or disruptive behavior.

Q.   **Well, the disruptive behavior is not enough, correct?**
MR. FREUND: Objection. You can answer.

A.   I mean, disruptive behavior as defined – from what I understand in the code, yes, it is required.

Q.   **Is required, but that in and of itself is not enough?**

A.   Yes, it is…

Q.   **You as the superintendent understand that students could not – should not be placed into the program just because principals wanted them placed in alternative education, right?**

A.   I understand that, and I think the principals understand that too. They had to have a reason. I mean, a reasonable situation to do that. They couldn't just arbitrarily do it.

Q.   **And it wasn't just a specific reason, it had to be a reason defined in the regulations, correct?**

A.   They had to be reasons defined by law and the recommendations in here, yes. That was the intent.

Q.   **And now, do you remember a meeting with Jose on November 2011 complaining about accusing him of interfering with placements requested by the principals?**

A.   I remember a meeting I had with Jose. I don't remember that that was the specific topic alone.

Q.   **Was that ever discussed with him?**

A.   What part?

Q.   **Did you ever discuss with him that principals are complaining that he was not honoring their request to place students in alternative education program?**

A.   If I discussed with him it would have been that the procedure was not clear, and that there was a feeling that he remained distant and aloof from his responsibilities and not communicating with the principals and making it clear what the expectations were.

Q.   **Shouldn't the principals know what the standards were?**

A.   Yes.

Q.   **And did they know?**

A.   I'm assuming that it was confusing because of the way it was being handled by Jose. And Jose would be the expert in that area, and the one responsible for coordinating and making sure it was clear to them.

Q.   **What was he doing wrong?**

A.   What was he doing wrong?

Q.   **Correct.**

A.   How about what was he not doing, how about if I answer that?

Q.   **He was not doing anything wrong then?**

A. He was not communicating. He was not making it clear across the board to all principals what the expectations were, what the purpose of alternative education was. And he was not offering assistance in trying to help them understand as well as coach them through the process.

Q. **I thought you said earlier that they as principals should have known what the regulations were?**

A. I did say they should have known, but there was no one telling them.

Q. **So they didn't know?**

A. Apparently not, because he was not telling them.

Q. **But this was not something Jose unilaterally determined what the standards were, correct?**

MR. FREUND: Objection to form.

Q. **Let me try it this way. The standards were not Jose's, the standards were the standards established by the Pennsylvania Department of Education, correct?**

A. Jose was supposed to know whatever the standards were. He was the person we hired as a staff person to be responsible for keeping up with any changes as well as what the current expectations were, and to make sure principals understood what those were.

Q. **But the principals were confused?**

A. I think the principals were confused by Jose, because I think he was inconsistent and limited in his communication with the.

Q. **So it was just a communication problem. He didn't do anything wrong, did he?**

A. No, I think it's an accountability problem if you want to get to the heart of the matter, a responsibility problem.

Q. **Did you order him to transfer all the students into the education program?**

A. All of what students?

Q. **At that meeting you had with him in November of 2011, did you say you wanted all the students who the principals had recommended for placement in the alternative education program to be transferred into the program?**

A. I can't believe I would have said that, no. I don't recall all the specifics of the meeting, but I can tell you I would not have said something like that.

Q. **Why would you not have said something like that?**

A. Because they have to be considered on a case-by-case basis.

Q. **And it would be illegal, correct?**

A. It would be unethical. It may also be illegal, but it depends on what part of the law and what you're talking about illegal. Everything in this book is not based on law, in this manual I'm referring to. Some of it is based on what we encourage principals to do with the procedures...

Q. **Well, doesn't – the regulations say the districts may refer students to alternative education only if at the time of the recommendation they demonstrate a marked degree of one of the following conditions: Disregard for school authority, employ or use of controlled substances, violent or certain behavior, possession of a weapon, commission of a criminal act, misconduct that would merit suspension or expulsion, and habitual truancy?**

A. And that is quoted almost from the code, I believe, yes, that's the law.

Q. **That's the law?**

A. That's why they are admitted.

Q. **And the district was supposed to be following it, correct?**

A. That's right.

Q. **And the responsibility of documenting that rests with the principals?**

A. Yes.

Q. **And if the principals weren't documenting it, you're saying that's Jose's problem?**

A. I'm saying the principals were documenting it.

Q. **Did you ever examine any of these applications to see if that's accurate, or you accepted somebody's word that it was accurate?**

A. I'm accepting the principal's word when they were asked by me and staff telling me what was happening.

Q. **So you have not seen any documents which indicated that the principals were preparing the correct documentation?**

A. I haven't seen – I didn't look at every document, no.

Q. **Did you ever see any document where the prepared documentation was presented and given to Jose and he refused to transfer a student?**

A. I would not have seen such a document anyway ordinarily.

Q. **Well, if there was a problem did you check to see if there was such an instance?**

A. Well, I had the word of our principals that I had spoken with, and their concern, and the collective concern of several of the staff...

Q. **After the meeting did Jose transfer the students?**

A. I don't know.

Q. **Did there come a time when the Pennsylvania Department of Education came in to the school district to determine whether or not those transfers were proper?**

    MR. FREUND: Objection to form. You can answer.

A. I don't know exactly why the Department came in, but they did come in I know now, but not at the time, until after the audit.

Q. **And they came in to audit whether the transfers were proper, correct?**

A. I'm sorry?

Q. **They came in to determine whether the transfers were proper?**

A. I don't know why they came in.

Q. **Well, did they in fact audit to see if the transfers were proper?**

A. Yes, they did, but I don't know if they were the transfers that I had talked about or that Jose claims that I had demanded or said he should transfer all of them.

Q. **Did they find any students were transferred who should not have been transferred?**

A. I haven't read the report recently, so I think they did probably. But were they those kids, I don't know...

Q. **Okay. Who's supposed to make the determination as to whether or not the student should be transferred, the principal or Jose?**

A. Well, it didn't rest with one individual. It was supposed to be a joint decision...

Q. **Do you think that students had certain due process rights?**

MR. FREUND: Objection.

Q. **Concerning the decision to transfer?**

    MR. FREUND: Objection. Which students?

    MR. ORLOSKI: Any student that's being transferred.

    MR. FREUND: Okay. You can answer.

A. Students always have due process rights. It's fundamental.

Q. **And do you know if the principals were following them?**

A. I know the principals would have been following the due process rights, yes. I know they would have.

Q. **They should have followed, right?**

A. I know they would have...

Q. **Before a student can be transferred to the alternative placement education process there's supposed to be a due process –**

A. Hearing.

Q. **– Hearing involving the parents where the parents are told about the problem, and there's a check-off sheet that such a hearing happened, correct?**

A. I don't know. That probably is in the manual, but I can tell you sometimes if you could not get the parent to come in, you can do it by phone.

Q. **And it's not Jose's responsibility to prepare that, it's the principal's responsibility to prepare that, correct?**

    MR. FREUND: Objection. You can answer.

A. I think that depends on the communication and what they worked out. Sometimes it might be better if the alternative administrator, school administrator does it. But generally the initiation of that process is the principal's responsibility.

Q. **And if the principal doesn't do it then the student should not be transferred, correct?**

    MR. FREUND: Objection. You can answer.

A. If the principal doesn't do what?

Q. **Doesn't go through the due process rights of the student –**

A. Right.

Q. **– Jose cannot accept that student into the transfer, right**

    MR. FREUND: Objection. You can answer.

A. Students have the right to due process. I expect every principal to do due process.

Q. **And if due process doesn't happen in this transfer process, then Jose should not accept them into the program?**

    MR. FREUND: Objection. Are you talking about regular kids or special ed kids?

Q. **I'm talking about regular.**

A. Jose should then inform them that we have not met the due process requirements, if you want me to help you, assist you, support you, I need you to make sure you've done this.

Q. **So you're giving him the responsibility to do the principal's job, right?**

A. No. I'm giving him the responsibility of being gatekeeper.

Q. **And the gatekeeper is supposed to protect the students, correct?**

A.   The gatekeeper is supposed to make sure that due process is properly executed…

Q.   **I show you what's been identified as Mayo Number 1. Can you tell me what that is, please?**

A.   It is a Focused Assistance Plan dated August 16, 2013, addressed to Jose Rosado, Senior, Director of Alternative Education, from David M. Wildonger, Chief Operations Officer.

Q.   **Is this the first one or the second one, or you don't know?**

A.   I believe this would be the second one, Second Focused Assistance Plan.

Q.   **Okay. Look at Mayo Number 2, please.**

A.   Okay.

Q.   **What is that?**

A.   That is a Focused Assistance Plan dated May 4, 2012, to Jose Rosado, Senior, from Susan Lozada, Executive Director of Community and Student Services.

Q.   **Is that the first one?**

A.   This would be the first one I would assume, judging from the date.

Q.   **Now, on its face it says it's from Susan Lozada. Do you see that?**

A.   Yes.

Q.   **Did you tell Susan Lozada to prepare this Focused Assistance Plan over her objection?**
     MR. FREUND: What was the question, did you tell her over her objection?

Q.   **Did you direct Susan Lozada to prepare this focused assistance program?**

A.   I don't believe I would have directed her to do that. I believe that either her supervisor would have, or she would have decided to do it herself, of course, with the collaboration of her supervisor.

Q.   **Her supervisor would be?**

A.   David Wildonger, Chief Operations Officer.

Q.   **So you don't know if this was his idea or her idea?**

A.   Well, I know I'm aware when any supervisor is concerned about performance. It could have been the collective idea of all three of us, but executed through David Wildonger, and by Susan Lozada.

Q.   **Anywhere in this Focused Assistance Plan do you specifically suggest that there was a problem with communication with principals about alternative placement, alternative education placements?**
     MR. FREUND: Objection. Did he suggest, or does the plan suggest?
     MR. ORLOSKI: Let me rephrase it. I'm not sure I got your objection.

Q.   **Is there anywhere in this Focused Assistance Plan where there's anything discussing lack of communication with principals about the alternative education placement program?**

A.   If you look under performance expectations on the May 4, 2012 document –

Q.   **Page 1?**

A.   That's page 1 on the front. Under performance expectations, letter A. You manage difficult or emotional situations judicially.

Q.   **I think it says judiciously?**

A.   I'm sorry, judiciously. I stand corrected. Yes, that implies that in his communication with principals and others he can become very emotional very quickly.

Q. **Well, read the first sentence, read the first paragraph of this Focused Assistance Plan.**

A. Out loud?

Q. **Yeah, read it out loud.**

A. "This document serves as a Focused Assistance Plan. This plan covers the period from April 20, 2012 through June 29, 2012. This plan is based on the outcome of the investigation into a complaint against you by a staff member. My hope is that this plan will improve your understanding and increase your chances for success as an administrator and principal. The directives in this plan must be followed until and unless directed differently by me as your supervisor."

Q. **Now, so on its face this document says there's one staff member who complained about him, correct?**

A. On its face, yes.

Q. **Who's that staff member?**

A. I do not know.

Q. **Do you recognize the name, Ryan Miller?**

A. I do recognize that name.

Q. **Who is Ryan Miller?**

A. As I recall, Ryan Miller was a teacher at the alternative education school.

Q. **Is he the person who complained about Jose Rosado that's discussed in this Focused Assistance Plan?**

A. I do not know. But you could eliminate that possibility by simply looking at the date of when his complaint was filed. He did file a complaint against Jose Rosado, but I'm not sure whether it was pre-May 4, 2012, or post.

Q. **So on its face you don't know what this specific person who complained about Jose Rosado, you don't know who the person was?**

A. I do not know who the person was, and I would tell you one person would not trigger a Focused Assistance Plan. It would be the final straw…

Q. **Okay. You just said there's a standard – there's a standard that one complaint by one person would not generate a Focused Assistance Plan, correct?**

A. It would not ordinarily. It might be the final straw that breaks the camel's back. And it might be the thing that's mentioned in a Focused Assistance Plan prompting it. But typically one isolated incident, isolated I emphasize, not ongoing, or other kinds of complaints would not trigger a Focused Assistance Plan…

Q. **You do remember a complaint by Ryan Miller, correct?**

A. Yes.

Q. **Do you remember what his complaint was?**

A. Harassment.

Q. **Now, let's look at Mayo 1, which is a second Focused Assistance Plan. What generated this Focused Assistance Plan?**

A. It's based – according to the first paragraph; this plan is based on your 2012-13 evaluation highlighting the specific performance expectations listed below.

Q. **Okay. Now, who did the evaluation that's referred to in this instance, do you know?**

A. It says your evaluation, so I'm assuming since it's addressed to Jose it's his evaluation.

Q. Who do it?

A. Oh, I believe Susan Lozada did it.

Q. Well, she should have done it, right, because she was the supervisor?

A. She actually did it along with Dave Wildonger together I think.

Q. Who signed it?

A. I don't know.

Q. So if the document shows that David Wildonger alone signed it, what makes you think Susan Lozada agreed with it?

A. Because I was monitoring this situation as it was developing.

Q. You were monitoring who was doing his evaluations?

A. Yes.

Q. Who was his supervisor?

A. His immediate supervisor was Susan Lozada.

Q. Why was she usurped and David Wildonger given the authority to evaluate him when he was not Jose's immediate supervisor?

A. That didn't happen. As I mentioned earlier, he was a part of the evaluation. He evaluated the positions he was familiar with. She evaluated the portions she was familiar with.

Q. Did she sign off?

A. I don't know.

Q. And if she evaluated, she should have signed off, right?

A. I'm sorry?

Q. If she was his supervisor and she evaluated him she should have signed it, correct?

A. Not necessarily. The ultimate supervisor was Dave Wildonger, but I would have wanted both to sign it, yes. And I know they both had input because I'm very familiar with this evaluation, which led to this. I had forgotten about this earlier Focused Assistance Plan...

Q. Now, in the instance of Jose Rosado, a Hispanic administrator, he had somebody who was not his immediate supervisor, David Wildonger, participate in the evaluation and sign off, correct?

    MR. FREUND: Objection. You can answer.

A. He was his supervisor.

Q. Not immediate supervisor?

A. Not the immediate supervisor, correct...

Q. How many principals have had Focused Assistance Plans prior to Jose Rosado's Focused Assistance Plan?

A. Gosh. Are you talking about in my tenure as superintendent?

Q. Yeah, in your tenure?

A. Or in the years I've worked in the district?

Q. Your tenure.

A. As I said, they're rare. I can't think of any immediately. I can think of a principal or two who have quit who were moving in that direction.

Q. But they didn't have the Focused Assistance Plan?

A. No...

Q. Now, at some point did Ryan Miller make a complaint against Jose Rosado, which the school district determined was bogus?

MR. FREUND: Objection. You can answer.

A. No. At least based on my recollection the answer is no to that.

Q. Was Ryan Miller ever disciplined for making false claims against Jose Rosado?

A. I'll tell you what I remember, that he was not because the complaint was founded as I recall. You said Ryan Miller complaining against Jose Rosado, right?

Q. Right, resulting in Ryan Miller being disciplined for filing a false charge against Jose Rosado?

A. If we're talking about the same complaint, which was a harassment complaint that was founded. Investigated by Rita Perez. If you and I are talking about the same situation. That was founded, and he actually received consequences as a result.

Q. Who received consequences?

A. Jose Rosado.

Q. And the consequences were what?

A. I believe he had suspension without pay.

Q. And at some point there was a second complaint by Ryan Miller against Jose Rosado, correct?

A. If there were, I don't remember the details of it. And as I recall, it may have come on the heels of one by Jose against Ryan Miller, which followed Ryan Miller's first one against Jose.

Q. And do you remember in the second complaint Ryan Miller was disciplined for filing false charges against Jose, do you remember that?

A. I don't remember that, because I don't remember well the second complaint, if there was one, of Ryan Miller. I do remember that Jose Rosado turned around and filed a complaint against Ryan.

Q. Do you remember the union filing a grievance, going to a grievance arbitration hearing about the discipline of Ryan Miller because the school district determined he filed false charges against Jose Rosado?

A. I don't remember it clearly, but I think that was possible. If there were a second complaint by him, I think it's entirely possible that was the outcome, because it became pretty clear there was a kind of tit for tat going on there possibly.

Q. And do you remember Jose asking you and the school district to remove the first Focused Assistance Plan because it was based on Ryan Miller, and Ryan Miller was found to be lying about Jose Rosado?

A. I do not know about that. I don't remember it, and was not aware of it that I can recall.

Q. If there was a determination that Ryan Miller was filing false charges against Jose Rosado, would that have been a legitimate basis for removing the first Focused Assistance Plan?

A. No. They're two separate incidences, two separate cases, and they rise and fall on the merits of one and the other separately.

Q. You don't remember what Ryan Miller's first charge was, just harassment?

A. It was harassment, yes. Under our board policy harassment is investigated, et cetera, and we have a procedure...

> **MR. ORLOSKI: This has been marked 44, but we're going to mark this as Mayo 3.**
>
> **(Mayo Exhibit 3, E-mails and Documents Regarding IBEAM, marked for identification.)**

Q. **Do you recognize that sequences of documents?**

A. Yes. I don't recognize the e-mails. I didn't see the e-mails prior to now, but –

Q. **What do you recognize, the audit report?**

A. Yes.

Q. **And what does that audit report say?**

A. The audit report is of the AEDY program, which is one component of alternative ed. There are a list of deficiencies...

Q. **What were the deficiencies?**

A. District placed students in this program do not qualify for AEDY placement...

Q. **So to the extent that Jose says those are the students you told him to transfer –**

A. No, I'm saying –

Q. **To the extent that Jose says that, you cannot contradict him because you don't know what students were –**

> MR. FREUND: Objection.

A. Well, first of all –

> MR. FREUND: Objection. You can answer.

A. You seem to be assuming that I know the students he claimed that I demanded he transfer or told him to transfer in. I'm not aware of any students that I told him to transfer. And I don't know what students these refer to...

Q. **Okay. I show you what's been identified as Mayo Number 4. Do you recognize that?**

A. It's a memorandum from Rita Perez dated April 2nd, 2012. And it appears to be her findings from her investigation of the complaint of harassment against Jose Rosado by Ryan Miller.

Q. **You got to read better than that.**

A. I wasn't reading it. I was just saying what I thought I remember it to be.

Q. **Well, it's the complaint – it's her investigation relative to Jose's complaint against Ryan Miller, and Ryan Miller's complaint against him.**

A. Can I read the first paragraph out loud?

Q. **If you want.**

A. "On March 9, 2012, I informed you of a harassment complaint filed by Jose Rosado, Principal of Record at the IBEAM Academy against IBEAM Academy teacher Ryan Miller. On March 13, 2012, I received a harassment complaint filed by IBEAM Academy teacher Ryan Miller against Jose Rosado."

Q. **So she was investigating both, correct?**

A. I received harassment – it appears, yes, yes. That's my understanding now.

Q. **And she makes a recommendation, correct?**

A. Yes.

Q. Read it out loud.

A. Yes. Both parties – the recommendation is, "both parties need to learn strategies for dealing with conflict, differences of opinion, and anger.

Ryan must understand that he is being insubordinate for his continual refusal to comply with the IBEAM philosophy. If he intends to remain an alternative education and/or Allentown School District teacher he must implement district curriculum in the Code of Conduct and use professional and appropriate mechanisms for addressing concerns and facilitating change.

Jose must provide focused and structured leadership for all alternative education programs. This includes regular staff meetings that focus on learning the IBEAM philosophy with opportunities to problem solve, plan and learn new strategies. Regular classroom supervision must include formal classroom observations, administrative walkthroughs and learning walks for teachers to see the implementation of the IBEAM philosophy.

Finally, a quantitative approach with VisionQuest " – which was a third party outsourcing group that ran the program –"and IU21 Sites Program must be initiated. While IBEAM is an ASD program our partners contribute to our success. The IBEAM philosophy has much potential and must be attended to in order to achieve success."

Q. So she determined that Ryan Miller was insubordinate, correct?

MR. FREUND: Objection. You can answer.

Q. Isn't that what you just read?

A. I saw a recommendation. I didn't see a conclusion. He has – Ryan has to understand– yes, he is being insubordinate, yes, you're correct.

Q. And Ryan Miller is a white male teacher, correct?

A. As I recall, yes.

Q. And Jose is his boss, right?

A. Yes.

Q. What punishment if any was give to Ryan Miller for being insubordinate?

A. I don't remember.

Q. So if there was none there would be none to remember, right?

A. Well, if there were none there would be none to remember, but if there was some and you didn't remember doesn't mean –

Q. Okay. You're not saying you know there was punishment directed against Ryan Miller, if there was you don't remember what it was?

A. I'm saying I don't remember whether or not there was punishment, or consequences as we call it.

Q. Insubordination is a reasonably serious charge, right?

A. Yes.

Q. And there was no conclusion by the investigator that Jose Rosado was insubordinate, correct?

A. I'm not sure this is the complete document or only document on the investigation. I'm not sure. Jose must – reading from that next to last paragraph, "Jose must provide focused and structured leadership for all alternative programs." And then she went through some of his responsibilities, which at the time he was not fulfilling.

Q. She didn't say that?

A. That's why it's on there.

Q. You interpret that that she's saying –

A. I'm not interpreting it, I know.

Q. She says that in that document?

A. The document is addressed to me. When there's a Focused Assistance Plan and investigation like this I'm involved. That is, in a loop, keeping up with it.

Q. Well, the Focused Assistance Plan didn't come out yet, right?

A. I don't know. The date on this is April 2nd, 2012.

Q. Where in that recommendation, or where in that document, which we've identified as Mayo 4, does the – is there a recommendation that he should be suspended, that Jose Rosado should be suspended?

A. I don't see that under the recommendations in this document.

Q. So to read that document, and accept it as her conclusions, there's no recommendation that he should be suspended, correct?

A. Not in this document, no.

Q. Do you think there is a document where she recommends suspension? I'll tell you we haven't seen it.

A. If you can give me a minute to read this first paragraph again and check these dates.

Based on what I'm remembering, this – this happened in reverse. I was thinking that Ryan Miller filed the first complaint. But it looks like based on this, March 9, Jose Rosado filed the first complaint against Ryan Miller. And then four days later Ryan Miller filed against Jose. I did not remember it that way. So if we're talking about the same situation, I was wrong about the sequence of events.

Q. But Jose Rosado was suspended for three days because of Ryan Miller's complaint, correct?

A. I'm not trusting my memory now after seeing this. But I thought he was suspended for some complaint. The one I remember most was Ryan Miller, so I'm tying the consequences to the Ryan Miller complaint. But it may have been a different complaint. I just don't remember now after seeing this and realizing I've reversed the complaints.

Q. Who made the decision to suspend him?

A. The initial decision to suspend occurs with a conversation with me and a recommendation to me, usually based on consultation with our attorneys, me, and whoever is making the recommendation.

Q. You have no piece of paper where anyone recommended the suspension, do you?

A. I can't say that I don't, no. I have not been through all of my records. I didn't know that was a question.

Q. So the papers available to use suggest that you and you alone initiated the idea of suspension, the three-day suspension?

A. The papers that you have suggest that?

Q. Right.

A. You might want to show me where, because I'm not clear.

Q. Well, let's look at –

A. I haven't told you that, and I haven't read it anywhere. So I'm not clear on what that means.

Q. **In the written recommendation there's no mention of suspension, correct?**

A. Under this memorandum that you've shown me, Mayo Number 4, I see no recommendation for consequences, period. I only see recommendations for changing behavior.

Q. **And that's what she – the investigator thought was appropriate, correct?**

A. I assume so.

Q. **And somehow it ended up in no consequences that you're aware of to Ryan Miller who was guilty of insubordination, but a three- day suspension to your administrator who happened to be Hispanic?**

A. I can't – I can't agree that that – with what you're saying, because now I don't remember whether his suspension was connected to this particular complaint.

Q. **Did you ever use terminology of fast tracking students into the alternative education program?**

A. I don't remember using that term…

   MR. ORLOSKI: Mark this as the next exhibit.

   (Mayo Exhibit 5, Newspaper Article, marked for identification)

   MR. FREUND: Off the record.

   (Discussion off the record.)

BY MR. ORLOSKI:

Q. **Mayo, 5 do you recognize that document?**

A. No, I don't. That's why I was asking the source of it. It looks like it's probably picked up from the media, an article that ran recently maybe.

Q. **It looks like you're the author of that article.**

A. No, no.

Q. **You did not author that article?**

A. Well, I don't know. Let me check.

Q. **You're quoted – you seem to be quoted extensively in there.**

A. No, I did not write this.

Q. **Okay. There's a quote there by you about fast tracking. Is that you?**

A. I don't remember saying that. If I knew who the author was, or the reporter, or whatever, I might recall a conversation with them, because this is in quote marks, which to me implied I actually said it. But fast tracking though means expediting the due process. It doesn't mean just pulling kids out of school and putting them in alternative ed program, if that's where we are going with this.

   MR. FREUND: Do you have a copy of that?

   MR. ORLOSKI: That's yours.

   MR. FREUND: It came from you.

   MR. ORLOSKI: I know. Show him the blue cover.

A. It looks strange – it looks strange because it's – it looks almost cut and pasted. It looks like – on the one hand it is by what appears at the bottom of the page, it looks like it comes from Allentown website. But I'm assuming it's an article that was picked up. I did not write this, no. I can tell you I did not write this.

    MR. ORLOSKI: Let's do Mayo 6.

    (Mayo Exhibit 6, Handwritten Notes, marked for identification.)

Q. **I'll represent to you that that was presented to Mr. Rosado at his deposition, and those are his handwritten notes.**

A. I will tell you that they were not written while in the meeting with me.

Q. **You see – can you read it?**

A. At the top it says, meeting, W slash, with Dr. Mayo and – it looks like Susan, probably Susan Lozada, on 11/2/11, November 2nd, 2011, asterisk, Mayo, quote, fast track students into alt ed.

Q. **And a quote, right?**

A. Right.

Q. **And a star by that?**

A. Correct.

Q. **Now, on its face he's attributing those words to you?**

A. On its face to me, he would be, yes...

Q. **Read the rest of it.**

A. "I informed of AEDY regional meeting regarding Drew Schuckman interventions. Mayo replied, we are operating under a state of emergency, " it looks like.

Q. **And did you say that to him?**

A. I don't know. I don't remember.

Q. **Do you recognize the name Shuckman?**

A. I don't – I do now after having seen the audit that was done.

Q. **And do you remember what – what he was referring to when he used that name?**

A. I don't remember his using that name or telling me that?

Q. **So if he says, I told Mayo he just had a meeting with Schuckman and we have to follow these standards, and you're saying we are operating under a state of emergency, did you say that, we're operating under a state of emergency?**

A. I don't remember that.

Q. **Does it make any sense to say that?**

A. I don't – I don't know. I would have to remember what times were. I just don't remember it...

Q. **At some point was the idea for terminating his employment discussed?**

    MR. FREUND: Objection. You can answer.

A. Yes.

Q. **Who initiated those discussions?**

A. Do you mean who said the word first?

Q. **Yeah, whose idea? Was it your idea, was it –**

A. It was an evolution. When you have a Focused Assistance Plan ultimately concluding termination is appropriate, it becomes obvious to those involved with supervising and monitoring that Focused Assistance Plan.

Q. There's nothing in the Focused Assistance Plan saying you're going to terminate him, is there?

A. No – well, yeah, if you don't meet the Focused Assistance Plan. I mean, that it could lead to termination.

Q. Who first came up with the idea Jose Rosado's employment should be terminated?

A. I could not tell you that because it's an evolutionary process. It's a process of reviewing the Focused Assistance Plan, that they go over it with him, they report to me, here's where we stand. I ask for a recommendation. Who said it first, I couldn't tell you. I couldn't tell you who said it, whether it was HR, or whether it was Wildonger, or – I couldn't tell you. I mean, it becomes pretty obvious to an experienced administrator if someone is not performing, they're not meeting their Focused Assistance Plan, they've been given support, it doesn't take a rocket scientist to say this person is either unwilling or unable to change.

Q. Okay. At some point you made the decision?

A. I made the decision that I would recommend to the board that, yes. That is my responsibility. As far as who initiated it or came up with the idea, as you say –

Q. And at some point it was communicated to him, correct?

A. Yes.

Q. How was it communicated?

A. It was done, as I recall, by David Wildonger.

Q. Orally?

A. Well, initially it would have been.

Q. Was he given a Loudermill hearing?

A. He was at least offered one if not given one. He had the opportunity to waive it.

Q. Do you know if he was given one?

A. I think he was. But, again, I'm not trusting my memory after looking at the order, the sequence of those complaints with Ryan Miller.

Q. He certainly was entitled to one, correct?

A. He's entitled to a Loudermill, yes.

Q. And prior to the Loudermill hearing you're supposed to have a – a written list of charges, correct?

A. Yes.

    MR. FREUND: Objection.

Q. Do you know if that happened?

A. If there was a Loudermill there was a letter of charges…

Q. Your understanding is, you filed a written list of charges, then you had the Loudermill hearing, correct?

    MR. FREUND: Objection.

A. You file it – you mean like notify the person?

Q. Yeah, if you have the hearing he has to know what he's charged with?

A. It's all part of the same letter typically.

Q. Did that happen here?

A. I don't know. I assume it did…

Q. **How did you explain that the written list of charges came after the Loudermill hearing? How do you explain that?**

A. I can't explain it because I don't remember the order of it, because I was not directly handling it.

Q. **Who was directly handling it?**

A. David Wildonger...

Q. **After his, the letter of termination, he requested a hearing before the school board?**

MR. FREUND: Objection. That's not – that's not an accurate statement. You can answer.

Q. **How do you say it happened?**

A. I don't know the sequence of letters and mailings and whatever. He did request a hearing before the board.

Q. **And did you understand once the board was in position – once the hearing was requested, you were not permitted under the law to discuss the termination with the board?**

A. Yes.

MR. FREUND: That's not accurate entirely.

Q. **You understood that, right?**

A. I know there's limited discussion that has to take place if any.

Q. **You think limited discussion is permitted?**

MR. FREUND: Objection. You can answer. You can answer that.

A. I think there is a limited amount of discussion when the board asks questions, but not a lot of detail can be shared because they may ultimately be the people who decide.

Q. **Did you share any information with the board before the hearing?**

A. Well, they would know the charges.

Q. **Other than the charges, the written charges, did you discuss anything with them?**

A. I don't recall anything beyond the charges.

Q. **You were discussing the charges with the board members after the request for a hearing?**

A. I don't know the sequence.

MR. FREUND: The charges go out before there's a request for hearing...

Q. **Did you ever discuss the basis for the charges to the board members?**

A. I don't recall discussing it with them, but I can tell you that they would have known about the complaints that you've already asked me about. They would have known – I mean, a board hears all kinds of things about all of us that work in the district, but they wouldn't have heard it directly from me necessarily.

I think the charges were self- explanatory, frankly. He wasn't doing his job.

Q. **Well, there's a suggestion of certain board members that you discussed the merits of the case with them.**

MR. FREUND: Is that a question?

Q. **Do you remember doing that?**

MR. FREUND: Objection. You can answer.

A. I don't remember discussing merits, and I'm not clear on the definition of merits in your jargon.

Q. **Did you ever say to anyone, if he stays I have to go?**

A. No.

Q. **Never said that?**

A. No.

Q. **A hundred percent sure?**

A. Absolutely.

(Mayo Exhibit 7, Test Message of 8/29/14, Mayo Exhibit 8, Test Message of 11/14/14, and Mayo Exhibit 9, Test Message of 11/30/14, marked for identification.)…

BY MR. ORLOSKI:

Q. **Okay. Can you read Mayo 7 into the record, please?**

A. – With text on. It's not clear to me who or where they're from. "Just got spoke with Ce-Ce. It's all-good. Shared ultimatum. Wow wee. Contacting Bob Smith after work. Will ask appropriate questions at tonight's meeting. Also shared with me, Ellen Bishop asked how could there be impartiality and unbiased if they have to go to Freund and Mayo for any questions relating to your case. Excellent sign."

Q. **That's sheet one. What was the second sheet?**

A. The second sheet, "I asked Ce-Ce about meeting. Here is her response. Ce-Ce, grievances. Jose hearing. Charter school transportation. Gender discrimination with field hockey. As expected not much said. Ellen asked about the potential conflict of interest. That was settled. We will have the hearing officer on call 24/7 and will not have to go to Freund for questions. Issue of impartiality of hearing officer not settled. Me. No. He won't settle that either. As usual he will just keep moving forward without ever addressing it. He'll just ignore it. Any further mention of ultimatum by Smith and/or other board members? Ce-Ce, by Bob, yes. Also board secretary told him that Mayo asked her to tell him everything that board members tell or send to her. Bob is pissed and said if Mayo wants to leave let him leave."

Q. **And do you know who wrote either of those documents?**

A. I have no idea.

Q. **There's reference to an ultimatum. Did you issue an ultimatum to Bob Smith?**

A. I did not, but I'd like to know more about what the ultimatum would have been. I can't think of any ultimatum I issued.

Q. **The ultimatum was that if they keep Jose Rosado, they vote to keep him, you were going to quit.**

A. No, I didn't say that.

Q. **Did you ever imply that?**

A. No. I would say I didn't. It doesn't make much sense that I would tell my boss that.

Q. **Now, you understand under the rules that would have violated the rules of keeping the board impartial, correct?**

    MR. FREUND: Objection. It's a misstatement of law. You can answer.

A. I don't know what one has to do with the other because I said it didn't happen.

Q. **Well, you said it didn't happen.**

A. I said it didn't happen.

Q. **Other people may say it did happen.**

A. I'm saying it didn't happen.

Q. **You understand that it should not have happened, correct, that you had no right to mention that to the board, correct?**

> MR. FREUND: Objection, Misstatement.

Q. **Or you think you did have the right to mention that to the board?**

> MR. FREUND: You can answer.

A. I'm not sure how to answer your question. I think I already have when I said I didn't give an ultimatum.

Q. **I'm asking you, assuming for purposes of this discussion that other people say you did tender such an ultimatum, do you agree that if such an ultimatum was issued it would be wholly improper under the rules governing the hearing?**

> MR. FREUND: Objection.

A. I would have to consult counsel on that because I don't know –

Q. **You don't know?**

A. I don't know all the rules, legal rules of that kind of thing.

Q. **So since you didn't know the rules is it possible you may have done it, said that to Bob Smith?**

> MR. FREUND: Objection.

A. I'm not sure. I don't see a connection between the rules and whether or not I remember doing it. No, it's not – I don't think it's possible…

Q. **Where is 9?**

A. Here it is.

Q. **Can you read that into the record?**

A. "From Ce-Ce. Is Jose's team still trying to get a third party to take over this because this Fisher guy is more than a hearing officer. District paid him to be one of its lawyers during the Central rape case. Have a good night."

> (The deposition was interrupted.)
>
> MR. FREUND: Just two minutes.
>
> (Discussion off the record, and the deposition was recessed at 3:51 p.m.)

* * *

MR. FREUND: I just spoke with counsel. We agreed that we will adjourn this for today, and it will be rescheduled for the balance of the hours that he's entitled to under the federal rules.

> (Deposition adjourned at 4:01 p.m.)

Unfortunately, Dr. Mayo's deposition was adjourned prior to further questioning regarding alleged ex parte communication with the board. The balance of time for him to be deposed was not rescheduled. Therefore, we were not able to hear how he would have responded to the following communications, which took place between a Board Member and another party:

Text message – November 14, 2014

Just got this from (Board Member):

Based on what we have been sent it will appear to the board members that Jose doesn't have a strong case

Rosado v. ASD (Federal law Suit) Claim no. 203261

We did not receive that whole document only that statement

Here is my response to (Board Member):

Wow. Let me get back to you. He's playing with fire if you ask me. Bob Smith will purger himself by denying/minimizing what Mayo said to him about how he will have to leave if you don't support to fire Jose. Bob said it to you and to Joanne AND, her husband. I'M not so sure you need much more. You said you will tell the truth.

(Board Member):

If I put my hand on a bible I damn sure ain't about to lie. Not trying to go to hell and burn my ass off all day

Me:

Lol. You got it!!! So go to this web site and see for yourself. Copy it and take it with you. Regardless of the facts of the czar, you could broker a deal to remove him based on what you know about the influence he tried to levy against Bob and Deb Lamb. Use Mark Fisher, your special hearing officer. DON'T use Fruend!!!!

His job is to defend Mayo.

Did you find anything out on our second visit from PDE? Another routine visit?

Email from Mayo to Board

The patterns emerging (in my mind, at least) are as follows:

1. Activity around this matter increases a few days prior to a Board Meeting;
2. The media blitz and opposing counsel tactics ran its course, and resulted in no changes in the process;
3. Every attempt is being made by the other side to usurp the process the Board has typically followed for the 10 years I have been here; and,
4. Much information from the other side seems to be fed to certain Board Members to promote the cause of the other side.

I must confess that when at least one Board Member is not perceived by me to be objective, and seems to be promoting the cause of the other side, it hampers my ability to communicate openly with the whole Board for fear of confidentiality being broken. Confidentiality in Board member responsibilities and mine are fundamental to this relationship.

While I know Board Members are wise enough to see these things, I felt that each of you should hear my perspective since some are getting the perspective of the other side.

Here's what I ask in being respectful of each other in our relationship. I ask that you be objective in this and any other matter. This is your value to the district, to me, and to our kids.

I ask further that on this particular matter that you as Board Members work through your elected President to handle matters with the hearing officer. This will keep the hearing officer from getting confused about requests and avoid usurping the normal process. As noted by our solicitor, their attorney should work directly with the hearing officer, as should the board. Just as dealing with me, having each of nine people make different request is difficult. You will receive all documents and information at the appropriate time by law. Nothing will be withheld.

I appreciate your understanding. There is too much emotion being generated around a topic that needs to be considered objectively by the Board.

See you Thursday night.

Russ

IN THE UNITED STATES DISTRICT COURT
FOR THE EASTERN DISTRICT OF PENNSYLVANIA

JOSE ROSADO,   : No. 14-cv-5794

        Plaintiff   :

        vs.   :

C. RUSSEL MAYO, Ed.D.,   :
DAVID WILDONGER and   :
ALLENTOWN SCHOOL DISTRICT, :

        Defendants   :

ORIGINAL

DEPOSITION OF DAVID M. WILDONGER

       Taken in the law offices of King, Spry, Herman, Freund & Faul, LLC, One West Broad Street, Suite 700, Bethlehem, Pennsylvania, on Tuesday, December 22, 2015, commencing at 9:52 a.m., before Thomas M. Gallagher, Notary Public of the Commonwealth of Pennsylvania.

* * *

GALLAGHER REPORTING & VIDEO, LLC
Mill Run Office Center
1275 Glenlivet Drive, Suite 100
Allentown, Pennsylvania 18106
(610) 439-0504   1 (800) 366-2980
gallagherreporting@verizon.net

PROCEEDINGS

DAVID M. WILDONGER, HAVING BEEN DULY SWORN, WAS EXAMINED AND TESTIFIED AS FOLLOWS:

EXAMINATION
BY MR. ORLOSKI:

Mr. Wildonger, my name is Rick Orloski. I represent Jose Rosado. He has filed a lawsuit against you, Russell Mayo, and the Allentown School District concerning his voluntary departure from the Allentown School District.

We're here today to ask straightforward, easily understood questions and get honest answers.

Q. What's your full name?

A. David Martin Wildonger. ...

Q. Now, what is your educational background starting with high school, where did you go to high school?

A. I attended William Allen High School.

Q. Did you get a diploma from William Allen?

A. I did.

Q. What year did you get your diploma?

A. 1971

Q. After Allen High School any further education?

A. Yes

Q. What did you do next?

A. I attended East Stroudsburg University.

Q. How long were you at East Stroudsburg?

A. I graduated - - four years. I graduated in 1975.

Q. And what degree did you get?

A. A degree in health and physical education.

Q. Did you get any type of teacher qualification?

A. Yes, I did.

Q. What type of teacher qualification?

A. K to 12, health and physical education.

Q. Basically a gym teacher, that's the concept?

A. Concept, yes. ...

Q. Any education after your degree in health and human services?

A. My degree – after college?

Q. After college.

A. Yes.

Q. What degree?

A. I received a master's equivalency. I took - - and my administrative cert.

Q. Now, a master's equivalency is not a master's, correct?

A. It is a mater's without the thesis. It's classes.

Q. Did you literally get a master's degree from any institution?

A. By the state, yes, I did. A mater's equivalency is the same as a master's by the state.

Q. **But where did you do the credit work for the master's equivalency?**

A. Marywood and Penn State.

Q. **And neither one gave you a master's?**

A. No. The state issued the equivalency.

Q. **Then you said you got an administrative certificate?**

A. Yes.

Q. **What was your certificate for?**

A. That was in - - what was it for?

Q. **To be a school superintendent?**

A. No, a school administrator. I do not have a letter of superintendency. That is a separate - -

Q. **Could you be a principal with your administrative certificate?**

A. Yes.

Q. **What was your first job after college?**

A. I substituted for two years in five school districts.

Q. **What geographic area, Lehigh Valley, Jersey?**

A. Lehigh Valley.

Q. **After your two years of substitute teaching, what next?**

A. I was hired by the Allentown School District.

Q. **What capacity?**

A. As a teacher in health and physical education.

Q. **When were you first hired?**

A. I was hired in 1977.

Q. **Where did you actually teach?**

A. I taught at William Allen High School.

Q. **What grades?**

A. Nine, ten, eleven and twelve.

Q. **How long did that last?**

A. That lasted until 2000 – 2001. 2001

Q. **So from 1977 till approximately 2001 you were a gym teacher at William Allen High School, correct?**

A. That is correct.

Q. **What happened in 2001?**

A. 2001 I went to the administration. I was brought to the administration building as a coordinator of academics.

Q. **And who made that decision?**

A. I believe that was Dr. Scott. …

Q. **What did you actually do as coordinator?**

A. Coordinating was to have the two high schools –part of the grant was to transform an educational direction in the two high schools into academies where the program of studies would - - where students would have a choice within the program of studies of selecting a career pathway. And career pathways were being developed. And the grant was specific in saying all students in the high schools over a four to five year period of time, I'm not sure, four or five, the life of the grant, all students would be into academies.

Q. **And the two high schools were Allen and Dieruff?**
A. Yes.
Q. **Does that program still exist today?**
A. Not in entirety, no.
Q. **Do the academies within the schools still exist today?**
A. The arts academy does.
Q. **How many academies were there?**
A. I believe the direction was five at Allen and four at Dieruff.
Q. **How many exist today at Allen?**
A. I believe just the arts academy.
Q. **And how many at Dieruff?**
A. I don't believe any.
Q. **All in all that program failed, correct?**
　　MR. FREUND: Objection.
　　You can answer.
Q. **Would you agree with that characterization?**
A. No.
Q. **Were you always the coordinator of the academies while they were doing the program?**
A. As the grant ran, yes.
Q. **After the grant ran out what happened with your employment?**
A. That position - - the position?
Q. **With your employment. I mean it's a four or five year grant, I believe you told me, correct?**
A. Yes. Then I became administrator on special assignment, high school reform. That was for two years.
Q. **So approximately when were those two years?**
A. 2005 to 2007
Q. **Special assignment for what?**
A. High school reform. Administrator on special assignment, high school reform.
Q. **Does that program still exist today?**
A. Yes.
Q. **Who has it today?**
A. There is no one overseeing. The program was to institute ninth grade as a separate entity of the high schools.
Q. **Who gave you that job?**
A. I believe that was Dr. Angelo.
Q. **What job did you have next?**
A. Executive Director of secondary education until 2012.

Q. So 2007 to 2012 you were executive director of secondary education of Allentown School District?

A. That is correct.

Q. What did that involve?

A. That involved coordinating a program of studies between two high schools. It involved the high schools and middle schools, overseeing them. It involved being liaison to LCTI.

Q. What's LCTI?

A. Lehigh Career and Technical Institute. It involved liaison to LCCC, Lehigh Carbon Community College. I also oversaw athletics.

Q. What percentage of your job was overseeing athletics?

A. I'd say maybe 10, 20 percent.

Q. Does that job exist today?

A. No.

Q. But you never competed the course requirements to receive a master's in any education of any sort, right?

MR. FREUND: Objection.

You can answer

THE WITNESS: I did receive a master's, a master's equivalency, which was by the state's requirements deemed a master's. It didn't involve a thesis.

Q. Do you really believe that a master's equivalency is a degree from an institution?

MR. FREUND: Objection.

You can answer.

Q. Because I know what a mater's equivalency is.

A. Yeah.

Q. So you have a degree from either Marywood or Penn State saying you have a master's?

A. No.

Q. That's 100 percent true, there is no degree issued to you, correct?

A. Would you ask the question again?

Q. You have no master's degree?

A. That is correct

Q. What you have is a master's equivalency that says if you completed X amount of courses for purposes of pay schedule, you will be treated as if you had a master's, which is why it's called a master's equivalency, correct?

MR.FREUND: Objection

You can answer.

THE WITNESS: As taking courses, it was simply done for course work.

Q. Course work for pay purposes?

A. It was course work. I just didn't do a thesis, which is required by a master's.

Q. How many courses did you take at Marywood?

A. I don't know offhand.

Q. How many courses did you take at Penn State?

A. I don't know offhand. That was a few years ago.
Q. **And the state doesn't issue a degree, correct?**
A. Pardon
Q. **The State of Pennsylvania did not say we're giving you a master's, correct?**
A. No. They gave me a master's equivalency.
Q. **They certify that you completed courses so for pay purposes you should be treated as if you had a master's, correct?**
A. Correct.
Q. **That's all a master's equivalency is, correct?**
A. Correct.
Q. **Now, after the executive director what was your next job?**
A. Chief operations officer.
Q. **Who gave you that job?**
A. I was approved by the board of education for that position.
Q. **Who recommended you from the board for that?**
A. Dr. Mayo.
Q. **What's your relationship with Dr. Mayo before he recommended you to that position?**
A. Professional.
Q. **What does that mean?**
A. He is - - he was - - before my appointment? He was basically over me in the hierarchy of the administration.
Q. **What were you expected to do as a chief operations officer?**
A. My job description?
Q. **Right.**
A. Oversee multiple departments, student services, HR, IT.
Q. **What background do you have in IT?**
A. Limited.
Q. **How limited?**
A. Very limited. …
Q. **What qualified you to oversee anybody in IT?**
A. It's always been my belief that you don't necessarily need to know everything about a department to be a leader of things. It comes to leadership. And I believe that's true of everything. You don't know everything about everything.
Q. **Do you know anything about IT other than to use a computer for word processing?**
A. I know what an explanation – when people explain things to me I hope I can understand what they're explaining and have a common direction or understanding of it.
Q. **But you agree that by education you have no specific education in IT?**
A. Yes.
Q. **Who were you supervising in the IT department?**
A. Now it is Tom Derhammer.
Q. **What's his background?**

A. He actually was coordinator of the IT academy at Dieruff who worked with Microsoft, the corporation. Not that he worked - - excuse me, I want to be very clear, not that he worked there. He worked with them into Dieruff High School.

Q. **Explain to me what you just said.**

A. When I said he worked with Microsoft, I did not mean that he worked at Microsoft directly.

Q. **What does that mean?**

A . Within the academy itself Microsoft had worked with his academy and kids where he worked directly with people from there in order to instill certain things.

Q. **What's his background? Does he have a degree?**

A. Does Tom have a degree?

Q. **Yeah.**

A. In?

Q. **IT, computer science.**

A. I honestly don't know.

Q. **So you supervise him in the IT department and you have no idea what his background is?**

A. I don't know what his - -

Q. **Educational background is?**

A. That's correct.

Q. **You don't know if he's an engineer?**

A. No.

Q. **You don't know if he's a programmer?**

A. No.

Q. **Did you get a raise when you took this position?**

A. I had a change in pay from the position I was in to this position, a higher pay.

Q. **How much more?**

A. I believe it would have been somewhere - - I don't know exactly, but I'd say probably $20,000, in that range.

Q. **Was the position bid, was it open, or did Mayo come to you and say I got a job for you?**

A. My understanding was Dr. Mayo was restructuring the administration building and he spoke to me about the position. And then I believe I was interviewed by board members or the board.

Q. **No other candidates for this job which had a $20,000 pay raise?**

A. Not that I'm aware of.

Q. **So this is an inside baseball thing, Mayo wanted you, you didn't know a thing about IT, but you're now going to oversee the IT department, correct?**

MR. FREUND: Objection.

You can answer.

THE WITNESS: That was part of my responsibility, yes...

Q. **What was your father's name?**

A. Kenneth Titus Wildonger.

305

Q. Did he have any relationship with the Allentown School District?

A. Yes, he did.

Q. What was his relationship?

A. He was a health and physical education teacher and coach for William Allen High School.

Q. How long was he a coach?

A. My best I would say is 38 years, 38 to 40 years. And that was not only William Allen High School, it was then Allentown High School.

Q. And he had a very successful tenure as a coach?

A. I believe so.

Q. When did he leave Allentown School District?

A. 1977 he retired.

Q. Now, today you're the chief operations officer, correct?

A. That is correct.

Q. What's your salary, what are you paid for that position?

A. A range of $133,000.

Q. Have you ever been a principal?

A. No, I have not.

Q. Have you ever been an assistant principal?

A. No, I have not.

Q. Have you ever supervised principals?

A. Yes.

Q. And your statement you don't have to know everything about a job in order to supervise people, is that similarly true for supervising principals?

A. You need to know about the job. But I don't believe you need to be in one to do it.

Q. And the executive director, was that another position that was given to you without going through a bid process, other people applying for it?

A. I believe - - again, I believe for that I was interviewed by the board also.

Q. Were there other candidates?

A. Not that I'm aware of.

Q. So you've had the good fortune in your last two positions of not having any candidates competing against you, correct?

    MR. FREUND: Objection

    You can answer.

    THE WITNESS: Not that I'm aware of.

Q. Is that how business is normally done in the Allentown School District?

    MR. FREUND: Objection

    Answer.

    THE WITNESS: In some cases I believe it is.

Q. In your case it was definitely true, correct?

A. In those situations I believe it to be, yes…

Q. Did there come a time when the Allentown School District hired Jose Rosado?

A. Yes.

Q. **When was he hired?**
A. The year I'm not clear on.
Q. **Did you play any role in his hiring?**
A. I did not.
Q. **Do you know what position he was hired for?**
A. Yes.
Q. **What position?**
A. Director of Student Services.
Q. **And that was for the alternative education program?**
A. That is correct.
Q. **And he was basically a principal of that school, correct?**
A. Principal of record, correct.
Q. **Who was his supervisor?**
A. Susan - - well, part as Susan Lozada. I don't know at the time of his hiring. I do know the time - - Susan Lozada was his supervisor at one time, yes.
Q. **And is it a fair statement that Susan Lozada was very satisfied with his performance? Do you agree that Susan Lozada was well pleased with Jose Rosado's performance as a principal?**
   MR. FREUND: Objection
   You can answer.
   THE WITNESS: No.
Q. **Did she ever say anything negative to you about his performance?**
A. Yes.
Q. **When did she first say anything negative about his performance?**
A. It would have been his 2011 evaluation.
Q. **Who did his 2011 evaluation?**
A. Susan Lozada.
Q. **Did you tell her what to put in there?**
A. No, not at all.
Q. **And it would be wholly improper for you to tell her what to put in his evaluation, right?**
A. I wouldn't tell someone to put anything into their evaluation. It would be discussed if that's what was agreed upon. But I wouldn't tell anyone to put it in.
Q. **How many evaluations were done on Jose Rosado during your tenure as his line of authority over him?**
A. I did the '12 – '13. I don't know if there was a '13 – '14. I know I did the '12 – '13.
Q. **Why did you do the '12 – '13?**
A. Susan Lozada was leaving the district, and I was requested to do his evaluation.
Q. **Who requested that of you?**
A. The superintendent and I had a discussion on that.
Q. **Who asked you to do it?**
A. The superintendent did.
Q. **Why?**

A.   I was asked to do it. She was leaving the district and I was asked to do the evaluation.

Q.   **She was his supervisor for the year, correct?**

A.   Direct supervisor, that is correct.

Q.   **And she was ready, willing and able to do the evaluation, correct?**

MR. FREUND: Objection

You can answer.

THE WITNESS: I don't know that.

Q.   **Was this part of the setup between you and Mayo, that you would supplant his supervisor and you give him a bad evaluation?**

MR. FREUND: Objection

You can answer.

THE WITNESS: No.

Q.   **Isn't that what happened though?**

MR. FREUND: Objection

You can answer.

THE WITNESS: I wouldn't do that.

Q.   **You wouldn't give him a bad evaluation?**

A.   No, I wouldn't be told by someone to do that.

Q.   **Did you do it?**

A.   I gave - - I did his evaluation.

Q.   **Was it good?**

A.   It was not where it should be.

Q.   **Because you made that determination, correct?**

A.   It was my determination.

Q.   **And you did not supervise him?**

A.   Not directly.

Q.   **And Susan Lozada supervised him?**

A.   Directly.

Q.   **And she was taken wholly out of the loop for purposes of the evaluation, right?**

MR. FREUND: Objection.

You can answer.

THE WITNESS: I wouldn't say taken wholly out of the loop.

Q.   **What would you say?**

A.   She did not - - there was a binder left, but she did not have that I recall an evaluation done or anything given to me to assist in the process.

Q.   **She didn't assist in the process at all?**

A.   Not his evaluation that year that I received anything from her.

Q.   **Because you told her you didn't want her input, right?**

A.   No, I did not.

Q.   **Did you ever go to her and ask her for her input?**

A.   I don't recall if I did.

Q. You don't recall if you went to the lady who was his immediate supervisor and ask her, I got to supervise this person who I haven't supervised, can you give me some help?

A. We had discussions during the year and at the end. But not directly handing me anything, no.

Q. **Who is Ryan Miller?**

A. Ryan Miller is a teacher in the Allentown School District.

Q. **And did he ever complain about Jose Rosado?**

A. I believe so, yes.

Q. **And as a result of that - - how many times did he complain?**

A. Oh, I don't know that. It could be multiple.

Q. **And at some point did you factor Ryan Miller's complaints about Jose Rosado into the evaluation?**

A. No.

Q. **You're sure?**

A. Yes.

Q. **Now, you understand that Ryan Miller was found by the Allentown School District to be lying about Jose Rosado, do you not?**

MR. FREUND: Objection

You can answer

THE WITNESS: I am not fully aware of all that, no.

Q. **Are you aware of it at all, if not fully aware of it?**

A. I've heard of it. I was not involved in that.

Q. **Who did you hear it from?**

A. I honestly don't remember.

Q. **What basis did you have, factual basis, for evaluating Jose Rosado in 2012 – 2013?**

A. In my position, I was overseeing Susan Lozada.

Q. **That's not facts. Let's talk facts. What facts did you have about Jose Rosado that enabled you to evaluate him?**

A. The meetings were being run prior to with I believe his name was Jeff Fries.

Q. **What meeting are you talking about?**

A. It was - - I don't remember the name of the group. It was over the - - we met regularly over a binder that was done for the direction of alternative ed. I was in all those meetings.

Q. **Wait, wait, wait. Is this the binder you're talking about?**

A. That is correct.

MR. FREUND: That's an exhibit in the Rosado case.

MR. ORLOSKI: This was Exhibit 2 as used in Jose Rosado's deposition.

Q. **So you did what about this binder?**

A. We were all involved in meetings over that binder during the time - - during this time with Jeff Fries. It was a review of the binder with all administrators. There were central office people. There were secondary principals. I was involved also in all grievances and any other disputes between faculty or the district. I was involved in those also.

Q. **You just told me you didn't know anything about the Ryan Miller grievance.**

A. I didn't - - there were - - I believe there were different grievances. Which grievance?. I wasn't - - my understanding - - if you could help me with which grievance and what time, what time frame. …

Q. **Did you ever attend a meeting with Jose Rosado about this binder?**

A. He was in the meetings.

Q. **All of them?**

A. I can't say all of them, but the majority, I will say that.

Q. **And what did he do in those meetings, was it positive, negative, what do you remember?**

A. Some of the meetings were positive. Some were negative.

Q. **Give me an illustration of one negative thing you remember about his interaction with this binder.**

A. It wasn't necessarily his interaction. It was the situations that were occurring in alt. ed. that he was in charge of that the other people in the room were bringing up for clarification and direction and change.

Q. **Because they wanted to dump Hispanic and black kids into that program without following the rules, right?**

MR. FREUND: Objection

THE WITNESS: No, not that I'm aware of, no.

Q. **You're not aware of that at all?**

MR. FREUND: Objection

THE WITNESS: No.

Q. **Do you agree the alternative education program has standards for being transferred into that program?**

A. Yes.

Q. **Do you agree that as a general rule it's a negative to be transferred into that program?**

MR. FREUND: Objection

You can answer.

THE WITNESS: I personally would not look at it as a negative. I personally would not.

Q. **Well, don't you have to be a disruptive student to get transferred into the program?**

A. There are - - there are directions to get in, yes. And one is disruptive, yes. Defined disruptive, yes.

Q. **I'm sorry, what did you say?**

A. As being defined as disruptive. …

Q. **Well, you understand you can't just put a student in that program because you want to, right?**

A. I do understand that.

Q. **You understand you can't put a student in that program just because he's black, you understand that?**

A. Oh, I do understand that.

Q. **And you can't just put a student in that program because he's Hispanic, correct?**

A. I do understand that.

Q. **And you can't put a student in that program just because he has special education needs, correct?**

A. I do understand that?

Q. **So it's designed for disruptive students?**

A. Yes.

Q. **And some people were complaining that Jose would not accept students that were referred to the alternative education program because he said they weren't meeting the standards, correct?**

> MR. FREUND: Objection.
>
> You can answer.
>
> THE WITNESS: He was saying they were not meeting the standards. They were not being - - there was either - - they were not going into the program or there was hesitation to let them in.

Q. **Because they weren't meeting the standards?**

A. I think it was on both ends?

Q. **What do you mean both ends?**

A. The administrators were saying that things were not - - the timely manner of students going in and out were not happening. There was also progress reports of students and success reports back and forth that were not happening.

Q. **You understand that the students had certain due process rights before they would be admitted into that program, right?**

> MR. FREUND: Objection. What program are you talking about?
>
> MR. ORLOSKI: The alternative education program.
>
> MR. FREUND: There is different alternative education programs. Some are AEDY. Some are not AEDY.

Q. **AEDY, do you know what that means?**

A. Yes.

Q. **What does it mean?**

A. Alternative education for disruptive youth.

Q. **And those students had certain due process rights?**

A. Yes.

Q. **And there is supposed to be contact between the principals and the parents?**

A. Yes.

Q. **And if the principals and the parents weren't doing that, should Jose Rosado have accepted them into the program?**

> MR. FREUND: Objection.
>
> THE WITNESS: I believe – pardon?
>
> MR. FREUND: You can answer.
>
> MR. ORLOSKI: Speak up. He's hard of hearing.
>
> THE WITNESS: I can't hear this way if I'm this way.
>
> MR. FREUND: I'll shout out my objections.
>
> THE WITNESS: Would you repeat the question, please?

MR. ORLOSKI: Mr. Gallagher, please repeat it.

(The court reporter read the following: Question: And if the principals and the parents weren't doing that, should Jose Rosado have accepted them into the program?)

MR. FREUND: And there is an objection.

THE WITNESS: Jose Rosado was responsible for the program, so he should have been working with those principals to make the access possible for those students.

Q. **So if principals weren't doing their job, you were blaming Jose Rosado, correct?**

MR. FREUND: Objection.

You can answer.

THE WITNESS: I think he directed the program and ran the program and should have been working with those principals in coordination with them.

Q. **And if the principals were making referrals that should not have been referred, you and Russ Mayo wanted him to take the black students and the Hispanic students into the program even though they weren't supposed to be there?**

MR. FREUND: Objection.

You can answer.

THE WITNESS: Did you say I can answer?

MR. FREUND: Yes, you can answer.

THE WITNESS: You turned away on me. Stay with me.

MR. FREUND: Sorry

THE WITNESS: No.

Q. **Didn't that actually happen, that Mayo told him to facilitate getting students into the program?**

MR. FREUND: Objection.

You can answer

THE WITNESS: Not that I'm aware of, no.

Q. **You weren't involved in that?**

A. No.

Q. **Didn't Jose Rosado tell you that and you ignored it?**

A. Not that I'm aware of.

Q. **So it may have happened, you just can't remember?**

A. I would have remembered something like that?

Q. **Well, do you remember that students were referred and after the referral the state came in and did an audit, do you remember that?**

A. There was an audit. I'm not sure what year that audit was. I am aware of the audit. I'm more aware of the - - that it was taken care of than what the audit was.

Q. **Well, didn't you find out from the audit that students that Jose Rosado said were not eligible were sent to the alternative disruptive program at the insistence of Mayo and the Pennsylvania Department of Education found the referrals were improper?**

MR. FREUND: Objection.

You can answer.

THE WITNESS: There was just too much to that question.

Q. **Okay. Do you know that in the audit the auditors specifically found that referrals were made that were improper?**

MR. FREUND: Objection.

Q. **Do you know that?**

MR. FREUND: You can answer.

THE WITNESS: I was made aware of that.

Q. **Do you know that those referrals that the state found were improper were referrals made - - were referrals that were accepted by Jose Rosado at the specific direction of Russ Mayo?**

A. I do not know that.

MR. FREUND: Objection.

Q. **Should Russ Mayo have been directing Jose Rosado to accept students who weren't eligible?**

A. I don't – he is the superintendent of the district that oversees everything. So I don't - - I wouldn't say yes or no to that.

Q. **You wouldn't say no to that?**

A. He does district – he's the boss.

MR. FREUND: Listen to the question.

Q. **Yeah, listen to the question.**

A. Go ahead.

Q. **You can keep the same answer. This is the question.**

MR. FREUND: Listen to the question. Can you ask the question again?

THE WITNESS: Can I have it again, please?

MR. ORLOSKI: Yeah. Read it back.

(The court reporter read the following: Question: Should Russ Mayo have been directing Jose Rosado to accept students who weren't eligible?)

THE WITNESS: I don't know if he did.

Q. **Would it be proper for him to do that?**

A. And it's against state regulations?

Q. **They didn't qualify under the regulations, should Mayo have told Rosado to get these kids into the program even though they're not eligible?**

A. Again, I don't know he did it. But I wouldn't think he would have done it. But I don't know if he did, but no, you don't force kids into things like that.

Q. **We know he did it. ...**

Q. **Do you know how many students the audit determined were improperly transferred?**

A. No, I don't know that either.

Q. **Do you agree that all principals that were referring students were white?**

MR. FREUND: Objection

You can answer.

THE WITNESS: I believe that to be correct.

Q. **Do you also know that the students that they were referring that Jose was saying were not eligible were predominantly either African American or Latino?**

A.   No, I did not know that.

Q.   **How would you know if there was discrimination taking place if you didn't have that basic information?**

MR. FREUND: Objection.

THE WITNESS: I didn't have that information. And it was being deemed upon, I would have thought, the requirements to go in and the students matching the requirements to go in. And that's how they entered the program. Whether it was on race, I didn't know that. I didn't know the racial background going into alt. ed.

Q.   **So if there was racial discrimination happening under your nose, you did not know it was happening?**

A.   I didn't know if it was happening if it was.

Q.   **Well, you know from the audit that students were being sent into the program who should not have been there, correct?**

MR. FREUND: Objection.

THE WITNESS: I knew from the end of the audit, yes, not the beginning of the audit.

Q.   **And did you know that all of those students that the audit found should not be in the program were students that Jose said should not be in the program but Mayo wanted in the program in order to put them in the program?**

MR. FREUND: Objection:

THE WITNESS: I'm not aware of that.

Q.   **You didn't know that?**

A.   No.

Q.   **Did you read the complaint?**

A.   Pardon?

Q.   **Did you read the complaint that you were served with?**

A.   Yes.

Q.   **Did you ever direct Jose Rosado to move special education kids into the AEDY program?**

A.   Not that I can remember.

Q.   **Okay. AEDY, did you ever have a meeting with Jose Rosado where you specifically instructed him that you wanted certain special ed kids into that program? Do you want me – to rephrase the question?**

A.   Would you, please?

MR. ORLOSKI: Let's mark this Wildonger 1.

(Wildonger Deposition Exhibit Number 1 was marked for the identification.)

MR. ORLOSKI: For the record, this document has been provided to you in discovery as number 44, but we're marking it here as Wildonger 1.

MR. FREUND: Read it through before you answer.

Q.   **Do you have –**

MR. FREUND: Let him read it.

Q.   **Oh, you haven't read it yet.**

A.   Yes.

Q.   **Have you seen that document before?**

A.   Yes...

Q.   **Let's look at it. There is an E-mail dated November 26, 2016 at 3:01 to Dave from Jose, correct?**

A.   Dave to Jose was November 26th.

Q.   **Okay, Let's see if we can put this into some context. Before this E-mail was sent there was a meeting, correct?**

A.   That is correct.

Q.   **And who was at that meeting?**

A.   There was a meeting with Tina Belardi, Belinda Miler, myself. And I don't know if it was one meeting or two, and I'm not sure if Jose was in the meeting. I'm not sure. I believe he was, but I'm not sure.

Q.   **And what was the purpose of the meeting?**

A.   The purpose of the meeting was Belinda Miller was overseeing - - she is the director of special education, and there wasn't compliance, I believe, if highly qualified. And the report was going in the next day. She recognized I believe.

Q.   **What did she recognize?**

A.   That we were out of compliance.

Q.   **What were you doing out of compliance?**

A.   I believe the situation was the teachers of special ed. were not highly qualified to be teaching what they were teaching.

Q.   **Was that Jose Rosado's problem?**

A.   Yes.

Q.   **He hired the teachers?**

A.   No.

Q.   **Who hired the teachers?**

A.   The board of education.

Q.   **Who put them in that position?**

A.   It's usually done - - I don't know who did that in this case, but it's usually done with the principal and whoever the director is or wherever they are coming from.

Q.   **Was there a furlough happening at that time?**

A.   I'm looking for the year on here.

Q.   **November 26, 2013.**

A.   I believe there was.

Q.   **So did Jose have any role in deciding which teachers to furlough?**

A.   Not at all.

Q.   **Not at all, right. So there was a meeting between special ed. teachers and you - - or special ed. - - let's back up. Who was at the meeting? You don't know if Jose was at the meeting, correct?**

A.   I believe he was, but I'm not sure. Tina Belardi and Belinda Miller and myself.

Q.   **And what was discussed at that meeting?**

A. What direction to take because I believe it was due the next day. Something was due the next day with highly qualified or something Belinda Miller had to do, that we were out of compliance and it needed to go to the state the next day.

Q. **Why were you out of compliance?**

A. Because the teachers were not highly qualified that were teaching special education in the alternative ed. building.

Q. **How does that involve Jose Rosado?**

A. Jose is in charge of that program and as principal of the building it goes - - HR sends out highly qualified, who is and who isn't, and how to rectify it. We need to be highly qualified across the district or we get fined.

Q. **Did they send it out to Jose Rosado?**

A. I believe they did.

Q. **Should they have sent it out to him?**

A. Yes.

Q. **Now if they didn't, whose mistake was that?**

A. That would have been between HR and special education.

Q. **And after that meeting did you give certain directives to Jose?**

A. I did. And I believe I did in the meeting.

Q. **And is that direction – what you told him to do, is that what prompted his letter dated November 26, 2013 at 3:01, the same day?**

A. I directed Jose to contact his contact at PDE, to get in contact with him. He said he had a contact there that he knows very well that he works with. I told him - - I directed him, get a hold of him. Because Jose's concern was he said, as I quote, I could lose my certificate over this.

Q. **What was he concerned about that would cause him to lose his certificate?**

A. That he was going against or out of compliance with what he had, what he was running.

Q. **So what were you specifically directing him to do?**

A. Check with PDE on what he was saying to see if we had time or we could work with them. And at the same time Belinda Miller, special ed., was calling PDE because we didn't want that to happen, as I stated to Jose.

Q. **Now the letter says - - do you have the letter in front of you?**

A. I do.

Q. **The option supported was to move the special education students into regular education classrooms and have the special education teachers co-teach with the regular education teachers. Is that what you told him to do?**

A. I believe – I believe that's what we agreed on would be the best direction, and from the advice of Belinda Miller, who was special education.

Q. **You definitely told him to do that then?**

A. I did.

Q. **And you thought that was proper and lawful?**

A. Again, that's why I had Jose call PDE and Belinda Miller, who was saying this is what we need to do, call PDE to make sure we could do this.

Q. **So you didn't know if it was lawful?**

A. No.

Q. **So you're telling him to do something that you didn't know if it was lawful or not?**

A. I was going under – what we wanted to do was find out. That's why they were instructed to call PDE, both of them.

Q. **And did Jose do that?**

A. **I believe he would have.**

Q. **Look at the third paragraph of his letter.**

A. I have contacted PDE.

Q. **And did Jose – read the second to last paragraph of the letter, I understand that.**

A. The third paragraph, I have not received any contact from PDE.

Q. **He says I left a message that they're seeking a waiver, right?**

A. Yes.

Q. **They haven't responded because they didn't get back a voicemail, right?**

A. I don't know.

Q. **Isn't that what you understand that to be?**

A. That they would get back to him?

Q. **That he left a voicemail.**

A. That's what I understand, yes.

Q. **Now, read the next full paragraph out loud please.**

A. I understand that the NHQT concern is important. However, taking action that contradicts the district's AEDY application and violates the corrective action plan is also a concern. I cannot anticipate the response from PDE regarding a request for a waiver or revision of the application. Moving forward without the approval of PDE could lead to the district being placed on corrective action status.

Q. **Read the last paragraph.**

A. I am uncomfortable with this course of action. However, I will proceed if that is what you direct me to do. Please advise me accordingly.

Q. **Okay. Then at the top of this document is your response?**

A. That is correct.

Q. **What did you tell him to do?**

A. Please follow through with what was agreed upon at the meeting.

Q. **So you avoided responding to his concerns?**

A. Pardon?

Q. **You avoided responding to his concerns?**

    MR. FREUND: Objection:

    You can answer.

    THE WITNESS: Do I avoid his –

Q. **Did you just simply avoid responding to his letter?**

A. No.

Q. **Your response was what?**

A. Please follow through with what was agreed on in the meeting.

Q. **And what was agreed upon at the meeting was to transfer special education students into the regular classroom, correct?**

MR. FREUND: Objection. You're conflating two completely different things.

MR. ORLOSKI: I don't know, John. That's the purpose of the question. You tell me.

MR. FREUND: This highly qualified thing and the transfer of the kids in the program are completely unrelated.

MR. ORLOSKI: Do you want to testify, John?

MR. FREUND: Well, no.

MR. ORLOSKI: Let him testify.

MR. FREUND: It's an unfair question, but he can answer it.

Q. Let's try it again. The sum total of your response was please follow through with what was agreed upon in the meeting, correct?

A. That is correct...

MR. ORLOSKI: Mark this Wildonger 2, please. It's 121.

(Wildonger Deposition Exhibit Number 2 was marked for identification.)

Q. Have you had an opportunity to read what we marked as Wildonger 2, which is in discovery marked 121? ...

A. I have.

Q. It's a three-page exhibit?

A. I only read the first page that you handed to me. Did you want me to read all three?

Q. Yeah, read all three please. Have you had a chance to read it?

A. Yes, I have.

Q. Basically starting at the second page and going into the third, that's what we already discussed as Exhibit 1, correct?

A. You're correct.

Q. And this is Jose's response to what was happening, correct?

MR. FREUND: Objection.

You can answer.

THE WITNESS: Of what he was doing, yes.

Q. Now, earlier you told me you did not know about the Mayo directive about putting students in the alternative education program who didn't belong there, you didn't know about that?

MR. FREUND: Objection.

You can answer.

THE WITNESS: That's correct.

Q. But that is mentioned in the first pages of Exhibit 2, correct?

A. That is correct.

Q. So to the extent that he wrote it on November 26, 2013, you actually had notice of that?

A. By his writing, not knowledge, yes.

Q. Well, is it your testimony still that you didn't know about it?

A. No.

Q. Even though he told you about it in writing?

A. No. ...

Q. How does the evaluation procedure work at Allentown School District, it's based upon the academic year, correct?

A. Based on the academic year, you are correct.

Q. It's a written evaluation, correct?

A. You are correct.

Q. And the immediate supervisor does it?

A. That is correct.

Q. And Jose had an evaluation for the 2009-2010 year, correct, there should be such an evaluation?

A. There should be, yes.

Q. Did you ever look at it?

A. Not that I'm aware of, no.

Q. You were involved with the decision to terminate him, correct?

A. That is correct.

Q. You didn't bother to look at his evaluations?

A. Not that year, no.

Q. Why not?

A. I didn't look at that year. I looked at other years, but I didn't look at that year, no. ...

Q. I'm going to show you what we marked as 450, but we had this original, which we did not copy because supposedly the school district had it. Do you recognize that document?

A. Yes. I believe this is the binder that was left by Susan Lozada to me on Jose Rosado.

Q. Did you read it?

A. Yes.

Q. Did you discuss it with Ms. Lozada?

A. I don't remember doing that.

Q. Did you ask her to preliminarily prepare her evaluation?

A. Would you rephrase the question?

Q. Did you give her an evaluation form that says, here, fill this out as you would fill it out?

A. Her evaluation?

Q. Let's try it again. Did you give Susan Lozada a blank evaluation form and say I'm going to prepare Jose Rosado's evaluation, jot down the way you would prepare it, I'd like to see what your evaluation would be?

A. Not that I remember, no.

Q. Why not? The fix was in already, correct?

A. There was no fix....

Q. That book is Susan Lozada's record on how Jose Rosado was doing his job, correct?

A. My understanding from Susan was he turned the documents in. But this wasn't her record. It was his record.

Q. Where did you get that understanding from?

A. That was my understanding when Susan – I received this to go through, that he was giving the materials to be put in here.

Q. Did you receive it from her or did she just leave it there?

A. That I don't remember.

Q. But you know she played no role in his evaluation, correct?

A. In the writing of this, yes.

Q. He prepared a rebuttal to your evaluation, correct?

A. When you go down I can't hear you. I apologize.

Q. I'm sorry. My fault.

    MR. ORLOSKI: Mark this, 425, the next exhibit.

    (Wildonger Deposition Exhibit Number 8 was marked for identification.)

Q. 425 is his rebuttal, correct?

A. To David Wildonger from Jose, yes.

Q. And after you received this rebuttal you had documents, which you said you didn't have before, correct?

A. I don't remember saying that.

Q. What, if anything, did you do with this rebuttal?

A. What if anything - -

Q. Did you do with the rebuttal. What, if anything, did you do with this rebuttal?

A. I would have gone through the rebuttal to see if it made any difference.

Q. Did you do that?

A. Yes.

Q. How long did it take you to go through that rebuttal?

A. I don't know that.

Q. But claim to have done it?

A. Yes.

Q. When did you do it?

A. I don't know that either. I would imagine at the time that it was sent or very close to it.

Q. Did you share that rebuttal with anybody at the school district?

A. No.

Q. Why not?

A. It was my job to do the evaluation.

Q. Well, it wasn't your job. It was Susan Lozada's job to do the evaluation.

A. I was directed to do it.

Q. Who directed you to do it?

A. It was my job. I did it. And this came to me for rebuttal. So I handled it.

Q. Who directed you to do it?

A. Pardon?

Q. Who directed you to do it? Who said take Susan Lozada's job function away from her and you do it?

A. I believe I stated that earlier, that I met with Dr. Mayo, Susan was leaving, and I was directed to do her evaluation.

Q. By whom, Russell Mayo?

A. Yes.

Q. How many people did Susan Lozada supervise?

A. I don't have that answer.

Q. Did you do other evaluations for other employees that she supervised, or was it just Jose Rosado that received the special honor?

A. Just Jose Rosado's.

Q. And he's the only Hispanic person - - strike that. Jose Rosado is the only person ever subject to removal by Russ Mayo and you, correct?

A. In the Allentown School District, yes. Yes. I don't want to speak for him. But the two of us together, yes.

Q. And he happens to be a Hispanic male?

A. He happened to be - -

Q. He happens to be a Hispanic male?

A. Yes.

Q. So the Hispanic male not only got fired by you, but you had Susan Lozada not do the evaluation, even though she was doing it for other people, and you and you alone did that evaluation?

   MS. KELLY: Okay, Objection ...

Q. Okay. Susan Lozada was doing other people's evaluations that she supervised even though she was leaving, correct?

A. To my knowledge she should have been.

Q. You only did Jose Rosado for her?

A. Correct.

Q. You never interacted with her about what her opinion was?

A. You asked the question before. I said I wasn't sure. I know we discussed issues, yes, we did.

Q. In the course of that academic year how many times did you see Jose Rosado?

A. I would have no idea of that. ...

Q. Did you ever in that year interact with him concerning his job in writing?

A. I don't - - I don't know that. ...

Q. Do you have exhibit 9 in front of you?

A. Yes, I do.

Q. Do you remember getting that letter?

A. Yes, I would think I would have, yes.

Q. And it claimed that the information you had was inaccurate and incomplete, correct?

A. Or missing, yes.

Q. And you ultimately agreed with that?

A. Pardon?

Q. You ultimately agreed with that?

A. Agreed with - -

Q. That the information was inaccurate and incomplete.

A. No, I didn't agree to that.

Q. You're sure?

A. That the information that I was given was inaccurate or missing?

Q. Incomplete.

A. Incomplete, inaccurate, or missing?

Q. Right. That's true, correct?

A. I thought we met on it. He's asking for the meeting.

Q. If the information was inaccurate or incomplete, it was impossible to do a fair evaluation of him, correct?

A. Well, whatever information could be supplied I would want, yes, that would help.

Q. And properly you should consider it, correct?

A. Yes.

Q. But you didn't do that?

A. Anything that was given to me I reviewed.

Q. After you found out the information was incomplete you made a specific decision not to change your evaluation even though you knew the information was incomplete, correct?

A. It's whether the information that was given would have changed my opinion or what I was doing?

Q. That's not how you handled it, is it? Is that how you handled it, the way you just said?

A. Any information I received was reviewed. And whether it should correct anything, it would be corrected. But if it didn't change anything, then it wouldn't have changed. But if it would have changed something, then I would have changed it, or did.

Q. But that's not how you handled this situation with this Hispanic male who you wanted to fire, correct?

A. No, that's not correct.

Q. Look at 24. Read the last sentence on the first page.

A. Based on what you provided me at our meeting on October 9th, 2013, it seems that what Ms. Lozada gave me in June 2013 was incomplete.

Q. So you did agree that the information was incomplete?

A. Based on what she provided it was incomplete from what she did. That's what it's saying.

Q. Then read the second sentence on the second page.

A. However, I have decided not to change any of the ratings on your '12-'13 performance evaluation report as a result of your submission of this additional documentation because this documentation should have been submitted in June 2013 when it was first requested. At worst you should have given it to me at or shortly after our August 16, 2013 meeting when we met to discuss your performance evaluation report.

Q. So you didn't say the information doesn't change my mind because it doesn't make a difference, you said I'm not going to consider it because you're late, that's what you said, correct?

A. This says that the information was given late. It should have been given when it was requested in a timely manner, which is part of the Focused Assistance Plan.

Q. And I'm not going to consider it because it's late, correct, that's what you said?

A. That's what this is saying.

Q. And have you ever done that to white subordinate?

A. I've never done this before to anyone.

Q. So Jose Rosado got the benefit of being the first person you treated in this fashion?

A. That I - - I didn't hear the last part of your statement.

Q. I'm sorry. Jose Rosado is the first person you got to treat in this fashion, one, you didn't let Susan Lozada do the evaluation, you did it, and when the information was late you weren't going to change your evaluation, correct?

A. I think there were multiple questions there.

Q. Well, name me one white person who was treated by you similarly to the way you treated Jose Rosado?

A. This was the only FAP I've done on anyone. I haven't done any before. ...

Q. What's your relationship with Russ Mayo today?

A. He is my supervisor.

Q. Are you friends?

MS. KELLY: Objection. I don't think this is relevant to anything.
But you can answer the question.
THE WITNESS: He is my supervisor. And we do not socially do anything together per se as far as dinners together or families together or anything that way. Depends on the definition of friend.

Q. Who made the decision to terminate Jose Rosado?

A. That decision was made between Dr. Mayo and myself and then the attorneys.

Q. Which attorneys?

A. This law firm.

Q. And this law firm, there is an attorney by the name of Elizabeth Kelly who is sitting by your side today, correct?

A. That's correct.

Q. And not only was she an attorney, she was the interim director of human resources, correct?

A. You're correct.

Q. And she had that position when Jose Rosado was fired?

A. That's correct. ...

Q. Let's work backwards. When was he terminated? He was suspended with pay, correct?

A. Everyone - - just about everyone - - well, everyone that I know that I've ever been involved with or knew is suspended with pay.

Q. When did he get suspended?

A. I don't have that information off the top of my head.

Q. If I told you May 6th, 2014, would that sound right?

A. I'll go with what you say. I don't know. Without showing me - - I'll go with what you say.

Q. Was he provided a reason for the suspension in writing?

A. A reason for the suspension?

Q. Right. Correct.

A. Should have been, yes.

Q. **So do you think there is such a reason - - there is such a writing relating to the suspension on May 6th, 2014?**

A. I'm not following your questioning.

Q. **You're saying there should be a writing concurrent with his suspension with pay on May 6th, 2014, it should have been in writing?**

A. Well, I would imagine - - well, HR - - whether he's brought in, gone over what it is, it's not simply you're gone. And it's with pay. It's starting an investigation and moving through that.

Q. **But there should be some type of notice to him?**

A. That he's suspended.

Q. **Why he's suspended?**

A. Pardon?

Q. **Is it just you're suspended, no reason given, or is it you're suspended, here's why?**

A. I don't know. I don't know. I can't remember.

Q. **Well, why - -**

A. I don't want to be inaccurate.

Q. **Why was he suspended, do you know why he was suspended?**

A. When he was going through termination?

Q. **No, On May 6th, 2014, he was in fact suspended with pay?**

A. Okay.

Q. **You were a decision maker?**

A. I was one of them, yes.

Q. **Why was he suspended on May 6th, 2014?**

A. I don't know off the top of my head. If I could see a document that would refresh my memory - - I just don't know off the top of my head. But I know any suspension that would have happened would have been through HR and myself. …

Q. **So sitting here today you have no independent recollection of what led to his suspension with pay?**

A. I don't remember that suspension, when it took place or what background, no, I don't.

Q. **So sitting here today you cannot give us a good reason for suspending him in May 6th, 2014?**

A. If I saw the process that was taking place, I could put it into the process.

Q. **Sitting here today using your recollection you cannot articulate for me why he was suspended?**

A. If it was part of the process - - I would be happier seeing documentation. But if it was part of the process within termination then that was the process that took place towards a Loudermill, towards a Loudermill hearing.

Q. **In your understanding before the Loudermill hearing should he have been given a written notice of the reasons for the suspension?**

A. Charges?

Q. **Right. Before the hearing.**

A. My understanding, I'm not an attorney - -

MS. KELLY: I'm going to object because you're asking what's legally required under the school code. This witness is not at attorney.

Q. I'm asking your understanding of the way it works in Allentown. Do you get a written notice of charges before the Loudermill hearing?

A. My understanding is as I would - - I use legal for those things. My understanding, I'm not legal, is that the charges are after. I'm not legal. But I follow legal.

Q. Now, do you understand that at some point he was suspended without pay?

A. That is correct.

Q. Were you a decision maker on that?

A. That would have gone through myself, Dr. Mayo, and the attorneys, and then to the board.

Q. Why was he suspended without pay, what did he do wrong that caused him to be suspended without pay?

A. For termination?

Q. Yeah.

A. Out of the Loudermill? That was the two FAP plans and his evaluations. That was his performance.

Q. You understand that one of the reasons for the FAP was the complaint by the teacher, Ryan Miller, right, or don't you know that?

A. Could you rephrase that?

Ms. KELLY: What's the question?

THE WITNESS: I don't understand the question.

Q. He had two FAP plans, correct?

A. I believe one was issued by Susan Lozada and one was issued by myself.

Q. And was Susan Lozada told by you or Russ Mayo to do the FAP plan?

A. I did not tell Susan Lozada to do the FAP plan. …

Q. Are you an assistant superintendent?

A. No, I am not.

Q. Do you have the credentials to be an assistant superintendent?

A. No, I do not.

Q. But yet Russ Mayo has carved out a position for you which basically is the de facto assistant superintendent, correct?

A. I was offered a position with what credentials I had as - - when he realigned he went into officers, and under the officers I didn't need it.

Q. He realigned - - he eliminated the position of assistant superintendent, correct?

A. That title, correct.

Q. Because you aren't qualified to be an assistant superintendent?

A. I don't know that.

Q. Don't you need a certificate from the State of Pennsylvania to be an assistant superintendent?

A. You do.

Q. And you don't have it?

A. No, I do not.

Q. So you cannot be an assistant superintendent anywhere in Pennsylvania?

A. That is correct.

Q. And that includes Allentown?

A. That is correct.

Q. And yet you are functioning as an assistant superintendent in Allentown?

A. Well, I'm functioning as an officer to the board. I'm not - - I don't have the credentials for an assistant superintendent so I can't say that I am one or functioning as one. I'm functioning in the capacity the board directed me to that approved me into. ...

Q. Did you have an FAP where you were supposed to supervise Jose Rosado?

A. Did I?

Q. Was there an FAP where you were the person who was supposed to meet with him to discuss his performance?

A. Yes.

Q. Which FAP was that?

A. The second.

Q. Did you do it?

A. We met in my meetings every Monday to bring up any topics that need discussion or stay with me to discuss anything as I had told him any time to meet with me.

Q. You just said every Monday you had meetings?

A. Department meetings, that's correct.

Q. Not a special meeting with Jose Rosado?

A. It wasn't special. It was a part of everything happening within those departments for anything that needed to be corrected or gone over and assisted as a group.

Q. So you would do an FAP meeting as a group?

A. No.

Q. You didn't do them with him, correct?

A. Pardon?

Q. You just didn't do them, correct?

A. Individual meetings, no. We met to go over the materials. But they were not individualized meetings.

Q. They were group meetings - -

A. Every Monday as a department.

Q. You never assigned any special time to meet with him for the FAP?

A. Not that I'm aware of.

Q. And did you understand that's what you were supposed to do? Did you understand that?

A. I don't understand that I needed to meet with him on just the FAP separately. ...

Q. Page three, the last paragraph says please understand that I will be working closely with you in the next year to support your efforts to improve. Do you see that?

A. Yes.

Q. Did that happen?

A. Yes.

Q. Tell me how many times you met with him one-on-one to discuss his performance?

A. I don't - - I don't have - - I don't know that information. I don't know that off my head.

Q. **So the answer is zero, you don't know if that's true or correct?**

A. I said I don't know.

Q. **If Jose said not a single time did you meet with him one-on-one to discuss his performance, are you in a position to dispute that?**

A. I'm saying I don't know.

Q. **You wouldn't dispute it, you just don't remember.**

A. Pardon?

Q. **You don't ever remember doing it?**

A. I'm saying I don't recollect it. ...

Q. **I'll show you what's been marked Exhibit 12. Do you know who wrote that letter?**

A. Christina Mazzella.

Q. **And that shows he was suspended immediately without pay - -**

A. With pay.

Q. **- - with pay as of May 6th, 2014?**

A. The letter is May 6th. Yes, assigned administrative suspension status. This letter serves as notice that you are hereby assigned administrative suspension status with pay.

Q. **And even in that letter they say you may have engaged, correct, it didn't accuse him of anything specific? ...**

A. Yes.

Q. **Even in that letter they didn't - - the school district didn't say what he did wrong, correct, it says you may have engaged in something?**

A. May I read the two paragraphs? I didn't read the entire thing.

Q. **Read the whole thing then.**

A. All right. I read the entire thing.

Q. **Based upon reading that letter can you tell us what he did wrong?**

A. It simply addresses the decision to place you in this status upon discovery indicating that you may have engaged in willful neglect of your duties.

Q. **Does that mean anything to you specifically?**

A. His duties would have been fulfillment, I would imagine, of the FAP plan.

Q. **Does it say that?**

A. It doesn't say that word for word, no. ...

Q. **According to your letter of May 19th, in the meeting of May 6th, he's saying what did I do wrong, what are the charges, correct?**

A. He inquired about information regarding the school code charges, correct.

Q. **And what was your answer to what charges were brought against him?**

A. At this time no such charges have been brought against him. However, the district may consider such charges in the near future.

Q. **So he was terminated without any charges, correct?**

A. No.

Q. **What were the charges?**

A. You asked me previously if I remember - - I said the charges would come after the Loudermill hearing. That's what I took it as. But I'm not an attorney.

Q. So you're going to have a Loudermill hearing. This was all a bluff, wasn't it?

A. No it was not. This is very serious stuff. It's not a bluff. I don't know what you're talking about.

Q. You don't file any charges, you tell him he's terminated with pay, you may bring charges in the future, let's have a Loudermill hearing on the nonexistent charges, it was all a bluff, it was a strategy decision that you and Mayo decided to see if we can get this guy to resign, isn't that accurate?

A. No, it is not.

Q. But when you wrote the letter on May 19th, 2014 saying no charges have been brought against you, that was the truth, correct, no charges were brought against him, correct?

A. My understanding was charges come after the Loudermill hearing. Again I'm dealing with advice from counsel on direction and when things take place. ...

(Wildonger Deposition Exhibit Number 17 was marked for identification.)

Q. Number 17, Did Jose in fact respond with that rebuttal and that documentation?

A. He responded - - this is dated May 28th.

Q. What year?

A. May 28th, 2014 to the midyear evaluation, Focused Assistance Plan midyear evaluation, yes.

Q. Did you get that documentation?

A. May I review it?

Q. Sure.

THE WITNESS: Could I have the question, please?

Q. The question is did you get that document?

MS. KELLY: You're talking about Exhibit 17, this large stack of documents here?

MR. ORLOSKI: Right.

MS. KELLY: Okay.

THE WITNESS: The materials within, I can say I saw some of them that I recollect. I don't know whether I received the whole packet. I don't know that. But - -

Q. You recollect some of them?

A. The materials in going through all this, I can't remember exactly whether it was given to me, handed to me, or how I received it.

Q. But they look familiar to you?

A. Some of the things within it do.

Q. Can I see the front page of that?

A. Sure.

Q. Now, this says it's to you from Jose dated May 28th, 2014, it says rebuttal, 2013-2014 Focused Assistance Plan midyear evaluation. Did you get that memo?

A. I said I'm not sure.

Q. But you recognize some of these other documents?

A. I do recognize some of the documents within it. I don't recognize the packet itself.

MR. ORLOSKI: Let me talk to Jose.
(Discussion held off the record.)
MR. ORLOSKI: No further questions.
MS. KELLY: Nothing from defense.

(Deposition concluded at 4:15 p.m.)

IN THE UNITED STATES DISTRICT COURT

FOR THE EASTERN DISTRICT, PENNSYLVANIA

CIVIL DIVISION

* * * * * * * * *

*

JOSE ROSADO,   *

    Plaintiff   *   Case No.

    vs.   *   15-0252

C. RUSSELL MAYO,   *

ED.D., DAVID   *

WILDONGER and   *

ALLENTOWN SCHOOL   *   COPY

DISTRICT,   *

    Defendants   *

*

* * * * * * * *

DEPOSITION OF

SUSAN LOZADA

December 30, 2015

Sargent's Court Reporting Service, Inc.
(814) 536-8908

PROCEEDINGS

SUSAN LOZADA, HAVING FIRST BEEN DULY SWORN, TESTIFIED AS FOLLOWS:

EXAMINATION
BY ATTORNEY ORLOSKI:

Q. I represent Jose Rosado in the lawsuit he has filed against Dr. Mayo and others at Allentown School District concerning his departure from the district. You've been identified as somebody who has information concerning this matter, because apparently you were a supervisor of Mr. Rosado at certain times.
 We're here today to get honest answers to questions...

Q. **Please state your full name for the record.**

A. Susan Lozada.

Q. **Are you employed today?**

A. I am.

Q. **Where are you employed today?**

A. I am a principal at Reading School District.

Q. **When did you start that job?**

A. I started that job on February 2nd, 2015.

Q. **Now, before February 2nd, 2015, were you employed?**

A. No.

Q. **Was there a period of time you were unemployed?**

A. Yes.

Q. **And how long were you unemployed?**

A. From June 30th, 2013 to February 2nd, 2015.

Q. **Where did you work before June 30th, 2013?**

A. I was with the Allentown School District.

Q. **When did you start with the Allentown School District?**

A. October 23rd, 2001...

Q. **When did Dr. Mayo become your supervisor?**

A. In 2011.

Q. **What about David Wildonger, at any point was he your supervisor?**

A. Yes.

Q. **When did he become your supervisor?**

A. I want to say it was 2012 once Dr. Mayo became the permanent superintendent...

Q. **Now, when you left Allentown in June of 2012, what was your motivating factor in leaving?**

A. My motivating factor in leaving was to get away from Mr. Wildonger and Dr. Mayo.

Q. **Why did you feel a need to get away from Dr. Mayo and Mr. Wildonger?**

A. It was a toxic environment.

Q. **Did you say toxic?**

A. I did.

Q. **Can you tell me what you mean by that?**

A.   Very unhealthy, very negative.

Q.   **Dr. Mayo and Mr. Wildonger are both Caucasian; correct?**

A.   Yes.

Q.   **And I gather you're Puerto Rican?**

A.   I am.

Q.   **Was that a factor in the negative relationship between you and them?**

A.   I think it was a factor for any person of color.

Q.   **What do you mean by that?**

A.   I mean, that none of the administrators of color who started when I started or was there when I was there are still there.

Q.   **How many persons of color were there?**

A.   I believe there were five principals and directors.

Q.   **Do you remember their names?**

A.   So it would have been myself and Jose Rosado, Michael Rodriguez, Nick Perez. I'm blanking on the last person.

Q.   **Do you know the name Shannon Mayfield?**

A.   Oh, Shannon, yes.

Q.   **What's her ethic background?**

A.   He is an African American, and he was a principal.

Q.   **So any person of color that was working with you when Mayo came aboard is now gone?**

A.   Is gone.

Q.   **Do you know — I want to make sure this right, but I've been articulating a theory that what Wildonger and Mayo were doing was implicitly threatening Jose Rosado with the hopes that he would quit, and Jose wouldn't quit. Did you have that type of experience where they were intimidating you to get you to quit?**

ATTORNEY FREUND:

Objection, form of the question. You can answer it. There may be a number of questions, but you can answer the questions. The Judge will figure out whether or not the objection's valid later.

A.   I believe that was the strategy for most cases.

BY ATTORNEY ORLOSKI:

Q.   **Is that the strategy that you experienced?**

A.   Yes...

Q.   **You've given me the names of five people of color who were there and departed after Mayo and Wildonger came in. Do you remember you gave me you, Jose Rosado, Michael Rodriguez, Nick Perez and Shannon Mayfield. Do you remember which one -who was the first one to leave?**

A.   Mike Rodriguez.

Q.   **Do you know why he left?**

A.   I think it was the toxic environment, lack of support.

Q. Did any of the administrators complain to you that they felt they were subject to discrimination because of their race of ethnicity?

    MR. FREUND: Objection. You can answer.

A. Yes.

Q. Which ones complained?

A. I would say Michael and Shannon.

Q. Did Jose ever complain to you?

A. Yes.

Q. And by Jose I mean Jose Rosado.

A. Yes.

Q. And that was consistently your experience, that you thought that the toxic environment was related to race and ethnicity?

A. Yes.

Q. My client has a recollection of handwritten notes of a meeting of November 2nd, 2011 with Dr. Mayo, you and him where Dr. Mayo complained that my client was blocking students from being admitted into AEDY program. Do you remember that meeting?

A. Yes.

    MR. FREUND: Objection. You can answer.

Q. What do you remember about the meeting?

A. At that time Dr. Mayo desired more students to be placed in alternative ed and felt that the process was laborious and time consuming. So he wanted us to expedite the process and get more students into alternative ed.

Q. Now, the students that he wanted into the alternative ed, were they all primarily students of color?

A. Yes.

Q. Did he say why he wanted them in alternative ed?

A. He identified students as being troublemakers at the school and wanted them out of the schools and into the alternative ed program.

Q. Now, how did he conclude they were troublemakers? Did he do any investigation to your knowledge?

A. He did not do investigations. He went by the list of students that he was given.

Q. So the process, he acknowledged the process was laborious?

A. Yes.

Q. And did anyone say that's the system that's defined by the Pennsylvania Code?

A. Yes, both Jose and I did.

Q. What did he say about that?

A. He wanted the students removed from the schools.

Q. Irrespective of what the Code required?

    MR. FREUND: Objection. You can answer.

A. Yes.

Q. Specifically what type of directive did Dr. Mayo give either you or Jose about moving the students into the alternative education program?

A. He wanted the students moved.

Q. **Was there any discussion about whether or not it could be lawfully done?**

A. Yes. We tried to explain the process.

Q. **And how did he respond to your explanations?**

A. He wanted the students moved so it didn't matter what we said...

Q. **In the normal course of business did you write evaluations for any people you supervised?**

A. I wrote evaluations for all of the folks that I supervised.

Q. **How many people did you supervise that you wrote evaluations for?**

A. It varied each year. I had a team of folks working at the building. Jose and the community and student services team, there were about six folks who were basically department chairs of their areas. And my secretaries, there were nine secretaries. And that's it.

Q. **Now, when you left in 2013 at the end of the academic year, did Mr. Wildonger tell you that he was going to take charge of all the evaluations for all the employees you supervised?**

A. No.

Q. **Did he say that – did he take over the evaluations for any of the employees?**

A. He said he would take over Jose's evaluation.

Q. **Did he tell you why he wanted to take over Jose's?**

A. No.

Q. **Were you ready, willing and able to do the evaluation for Jose?**

A. I had already sent it to him.

Q. **You sent him written evaluation?**

A. Uh-huh...

Q. **Are you saying you actually finished the evaluation for Jose in June of 2013?**

A. In that year I believe I had to have a binder full of data and information for Jose. Everything was submitted. Any my findings were shared with David Wildonger.

Q. **What was you overall – your personal overall evaluation for Jose Rosado in June of 2013?**

MR. FREUND: Objection. You can answer.

A. He met the requirements of the action plan, and so he was satisfactory for the year.

Q. **Did you tell that to Wildonger?**

A. I did.

Q. **Did Wildonger agree or disagree, or just ignored it?**

A. I believe I was just ignored. I don't recall ever speaking with him...

Q. **Okay. Was Jose ever placed on a focused assistance plan?**

A. Yes.

Q. **And just briefly what's a focused assistance plan?**

A. It is a plan to help an employee with deficiencies in their performance, job performance.

Q. **Did you ever initiate the idea that Jose Rosado needs to be on a Focused Assistance Plan?**

A. I did not.

Q. **Did anyone?**

A. Mr. Wildonger.

Q. **And did he tell you why he felt Jose needed to be on a Focused Assistance Plan?**

A. Did he tell me why? He went through the paperwork that was submitted by Rita Perez who had done the original Focused Assistance Plan for Mr. Wildonger for Jose.

Q. **Now, that Focused Assistance Plan related to Ryan Miller complaining about Jose Rosado?**

A. That's correct.

Q. **And at some point the District determined that Ryan Miller was lying about Jose Rosado, correct?**

A. Yes.

Q. **And after the determination did they withdraw the Focused Assistance Plan based upon Ryan Miller's complaint against Jose?**

MR. FREUND: Objection.

A. They did not.

Q. **Should they have?**

A. Yes.

MR. FREUND: Objection.

Q. **And who made the decision not to withdraw it?**

A. Mr. Wildonger.

Q. **And did he then prepare a second Focused Assistance Plan?**

A. Yes.

Q. **Now, the second Focused Assistance Plan, who prepared it?**

A. It was prepared through the – through Rita Perez's office. She left in the middle of it. And it came to me from Mr. Wildonger.

Q. **Well, did Mr. Wildonger prepare it or did you prepare it?**

A. It came to me from Mr. Wildonger.

Q. **Did you agree that the second Focused Assistance Plan should have been done?**

A. No.

Q. **Who made the decision to do it?**

A. Mr. Wildonger.

Q. **And did he direct you to sign off on that Focused Assistance Plan?**

A. He did.

Q. **Did you do so?**

A. I did...

Q. After the meeting where Mayo told Jose to facilitate the transfers did that actually happen, do you know if he did it?

A. No.

Q. **Do you know he reported that to the Department of Education?**

A. Yes.

Q. **And how did you know he reported it to the Department of Education?**

A. We were audited within a week.

Q. **So was there ever any discussion where Wildonger or Mayo said they knew that the audit was a result of a complaint by Jose Rosado?**

A. Not at that point.

Q. **At any point?**

A. Later on.

Q. **What happened later on where they mentioned this?**

A. I don't recall.

Q. **So the timing of the event suggested to you that the audit was caused by Jose Rosado?**

> MR. FREUND: Objection. Objection.

Q. **Do you know that because Jose told you that?**

A. Jose told me.

Q. **Do you know if Wildonger or Mayo took any retaliatory action against Jose because of that?**

> MR. FREUND: Objection. You can answer that.

A. I believe they did…

Q. **After the second FAP that you were directed to sign off on by Wildonger did you have any discussion with Jose about that?**

A. Yes.

Q. **Did you say it's a set up, they're doing it to fire you?**

A. Yes.

> MR. ORLOSKI: I have no further questions. Thank you very much. He has the right to ask you some questions.

EXAMINATION
BY MR. FREUND:

Q. **Susan, the last question Mr. Orloski asked you, if I understand your testimony correctly you said that – you said to Mr. Rosado it's a set up, they're doing it to fire you?**

A. To terminate him, yes.

Q. **And you said that to Jose. When did you say that to him?**

A. With the second FAP.

Q. **And what facts do you have that led you to that conclusion?**

A. I was written up because I did not handle the meeting for the second FAP. I was told that the meeting needed to be scheduled. I scheduled the meeting. I brought all the folks that were supposed to come to the meeting. And I waited because I thought the FAP was coming from Mr. Wildonger. And I was informed that that was my meeting and that I was handling this FAP. And because of my reaction at that meeting I was written up.

Q. **Okay. Now, was this at the so-called second FAP that were talking about?**

A. Yes.…

Q. **Okay. Ms. Lozada, you have in front of you what I have marked as Rosado 9 and Rosado 10. For the record these haven't yet been put in this deposition, but for purposes of simplicity we'll keep these with his unfinished deposition. Do you recognize these documents?**

A. Yes.

Q. Okay. Now, the Rosado 9 document, is that what Mr. Orlsoki has been referring to as the first FAP?

A. This was under two months. That was done during Rita Perez. Yes.

Q. Okay. It's got your name on it.

A. Yes.

Q. It's from you?

A. Yes.

Q. All right. And do you know what the motivating factor for issuing this FAP was?

MR. ORLOSKI: I'm going to object to the form of the question. Whose motivating factor, her motivating factor or Wildonger's motivating factor?

MR. FREUND: Wildonger is not part of this. Perez is apparently.

Q. Hers or yours or someone else's, what motivated that FPA by whomever?

A. Okay. This was motivated due to Ryan Miller's complaint, and Rita's directions under Mr. Wildonger and Dr. Mayo…

Q. … Did he fulfill his obligation under number one?

A. He did according to me, yes.

Q. Okay. And was that your responsibility to make that determination?

A. At that point no one knew who was responsible for the evaluation at that point …

Q. Okay. So number 9 is about Ryan Miller, number 9 is about Ryan Miller?

A. Yes.

Q. Now, Number 10, is this the so-called second FAP?

MR. ORLOSKI: John, just to help you out here. They started with this and then they changed it. You have the first version of Number 10. There's a second version. And it says a compliant against you by a staff member. Jose said, if that's—if I win that appeal this disappears, so then they said no, and the they changed it, so there's another version of this document.

A. This was the first draft, so to speak.

Q. All right. Well, it has your name on it, right?

A. Yes, it does.

Q. So you wrote it, correct?

A. I received part of this, and I wrote the memo based on it…

Q. Okay. All right. Now, you said there was a meeting at which there was apparently some confusion on someone's part to go over this June 12, 2012 FAP. Did I understand that correctly from your earlier testimony?

A. Yes.

Q. And you said you were written up about it?

A. I was.

Q. What was the format of you being written up about it?

A. I did not handle my responsibilities correctly, according to Mr. Wildonger…

Q. Did you do an evaluation in 2012?

A. I did.

Q. Okay. And what, what primarily were the problems, the deficiency that this FAP was directed towards Mr. Rosado?

MR. ORLOSKI: Well, from her perspective or from Wildonger's perspective? She's saying she didn't agree with this.

MR. FREUND: She's a witness. Whatever she says. You can follow up. Her name is on it.

Q. **Your name is on it, right?**

A. My name is all over this.

Q. **Okay. Well can you explain what were the problems to which assistance was to be focused?**

A. They're listed there under competencies. And under each of those I needed to show that Mr. Rosado was showing improvement in every one of those areas.

Q. **Okay. Now, let's see. You said some of this was given to you and some of it you wrote. Did I understand that correctly?**

A. I supplied – I was given the competencies and I supplied the explanation.

MR. ORLOSKI: I'm sorry?

A. The explanation for the plan.

Q. **What is that?**

A. After the discussion with Mr. Wildonger and Mr. Cote.

Q. **Activities to address the objectives, is that what you supplied?**

A. Activities to address the objectives was basically given to me. The competencies were given to me. This was part of the discussion of the group as to having to have an FAP…

Q. **Okay. Now, on June – let me ask you this. On June 12, when the FAP was issued, did you know anything about Mr. Rosado contacting the Department of Education for any reason?**

A. By then if you're talking about the alternative ed audit that we had from PDE, I knew about that.

Q. **At that point, on June 12, you knew about it at that point?…**

A. Yes.

Q. **All right. What did you know about it?**

A. I knew that Jose contacted PDE about being forced to move students from alternative – from our schools into alternative ed.

Q. **Before he did that did he ever – did he ever mention to you that there was a problem, that he thought there was a problem?**

A. We talked about there being a problem with the movement of students.

Q. **Okay. Did he – did he ever mention anything to you about principals or assistant principals weren't completing their AEDY paperwork to his satisfaction?**

A. They weren't handing in completed AEDY referrals.

Q. **Okay. When you were his supervisor, right?**

A. Correct.

Q. **What did you tell him to do about it?**

A. We couldn't accept the referrals.

Q. **Well, how about going to the principals and saying fill out your paperwork like you're supposed to do?**

A. We did. Both Jose and I would talk to principals about the lack of paperwork completion.

Q. Can you tell me what specific principals you talked to about that?

A. All of the secondary principals, that's middle and high schools at that point, and their assistants.

Q. Well, at some point after the audit I understand that there was a general session where there was discussion about this, is that right?

A. Yes.

Q. I'm talking about before, before that, before any contact was even made with PDE concerning the perception that there was a problem?

A. There was a constant discussion with the assistants and the principals about their lack of completion of paperwork. They made Jose out to be the bad guy when they weren't completing the paperwork.

Q. Why weren't they forced to do that? Why weren't they forced to do that? Why weren't they forced to do that if the claim is that – ...

A. Their supervisors didn't force them to redo the paperwork. Mr. Wildonger was the supervisor. They were not being forced to redo the paperwork.

Q. But Jose was the Director of Alternative Education, correct?

A. Correct.

Q. And you were his supervisor?

A. Correct.

Q. Why didn't you do something about it?

A. I did do something about it.

Q. What did you do?

A. I spoke to the principals, and their supervisors.

Q. After the audit?

A. No, before.

Q. Well, who did you speak to before?

A. David Wildonger. Dr. Mayo …

Q. Okay. Do you remember when and how you communicated this concern to either of those gentlemen?

A. Whenever it was brought up, either by a principal, as a topic of conversation at cabinet meeting, I would always address it.

Q. What would you say to them?

A. People were not completing the paperwork correctly. They were trying to rush students in. We were getting incomplete paperwork and then they would claim they didn't know about it. So they knew what was happening …

Q. Okay. Ms. Lozada, did you talk to Mr. Rosado at all in preparation for this disposition today?

A. No …

Q. Okay. Number 49 says that in order to bypass the federal mandate that defendants Mayo and Wildonger ordered Mr. Rosado to label certain students with learning and/or emotional disabilities as disruptive students, even though such students were not disruptive and should not be so classified. Do you have any information that would support or deny that allegation?

A. If this happened in November of 2013 I wasn't there.

Q. **No, I'm saying at any time. It could have happened at any time, at any time.**

A. There was discussion about movement of students without regard to their classification, and just getting them out of the schools was the primary focus of those discussions with Wildonger and Dr. Mayo. So that was a constant throughout the time that I was there.

Q. **Okay. There was discussion about that?**

A. Yes.

Q. **Special ed students?**

A. There was no regard to their classification.

Q. **At any time did you become aware of any instance in which Dr. Mayo or Mr. Wildonger did anything, said anything, that someone could have construed as ignoring the requirements of the IDEA in the placement and programming of special education kids?**

A. Besides the November meeting, I mean, that was about the movement of the top disruptive students in terms of the number of behavioral issues that they had. There was no discussion about whether or not they were special ed, it was just, get them out of the building…

Q. **So do I understand, did you give Mr. Wildonger a three-ring notebook full of material?**

A. Yes. Jose had a copy and I had a copy. I gave Dave my copy.

MR. FREUND: Okay. So, Mr. Orloski, is that something that you produced to us in the 5,000 pages –

MR. ORLOSKI: I think it was in …

(Discussion off the record)

MR. FREUND: I don't have any more questions at this point.

MR. ORLOSKI: Let me ask some questions.

RE-EXAMINATION
BY MR. ORLOSKI:

Q. **Okay. Now, do you remember the audit?**

A. Uh-huh.

Q. **Did the audit find that there was a special education student who was transferred to the disruptive youth program that didn't belong there?**

A. Yes.

Q. **So that was an actual fact as determined by the Pennsylvania Department of Education, correct?**

A. Yes.

Q. **Now, you said several times their goal was to get students out of the building?**

A. Yes.

Q. **Can you elaborate on that? What were you talking about?**

A. They wanted to remove the students that they identified as disruptive as quickly as possible. If they could do it overnight they would do it overnight. It would just be a matter of that's the students placement come tomorrow, and notwithstanding the law and the process…

Q. I think that's Exhibit 12, the evaluations, do you have that in front of you?

A. Uh-huh…

Q. Then there's a comment. Jose has always demonstrated the ability to admit mistakes and learn from them. He has implemented leadership and policy decisions even when faced with great personal and professional challenges due to defending the district's policies and procedures. What did you mean by that? What does that refer to? Lets read the next sentence, maybe that will help you. Jose has been challenged this year due to his defense of the Comprehensive Suspension Program and its implementation in the district. What was the Comprehensive Suspension Program?

A. Under Jerry Zahorchak when he came in we completely revamped the discipline process for administrators so that they could understand progressive discipline, and so that they could keep track of how they implemented the discipline, to the degree that Jose even shared with them tracking sheets that they could use with the students. It was not looked upon favorably by the majority of the building administrators because they didn't want to have to be so accountable for the process. And that was something that happened under Jerry Zahorchak. But since he left after a year, it stayed within my department, came under the Director of Community and Student Services, and was seen as Jose's plan, when it really was the right thing to do for our students, and the right thing that other districts were doing. This was basically Bethlehem's plan and East Penn's plan. We were just starting it. But he got so much push back from the administrators and teachers with its implementation.

Q. What about the union, did the union push back on it?

A. All the time.

Q. Now, the Ryan Miller – there were students and parents complaining about Ryan Miller, correct?

A. Yes…

Q. And because of these complaints did Jose initiate an investigation into the complaints?

A. Yes, he did.

Q. And when he initiated the investigation did that generate a countercharge by Ryan Miller?

A. Yes, it did.

Q. And basically Ryan Miller was complaining that he was being investigated for being a racist, correct?

A. Yes.

Q. And that resulted in the first FAP?

A. Uh-huh.

Q. Correct?

A. Yes.

Q. And from your perspective Jose successfully completed that, right?

A. Yes.

Q. Now, at the time you did this evaluation did you have that first FAP, this evaluation which you've marked as Exhibit 12 dated June 11, 2012?

A. Yes.

Q. The fact that there was the FAP 1 against him at the time that you did this evaluation; did you factor that into these answers here?

A. I did.

Q. Now, if you knew what you know today that Ryan Miller fabricated false charges against Jose, would this evaluation be different?

MR. FREUND: Objection. You can answer …

A. Yes.

Q. More favorably towards Jose, correct?

A. I believe so, because he was proven out with the investigation.

Q. Okay.

A. Can I just add, due to this evaluation was the first time that I received a negative comment in my evaluation, because I was evaluated by Regina Cesario that year, and I was penalized in my evaluation for not giving Jose an unsat.

Q. And who's the one who did your evaluation?

A. Regina Cesario was the Interim Assistant Superintendent before Tina Belardi. Tina Belardi I believe signed off on this in July, but before her Regina Cesario was the Acting Assistant Superintendent. And I received a negative comment on my evaluation because of Jose receiving a satisfactory evaluation.

Q. Now, what about – you said as a result of the – let me start over again. You suggested that you were penalized for the way you handled Jose's FAP, correct?

A. Yes.

Q. How were you penalized?

A. Like I said, I received a negative mark on my evaluation, specifically for Jose receiving a satisfactory on his. And I was written up – actually the few times that I've been written up in my career have been with Wildonger and Mayo. But specifically for the handling of the FAP meeting, the original meeting.

Q. Okay. And in the write-up that you received, were you threatened with potential termination?

A. Yes…

Q. Was that a factor in you leaving?

A. Yes.

Q. You say you loved you job?

A. I loved my job.

Q. And yet you left the job you loved?

A. I left.

Q. And when you left you didn't leave for another job, you left for unemployment?

A. I left for unemployment.

Q. So you left a job you loved at a decent salary, correct?

MR. FREUND: Objection.

A. Yes.

Q. Because Wildonger and Mayo were that bad?

    MR. FREUND: Objection.

A. Yes.

    MR. ORLOSKI: I have no further questions.

RE-EXAMINATION

BY MR. FREUND:

Q. Mrs. Lozada, Regina Cesario was – was she a racist too?

A. I don't know. No.

Q. You said she – she gave you a write-up because you didn't – you didn't give Mr. Rosado an unsatisfactory. Did she have a reason for that, whether you agreed with it or not?

A. I don't recall the rationale. I understand she was in the same situation I was in.

Q. Which was what?

A. All of these forms that have my name on them were part of a group that worked on them. So I have no doubt that her evaluation of me also involved others.

Q. So what your testimony is, she was forced to tell you that?

A. I would say that she was required to tell me that. I don't know forced.

Q. Okay. Is that your – is that your feeling, or do you have some evidence that would support your belief?

A. That was the MO that was operating at that time, how things were being handled. People clustered together, worked together, and there was a spokesperson. She happened to be my supervisor. She got to do the write-up …

Q. Is that in your personal file?

A. I don't know what they did with it. I was just told to sign it. I got a copy.

    MR. FREUND: That's all I have.

    MR. ORLOSKI: Thank you very much.

    MR. FREUND: Thanks for coming on short notice.

(Deposition concluded at 5:20 pm)

CONCLUSION

⊰——⊱

On December 9, 2014, the morning of my fifty-first birthday, I sat in the Allentown School District boardroom alongside my attorney awaiting the start of my termination hearing. The room was full with administrators, family and friends, community leaders and other supporters as well as members of the media. As the hearing officer and board members took their places, Attorney Freund entered the room and signaled to my attorney to step out of the room with him just minutes before the hearing was to begin. A few minutes later, my attorney reentered the room and informed me "the District wants to settle." He explained that the District would withdraw all charges and suspensions, reimburse me for pay lost during the suspensions, and the separation would be effective in March of 2015. I would also retain my right to pursue a civil law suite against the District, Dr. Mayo and David Wildonger.

My initial thought was that I wanted to proceed with the hearing, but due to the ex parte communication, which had taken place between Dr. Mayo and the board, I did not trust the board. As such, I could not risk being found guilty of the charges and losing my certification. Further, if the board would have voted in my favor, Dr. Mayo had already assigned someone else to my job and Attorney Orloski informed me that I would be reassigned to another position.

SEPARATION AGREEMENT

The purpose of this SEPARATION AGREEMENT ("Agreement") is to establish an amicable arrangement for José Rosado, Sr.'s separation from employment with the Allentown School District ("District"). As set forth below, in return for the separation benefits listed, José Rosado, Sr. hereby agrees to resign from employment with the District under the conditions set forth in this Agreement.

1.   The District hereby withdraws all charges of misconduct against José Rosado, Sr., including any prior disciplinary actions of suspension and termination.

2.   Resignation Date. In consideration thereof, José Rosado, Sr. will resign from employment as of the end of the workday, on Friday, March 20, 2015 (the "Last Date of Employment"). A signed Resignation Letter is attached.

3.   Separation Benefit. In exchange for the mutual covenants set forth in this Agreement, the District shall provide José Rosado, Sr. with the following (the "Separation Benefit"):

   (a) The District shall withdraw the Notice of Hearing and Charges dated July 28, 2014, and vacate all prior discipline and suspensions.

   (b) The District shall reimburse José Rosado, Sr. for pay lost beginning on the date of his suspension without pay, July 21, 2014, and continuing up until January 5, 2015.

   (c) The District accepts the prior documentation José Rosado, Sr. submitted from his doctor and understands that he shall use up all of his available sick leave and, upon exhaustion of sick leave, shall permit him to use all of his available vacation leave until his Last Date of Employment, March 20, 2015.

   José Rosado, Sr. explicitly acknowledges that the Separation Benefits are not otherwise due or owing to him under any employment agreement (oral or written), policy or practice.

4.   COBRA. José Rosado, Sr. is entitled to continue certain health care benefits coverage under COBRA, regardless of whether he accepts this Agreement. His COBRA rights will be communicated to him separately.

{00194566}

346

5. **No Further Separation Benefits.** José Rosado, Sr. understands that the Separation Benefits constitute special consideration in exchange for the promises he makes in this Agreement, and that the District is not otherwise obligated to provide him with the Separation Benefits.

6. **Severability.** All parts of this Agreement are severable. If any part of this Agreement, or the application of any part of this Agreement is determined by any court to be unlawful, unenforceable, invalid, void or voidable, to any extent, for any reason: (a) the application of such part of this Agreement to any other person, circumstance, or claim, will not be affected, and (b) all other parts of this Agreement will remain in full force and effect to extent permitted by law.

7. This Agreement constitutes the complete understanding between the parties concerning the subject matter described herein and supersedes all prior negotiations, discussions, representations or agreements of any kind, written or oral, between José Rosado, Sr. and the District. This Agreement may only be modified by a written document signed by José Rosado, Sr. and the District's Board President.

DATE: 12/18/14

José Rosado, Sr.:

918 N. Bergen St.
Address Fountain Hill, Pa 18015

Address

DATE: 1/9/15

BY: Robert E. Smith Jr
Robert E. Smith, Jr., Board President

ATTEST:

Janet Morillo, Board Secretary

{00194566}   2

SETTLEMENT AGREEMENT AND RELEASE

IT IS HEREBY AGREED AS FOLLOWS:

JOSE ROSADO, for and in consideration of payments and other good and valuable consideration described more fully herein, does, hereby remise, release, and forever discharge the **ALLENTOWN SCHOOL DISTRICT, C. RUSSELL MAYO, Ed.D., DAVID WILDONGER and OLD REPUBLIC INSURANCE COMPANY,** as well as members of the School Board of Directors, administrators, officers, and their past, present and future School Board of Directors, administrators, officers, insurers, attorneys, agents, servants, representatives, employees, subsidiaries, affiliates, predecessors and successors in interest, and assigns, and any and all other persons, firms, corporations and entities, whether herein named or referred to or not, of and from all, and all manner of, actions, causes of action, suits, claims, debts, demands, dues, accounts, bonds, covenants, contracts, agreements, judgments, damages, delay damages, costs, expenses, loss of services, attorney fees, and any and all claims of whatever kind and nature whatsoever, arising out of or related to his employment, in law or in equity, especially pertaining to those claims and causes of action more specifically described in actions filed in the United States District Court for the Eastern District of Pennsylvania, docketed to number 15-0252, including but not limited to 42 U.S.C. Section 1983, Title VII, retaliation and for Breach of Settlement agreement, which Jose Rosado ever had, now has, or can, shall, or which his heirs, executors, administrators, successors, or assigns, or any of them, hereafter can, shall, or may have, for or by reason of any cause, matter, or thing whatsoever, from the beginning of the world to the date of these presents.

{00265570}

The Release of all claims and damages includes, but is not limited to any claims under any federal, state or local law, regulation or ordinance prohibiting race, sex, age, religion, national origin, disability or other form of discrimination. This Release includes, but is not limited to, Title VII of the Civil Rights Act of 1964 as amended, the Age Discrimination and Employment Act as amended, the Older Worker Protection Act, the Americans with Disabilities Act as amended, the Equal Pay Act and the Family Medical Leave Act. This Release also includes, but is not limited to, any claim of wrongful discharge, any claim under the Employee Retirement Income Security Act as amended, and the Pennsylvania Public Employee Relations Act as amended. The claims you are releasing also include, but are not limited to, claims for retaliation under any of the laws described above, any claims for breach of express or implied contract, any claims for pay not specifically recited in this letter, any claims for defamation and any claims for infliction of emotional distress as related to his employment.

IT IS AGREED AND UNDERSTOOD that Defendant agrees to pay a total of $135,000, as follows: $90,000 to Jose Rosado and $45,000 to the Orloski law firm for legal fees and costs. The total amount is inclusive of attorneys' fees, and is in full and final settlement of this matter to Plaintiff Jose Rosado. Plaintiff acknowledges that he will be responsible for payment of all taxes resulting from his share of the settlement award.

{00285570}

IT IS AGREED AND UNDERSTOOD that Defendant will provide Plaintiff Jose Rosado with a letter of recommendation from the School District on school letter head in the form attached as Exhibit A, signed by the Executive Director of Human Resources of the Allentown School District.

Plaintiff agrees to indemnify and hold harmless Defendant from any and all claims or liens to these funds made by healthcare providers and insurers, including, but not limited to, Medicare, Medicaid, worker's compensation carriers, private insurance carriers and other entities.

IT IS AGREED AND UNDERSTOOD that this is a full and final release of all claims of every nature and kind whatsoever and that it releases all claims for injuries, losses, and damages that are presently known or suspected and all claims for injuries, losses, and damages that are not presently known or suspected but which may later develop or be discovered.

IT IS AGREED AND UNDERSTOOD that the parties agree that nothing will be said by either party that will defame either party's professional or business reputation.

IT IS AGREED AND UNDERSTOOD that the consideration paid in exchange for this release is not to be construed as an admission of liability on the part of the Defendant herein, all liability being expressly denied, and that the said payment is made to effect a compromise of a disputed claim.

{00265570}

Jose Rosado agrees and represents that:

(a) He has read carefully the terms of this Agreement, including the General Release;

(b) He has had an opportunity to review this Agreement, including the General Release, with an attorney;

(c) He understands the meaning and effect of the terms of this Agreement, including the General Release, which waives, among other claims, any claims for damages for age discrimination under the Age Discrimination in Employment Act;

(d) He was given a reasonable time to decide whether to enter into this Agreement, including the General Release;

(e) The entry into and execution of this Agreement, including the General Release, is his own free and voluntary Act without compulsion of any kind.

IT IS FURTHER AGREED AND UNDERSTOOD that this release contains the entire agreement between the parties hereto and that the terms of this release are contractual and not a mere recital.

_____
JOSE ROSADO

_____
DAVID F. ZIMMERMAN, PRESIDENT OF BOARD OF DIRECTORS
On behalf of Allentown School District

DATE: 2/18/16

{00285570}

351

SETTLEMENT STATEMENT

After careful consideration and consultation with my attorney and family, I have decided to accept a settlement agreement offered to me by the Allentown School District regarding the federal law suite I filed against the district.

Although I have accepted the negotiated settlement agreement, I steadfastly maintain that I did my job in an ethical manner and in compliance with Pennsylvania School Code.

I am pleased that the negotiated settlement agreement does not include a "confidentiality clause"; therefore the record is NOT SEALED.

I encourage the Allentown School District Board Of Directors and any and all other parties that may have an interest in the facts of this case to obtain and review all of the evidence introduced "for the record"; including discovery documents and sworn statements given during depositions. By doing so, they can base their conclusion on the evidence.

Jose Rosado

In June of 2016, the Allentown School District approved a one-year sabbatical for Dr. Mayo - the final year of his contract. And although he does not possess a superintendent letter of certification, the school board approved David Wildonger to serve as acting superintendent. He was eventually reassigned to acting deputy superintendent.

On April 15, 2014, I contacted Attorney Lapp (Education Law Center – PA) regarding alleged AEDY violations in the Allentown School District. Attorney Lapp referred me to Zoe M. Savitski, Trial Attorney with the U.S. Department of Justice, Civil Rights Division Educational Opportunities Section.

To:	David Lapp
From:	Jose Rosado
Subject:	Fwd: AEDY/Special Education – Compliance Concerns (Refusal To Comply With Directive)
Date:	April 15, 2014 9:35 AM

Attorney Lapp,

Please see the attached email below (November 26, 2013 Re: AEDY/Special Education – Compliance Concerns). As you will see, I refused to comply with the directive to move special education students in to the AEDY Program.

You will also see that I was given a similar directive by Dr. Mayo (Superintendent) in November of 2011. Although I complied with the directive issued by the superintendent, I reported the violation to Drew Schuckman at PDE in December. As a result of my report to PDE, a compliance visit was scheduled. The compliance visit resulted in 8 violations.

I am very troubled that the district continues to issue directives and follow a practice that violates the due process and civil rights of special education students.

Thank you!!!

Jose Rosado

On 2014-04-15 10:25, David Lapp wrote:

Jose,

Thanks so much for forwarding these emails. I can easily forward to DOJ, but it would be better if you would. I would also suggest that you ask to speak with them confidentially.

Thanks for your good work on behalf of kids.

All the best,

David

David Lapp – Staff Attorney
Education Law Center
1315 Walnut St., Rm 400
Philadelphia, PA 19107

From: Jose Rosado
Sent: Tuesday, April 15, 2014
To: Savitsky, Zoe (CRT)
Subject: Fwd: FW: District Non-Compliance (NHQT-Staffing & Special Education Students Assigned to Alternative Education)

Dear Attorney Savitsky and Attorney Zisser,

My name is Jose Rosado and I am the Director/Principal of Alternative Education Programs for the Allentown School District (Pennsylvania). I was provided with your contact information by Attorney David Lapp from the Education Law Center. I contacted Attorney Lapp regarding the compliant the ELC filed with the DOJ.

I have attached an email I sent to Attorney Lapp, followed by an email I sent to my supervisor regarding the process (illegal process) of moving special education students into the district's alternative education (AEDY) program.

Please consider this information in regards to the ELC complaint.

I will make myself available to speak and/or meet with you regarding this concern.

Thank you!!!

Jose Rosado

On 2014-05-22 11:30, Savitsky, Zoe (CRT) wrote:

Mr. Rosado,

Thank you very much for your email. My apologies for the delay in responding. We would like to arrange a time to meet with you to discuss these issues further. Please let me know when you are available in the next three weeks for a meeting. If meeting on a weekend or in the evening is better for you, that is fine.

Looking forward to speaking with you.

Sincerely,

Zoe

In June of 2014, Attorney Savitski, along with three of her colleagues for the U.S. Department of Justice, traveled from Washington, D.C. and came to my house to interview Susan Lozada and I regarding the Education Law Center complaint and the alleged AEDY violations in the Allentown School District. During the interview, Susan and I shared much of the information and documents included in this book with them.

As of my last communication with Attorney Lapp, in the winter of 2016, the U.S. Department of Justice was still in the process of its investigation regarding the Education Law Center complaint against the Pennsylvania Department of Education.

REFERENCES

1. "Fact Sheet: How Bad Is the School-to-Prison Pipeline?" Tavis Smiley Reports, Episode 6: Education Under Arrest, Feature By Carla Amurao

2. U.S. Drug Enforcement Administration – DEA History 1970-1975, Creation of the DEA, July 1, 1973

3. Politico, Reagan Declares "War on Drugs," October 14, 1982, By Andrew Glass

4. Legislative Analyst's Office - California, Policy Brief, The Federal Crime Bill: What Will It Mean for California? September 27, 1994

5. Sentencing Project, Trends in U.S. Corrections, U.S. State and Federal Prison Population, 1925-2014,

6. Drug Policy Alliance, The Drug War, Mass Incarceration and Race, February 2016

7. Rethinking Schools, Editorial: Stop the School-to Prison Pipeline, By the Editors of Rethinking Schools, Winter 2011-2012

8. Education Week, No Child Left Behind: An Overview, By Alyson Klein, April 10, 2015

9. Mathematica Policy Research, Evaluating Race to the Top and School Improvement Grants, Prepared for: U.S. Department of Education, Institute of Education Sciences

10. Education Week, The Every Student Succeeds Act: An ESSA Overview, By Alyson Klein, March 31, 2016

11. "Fact Sheet: How Bad Is the School-to-Prison Pipeline?" Tavis Smiley Reports, Episode 6: Education Under Arrest, Feature By Carla Amurao

12. USLEGAL.com, Loudermill Rights Law and Legal Definition

44012925R00205